C'est La Gar

by

Pete Larsen

authorHOUSE™

1663 LIBERTY DRIVE, SUITE 200
BLOOMINGTON, INDIANA 47403
(800) 839-8640
WWW.AUTHORHOUSE.COM

This book is a work of fiction based on actual historical events. People, places, events, and situations are the product of the author's imagination. Any resemblance to actual persons, living or dead, or historical events, is purely coincidental.

First published by AuthorHouse 02/17/05

ISBN: 1-4208-3021-X (sc)

Printed in the United States of America
Bloomington, Indiana

This book is printed on acid-free paper.

Comments and inquires are welcome at cestlagar@aol.com

DEDICATION

To all the B-52 gunners who flew missions from Anderson, Kadena and U-Tapao and to four gunners who are no longer with us.

Earl J Barnes was my instructor. He taught me to be afraid of the tail. He must have been right—he died in it.

Duane "Uke" Anderson. He flew 446 missions, including a hundred over North Vietnam, only to die in a motorcycle crash after his retirement.

Louie LeBlanc. He flew 352 missions, including 79 over the North. He was a POW from December 22, 1972 to April 1, 1973. He died of a heart attack on the island of Guam.

Charlie Poole. He flew 29 B-29 missions over Korea and 380 B-52 missions in Southeast Asia. He was shot down and killed December 19, 1972. His remains were discovered in 1996 and finally returned to his family in October 2003. I attended his memorial service held the same month.

PREFACE

Between March and September 1966, I flew forty-nine combat missions in the tail of a B-52, including the first bomber raid over North Vietnam. Looking back on it, it seems my best memories are of the fun parts, if war can ever be fun. In those days we didn't think much about the moral aspects of the war. Danger, although always in the back of the mind, was slight. There were a few divorces, if not caused, at least helped by the six-month separation, but for the most part, wives and families were "good soldiers".

Broken arms, stopped plumbing or transmissions that wouldn't shift somehow got fixed along with a few rubber checks that got covered. The one-dollar-a-day per diem the gunners received was a long way from the eight bucks our officers got, yet we managed. It took savings or a lot of skill at poker, but we were able to support our families and have a few bucks left over for beer. It was an adventure.

Seven years later the adventure was over. By 1973 the story was one of strained marriages, MIA's, POW'S and some damn brave people who flew an unprecedented number of combat hours. The officers I flew with were mostly promoted to staff jobs, which meant that for them, the war would sometimes not come around as frequently. The only promotion most of the gunners got was to higher-ranking gunner. It didn't get them out of the tail. Many of the gunners I flew with accumulated three, four, or more six-month tours of combat duty with assorted shorter stretches thrown in. Gunners with two and three thousand hours of combat time are not uncommon.

After I left the tail I spent a year as a civilian finishing my degree. I re-entered the Air Force and, after a six-month fight with the bureaucracy, I was finally accepted for Officer Training School. I was commissioned a second lieutenant and in time was promoted to first lieutenant and then captain. All this time the war dragged on. Many of my friends stayed in the tail and every year or so went off to war. It became harder and harder for them and their families. Their war wasn't glorious one. It meant family separation and a constant, well-founded, nagging fear that they were going to get killed. Many were.

I've kept in touch with many of the gunners I knew and much of this book comes from them. I've often wondered how they feel about old "Sundown," the poker player, part-time hell raiser and shade-tree gunner being an officer. I was probably as outspoken against those clowns who made us carry their bags as anybody, yet I'm sure that by the time I made lieutenant colonel I was classified as a gunner gone bad.

I need to tell you that gunners are my heroes and this story closely resembles the truth. The incidents did not always happen as told, but they did happen. Gunners by nature are storytellers and much of this book is based on stories told among them. Over time refinements may have been added, yet the basic story is true. Most of the characters are composites made up of many individuals, but they did exist. When real names are used I will swear they never drank or chased bar girls. I expect them to deny any tales about me.

Chapter One

After twelve hours in the tail, fifteen if you counted ground time, the balding technical sergeant was weary and his knees ached from lack of movement. It was no small pleasure pulling off the heavy boots and feeling the cool evaporation of trapped sweat. After two beers he wanted to talk about what a gunner's life was like once he was airborne in a B-52. Few people other than gunners themselves had any idea that directly behind and below the vertical fin of early B-52's the tail gunner sat in a small compartment no larger than the cockpit of a fighter. By looking through the windows above him, he could visually check the airplane taillight for operation and observe the movement of the tall rudder when one of the pilots 145 feet away pushed on his pedals. If the gunner moved his elbows only inches away from his body they would touch the side panels, and with the seat forward his knees straddled the control column for the guns. Depending on his torso height and seat adjustment, the clearance between his head and the top of the small space he rode in was less than the width of a deck of cards. Unable to stand and with no way to fully stretch without unbuckling himself from the harness holding him in place, a tail gunner was isolated from the five forward crewmembers by a long unpressurized fuselage main body. Unless emergency conditions existed he did not go to the front of the aircraft in flight and often spent twelve and sometimes more than twenty-four hours alone, without seeing another human being.

To enable a gunner to urinate in flight, the same fifty thou' a year engineers who designed the multi-million dollar B-52 thoughtfully designed a buck and a half arrangement. A small funnel connected to a rubber hose running thirty inches or so down to a two-quart can snapped into a panel alongside the base of the gunner's seat. This rig, cumbersome at best, never worked well in practice. Because it was filthy and smelled of stale urine, maintenance people didn't like to work on it. When clogged, the standard fix was to cut out the clogged section and slide the pieces together over a smaller tube. In time the tubes became so short that urinating became a test of aim and was no simple process. Gunners who wrote the relief tubes up for being too short could expect numerous caustic comments about just what was too short, so mostly they didn't write them up. A long tube worked better than a short one, but crimped easily. Then the procedure required the gunner to pinch himself off with one hand while he held the tube eye level to remove the crimp and let the funnel drain out. This method although standard, was complicated by turbulence.

The sergeant shifted on the makeshift desk, lit a cigarette and looked at the tall maintenance three-striper, in green fatigues who was standing alongside another gunner wearing a flight suit.

"Have you ever seen a ball of piss floating eye level?" he asked, and without waiting for an answer continued, "The damn relief tube wouldn't work and I'd already pissed all over my hands so I unsnapped the can from the side panel, put it in my lap and took the lid off.

"As usual it was about three-quarters full because somebody didn't dump it after the last flight and I was holding it between my legs trying to piss in it. At the time we were just starting refueling and coming up on the tanker. The next thing I know, the navigator tells the pilot our closure rate is too fast.

"The Ace tells the co-pilot to go to airbrakes two and the damn idiot slams it into airbrakes six.[1]

"The negative G's caused the piss to rise even with my visor. I sat there moving the can back and forth trying to get under it." He used hand gestures to describe his plight. "Then the damn idiot slams it into airbrakes nothing."

2

The tall maintenance troop in the fatigues almost doubled over in laughter when the gunner next to him said, "Yeah, but now you know why your peanut butter sandwiches taste salty. I'll tell you, anybody who thinks there is glory in flying has never held a plugged relief tube at eye level with piss running down their sleeve. It's as much fun as trying to shit in a flight lunch box."[2]

Airman First Class Sam Jackson, twenty-two, correctly suspected he was the designated audience of the war stories. Of the three men standing in the gray World War II vintage Bomb Squadron building on Ellsworth Air Force Base, South Dakota, he was the only one not in a flight suit. But he still managed to look good, even casual, in his starched fatigues, shined shoes and proper military haircut. Normally he didn't frequent this "ops" building, but lately he'd started hanging around, gathering intelligence about applying for gunnery school. Today he received the full treatment.

Sam listened to the banter with the laid-back expression and slight smile he worked to cultivate. Then he looked at his watch and realized it was time for him to get back to the flight line, but the gunner's tales weren't easy to leave.

"If you want to practice being a tail gunner, take a large metal garbage can to the top of a high set of stairs," the technical sergeant said. "Get in and put the lid on. Then have somebody kick it down the stairs.

"Sometimes it's so bad you have trouble hanging on to your teeth. If you like misery it's a good deal, but you're betting your flying pay you won't live to collect your retirement pay."

Gunners' stories, some as much legend as fact, helped explain why talk about riding in the tail usually brought a grimace or just a shake of the head from the ground maintenance troops like Sam. His title said assistant crew chief, but in reality he was not much more than a glorified service station attendant. Pump gas, wipe down leaks, inspect for obvious discrepancies, clean the cockpit and wash the windows. Not very satisfying on a day-to-day basis and Sam figured it was time to move on and become a gunner.

"As a start it's more money and probably a better shot at promotion," he thought. "It's got to be better than working weird shifts and fixing airplanes outside in the damn weather. If nothing else it's going to get me in a lot more poker games."

Sam learned poker from a master. As a young GI he played with the best distraction and creator of smoke screens he'd ever seen. Staff Sergeant Dana D. Robinson put on the darndest show imaginable. It took months before Sam figured out Dana D wasn't the dumbest Missouri country boy in existence. He could play twelve hours straight with nothing but a bathroom break and appeared to get stupider by the minute. But he could talk. God, he talked about everything under the sun. All in country boy homilies intermixed with awesomely classic foul language. He had twenty sex stories about his Daddy's mule alone. When he wasn't storytelling he was bitching about how he was losing his butt.

Dana appeared to have phenomenal luck and when he won it seemed to be with cards that weren't worth the ante. It got to the point people were afraid to go against him for fear he'd get a lock on the last card. Yet he was tolerated and in fact liked. So convincing was he about his continued losses, everyone considered him a big donor.

Sam's first clue came on a night when Dana was bitching about losing his usual amount and the game had to stop because nobody had any money. Even by trying to borrow from each other the other players couldn't raise any cash. "Where has the money gone?" Sam thought. "Nobody has left the table and there haven't been any holdups." After that Sam watched the country boy closely. He did crazy things like raise and fold. But Sam noticed his dumb moves usually came early in the hand where they didn't cost much. Many times Dana said, "I'm going to play without looking at my hole cards," then took a peek if the competition looked tough. When he bragged about his great high hand that usually meant he held baby cards. This fish was a shark. He made wages by diverting attention and keeping people's mind off the game.

Sam learned well, but good games were hard to come by and he didn't like taking money from the young troops he worked with. Too many of them were struggling already. This would change if he became a gunner. Gunners spent up to seven days at a stretch living on base with their crew and there was a game every night. Better yet, a lot of it was officer money. All he had to do was break the code on how to get on flying status as a tail gunner. But the application process began to look like a dead end. When Sam first applied for cross training a prissy NCO in military personnel told him to forget it.

"Only fire control technicians qualify and your career field is frozen which means nobody can transfer out of it. Unless you're married to some general's ugly daughter, you don't have much of a prayer. I'd say you better forget it."

"Okay, sarge. I understand you said no. Who can say yes?"

"You can try my major."

The humorless major spoke through scarred lips. "Airman!" he said. "Regulations are regulations. I'm tired of you three-stripers who think they can merrily waltz through the rules just because you think your case is special. You need to go back to the job you were assigned. If I see you again I'm going to be very unhappy."

As a last resort Sam visited the wing gunner who told him to disregard what the major said. "Go ahead and get a set up for a flight physical (class A), I'll make a phone call."

It's been said that chief master sergeants run the Air Force, and the wing gunner, Chief Master Sergeant Robert Bell, believed it. He picked up the black phone on his desk and told the base operator he would like SAC headquarters on a priority. He then told the SAC operator to dial extension 5335, the number of Chief Master Sergeant William (Billy) Bass, the Strategic Air Command gunner.

"Hey, chief," he said. "If I'm not calling in the middle of your afternoon nap, I need a favor."

"I guess if it's important enough for you to take your head out of your Superman comics, I better see what I can do," said Chief Bass. "Is this going to involve nefarious action on my part?"

"Nah, I'm just trying to get a kid into gunnery school and our sterling personnel office won't let him apply because he doesn't meet the prerequisites and his career field is frozen."

"Tell him to request a waiver."

"He tried that, but some major in tight drawers won't let it get off base. I thought about going to the wing king and decided that since you approve these things anyway, maybe you could use your magic. This is a good young three-striper. I've looked at his records and they say's he's sharp. He's not in avionics but he's got good AQE (Airman Qualification Exam) scores in electronics. You know we are going to be a couple people short up here…"

"I'll tell you up front that if your boy isn't a spark-chaser he's going to have a hard time getting through school. But if that's what you want, how about I just get the headquarters' Strategic Air Command director of operations (a two-star general) to send a message saying a request for waiver is approved. Then let your personnel toads figure out how that happened. Give me his name and number and I'll see if I can't work it in before my next nap."

The Gunners' Union worked fast. The next afternoon the prissy NCO phoned Sam about re-doing his application. When they finished the paperwork the sergeant said, "My major wants to see you before you leave."

In his office later that day, the major told Sam, "I don't know what you did or who you know, but assuming you pass the physical and get a clearance you've got your school slot. But let me tell you something about the personnel system. When you flunk out you don't automatically go back to your old job. You become my asset for reassignment and you can bet your next ten paychecks I'll remember your name. Just for the record you are going to have serious trouble with your lack of electronics background. I know of several people who didn't make it through survival school. So you might try to figure out what you know about Roads and Grounds."

This didn't bother Sam. Despite his casual manner he took a careful, analytical approach to things. He believed actions had reactions and that good things didn't happen through luck alone. You had to work for them. And he was prepared to do whatever it took to get through the required training.

Fifteen days later a clerk in his orderly room handed Sam orders putting him on flying status and transferring him to the 77th Bomb Squadron. His paperwork for a Top Secret Clearance granting him access to targeting information in the SIOP (Single Integrated Operations Plan) cleared and he prepared to attend the three schools that would make him a gunner.

Sam's wife Cathy, like her mother, always wanted things to be neat and clean and predictable. This was not always Sam's style.

He was more ambitious and pushed for advancement while she was comfortable with life in general and was happy being a stay-at-home housewife and mother. Even with their differences Sam adored her. He admired her beauty and the figure she kept in spite of being the mother of their two boys. They had known each other since they started ninth grade together, in a new, consolidated high school made up of students from several small, almost rural, county schools north of Minneapolis. Sam had had a car and this was what started their relationship. They'd gone intensely steady for most of their high school years.

Not that they didn't break up a few times. Once Cathy went to the junior prom with someone else, leaving Sam listening to Marty Robbins singing "White Carnation and a Pink Rose."

It was now March 1962, and Sam and Cathy were sitting in the living room of their small but nicely decorated two-bedroom house in Rapid City, about ten miles south of Ellsworth. Cathy as usual did not have a hair out of place while Sam's blond hair appeared to have been stirred with a rake. But Cathy was frowning. "I'm not sure I like the idea of you being a gunner," she said. "I've heard things about them and all the time they spend on alert. My idea of a husband is someone who comes home at night."

"I know it's going to be tough, but in the long run we'll be better off," Sam replied. "This will give us more money and provide some stability. More importantly, I won't have to worry about getting sent overseas. Gunners rarely go anywhere and then it's only for a few days. You know how many short tours maintenance people pull. As a gunner the odds of this happening are zilch. I can promise you going to school will be my last long TDY (Temporary Duty). That's one of the reasons I need to do this. The other is, I want to start going to school nights, and being a mechanic there's no way. If it makes you feel better, you can keep our entire check while I'm gone. I can live on my flying pay and per-diem."

"If you don't lose it all in a poker game," said Cathy, shaking her head.

Poker was something Cathy didn't understand. Sam could win at ten games in a row and make over three hundred dollars. However, if he lost eight bucks once, Cathy would say: "We could have used the money."

Sam's first stop was Stead Air Force Base in the foothills of the Sierra Nevada. Ideally located for both desert and mountain training, it housed the USAF Survival School, which was a mandatory requirement for all SAC crewmembers.

The ten-day escape and evasion exercise left Sam hungry enough to consider chewing the bark off trees. But except for the complete lack of mosquitoes it reminded him of camping trips he went on as a kid in Minnesota. Of course then he didn't have to avoid "enemy soldiers" or hide from searching helicopters.

The prison camp was another story. The sadistic Americans playing enemy guards allowed them to cut meat, chop carrots and peel enough potatoes to make a twenty-five gallon pot of stew. Cooked over a wood fire the overpowering aroma tantalized the so-called prisoners for several hours. Finally they lined up, carrying their canteen cups, and the first person in line was fed. Then the bastards kicked the pot over.

During three weeks in Kansas[3] Sam studied the guns and practiced tearing them down, something he would never do again in his career. Then Sam and his six classmates shot at targets individually with the fifty-caliber machine guns and the Vulcan Cannon[4] until each made a confirmed kill. This earned them a poorly copied certificate that proclaimed:

YOUR LUCKY HIT HAS MADE YOU
A CERTIFIED DEAD EYE

As advertised, the ground school portion of the Combat Crew Training School (CCTS), at Castle Air Force in California, turned out to be a real bitch. Tested on fire control electronics at the end of the first week, Sam received his grade and it was not good.

"I must have put in twenty-five solid hours of hard study only to get a high F," he thought. "That's scary."

At the end of the second week Sam was scheduled to see the course supervisor for counseling. This concerned him because he could see he was holding bad cards. His second test hadn't gone any better than the first and he started to feel he was in the wrong game. But he couldn't fold. There was no way he was going back to face that scar-faced major in personnel.

Nothing in ground school replicated what Sam knew from working on B-52's. He had trouble understanding why a gunner needed to know so much about electronic theory. He wasn't going to repair the system, just operate it. But he knew he wouldn't help his case if he complained about what the school covered. The best Sam could probably hope for would involve an ass-chewing and some sort of probation. For an expected ass-chewing the counseling session was surprisingly gentle.

"I've been looking at your test scores and I can see you're having a little problem with the electronics," said the pleasant master sergeant who sat casually behind a desk with his feet up on a side table. "Passing is seventy and you've got a sixty-seven and a sixty eight. It seems to me that both of these could be rounded off to the next zero. That puts you back in the green and I don't expect you to have any difficulty with the rest of the academics. The last two blocks are aircraft systems and as a former B-52 grease monkey there's no excuse if you don't ace them. If you bust out it's going to be in the flying phase. That's where the rubber meets the road."

Sam earned a pair of ninety-eights on the last two written exams. Now if somebody wanted to average his scores they could do it with a straight face. He hadn't paid too much attention to the instructors when they talked about gunners getting hurt or killed in the tail. To him that was kind of like hearing about highway accidents—they always happened to other people, not to him.

Simulators were next and learning the switches to operate the MD-9 fire control system boggled him for a while.[5]

Everything came together in the MD-1A gunnery simulator.

Azimuth and elevation limits made sense and Sam could see how you changed from one target to another. Shooting at dull blips on a gray background took eye-to-hand coordination and practice, but Sam got it down. He felt good about his new skill.

During the flying phase his flight instructor carefully walked him through all the steps in preflight of the tail. He finished with a short briefing.

"I'll be up front the whole time. You know your stuff, you've got nothing to worry about. Just remember what I told you about oxygen. You don't have anybody back there to watch out for you. Good luck, I'll buy you a beer when we get on the ground."

After an uneventful first flight, Sam's instructor told him, "It's minor, but some of your interphone calls were a little shaky and you were late in clearing three turns. No big deal, you'll get used to monitoring what they are about to do up front. You did all right. This is the last time I'm going to ride with you."

From there on the training concentrated on pilots and navigators. When the student pilots started practicing refueling behind the KC-135, Sam felt the effect of their erratic movement of the control columns.

Several times the airplane pitched up enough to make him queasy and Sam felt the hard slam he had been warned to expect. Student landings were the worst. For the last two hours of every flight a pair of lieutenants would take turns seeing who could smack the bomber into the ground the hardest. The first couple of times this hurt, but then he learned to lift up in the seat and take the shock with his legs. After six flights Sam was comfortable riding alone in the back of the large bomber although he would never get totally used to the lingering odor of burnt oil in the tail.

On flight seven Sam's bomber, flying a desert low-level route, climbed to clear a ridge and hit clear air turbulence. Debris filled the tail compartment and he violently bounced between both sides of the compartment. His flashlight whacked him in the mouth because he didn't want to release his grip on the handholds to put his oxygen mask on. His shoulders burnt from the harness digging into them and he felt like he was being shaken apart. It was over in ninety seconds or less and he heard the pilot on the radio say, "Reno 31 just experienced moderate turbulence coming out of low level."

"If that was moderate, I wonder what the hell severe would be," thought Sam.

Sam's last flight at Castle was a crew solo without instructors aboard. This graduated the student crewmembers and they made a big deal of it. Sam left the solo celebration thinking, "This must be an officer thing—I was solo from day one."

After graduation Sam put his fatigues away and began wearing a zippered flight suit. He didn't know why, but when he was on base people seem to show him more respect. He wondered whether that came from being on a B-52 crew or just because no one could tell his rank at a glance.

Now Sam's life was a lot different from when he worked unpredictable shifts and fixed airplanes. His flying and alert schedules were put together quarterly and it was possible to plan things around them. He usually flew three or four times a month, broken up by alert tours that ranged from three to seven days. It was not unusual for Sam to have twelve to fifteen days off every month.

When he was on the alert pad Sam continued to hone his poker skills. The game was seven-card high-low with two winners. Six cards dealt, two down—four up. Five players remained in the pot.

Sam didn't have squat so he bet and re-raised when he was raised. This ran two players out, leaving three. His Jack and a Queen in the hole couldn't beat the pair of Kings shown across the table if he could name his seventh card. This turned out to be a King that didn't change his front porch of three low cards and a ten. He rubbed his temples and thought about his cards. "I'm obviously a low player, just not very low with these hole cards. If I'm going to get any part of this pot I need position."

As the last raiser he declared first and called "Low," correctly expecting the Kings to go the other way. Sam's aggressive last bet bluffed the winning low hand into declaring "High." He got the back door win and half of the eighteen-dollar pot.

Two days after coming off this alert tour Sam was scheduled for a low-level night training mission against an arms plant just north of the Twin Cities. It routed him almost directly over the house where he grew up. He was trying to locate it in the dark when the "sidesteps" started. This violent climbing maneuver, which was designed to evade missiles, required rapid sixty-degree banks to the left and then to the right. Every time they hit the top of the loop Sam puked. There was nothing to throw up in except a helmet bag with a headset, checklist and flashlight in it. Spilled barf down the front of his flight suit produced an occupational challenge his high school friends would not understand. *They need to meet Jim Siedenburg who swears he got sick in the tail so often he could start an air sickness bag, fill it, tie it off and start another without spilling a drop.*

Sam remembered being in high school when a B-52 crashed near his home, killing all six crewmembers. After his uncomfortable puking experience he thought about that incident again. "Could the crew that crashed have been using the same arms plant as a practice target?" he thought. "Did they lose control attempting the 'sidestep' exercise we did tonight? Nobody ever talks about it, but I wonder how safe it is to wrestle a big bomber around in the dark. I'd like to see the statistics, although thinking about it might scare the crap out of me."

Sam thought about how dependent he was on the five officers up front. It was easy to think that they had it good, being able to move around, but in reality they spent most of their time strapped into ejection seats in less than luxurious working space. The navigator and radar navigator rode side by side on the windowless lower deck and the electronic warfare officer sat in a dark cubicle in the rear of the upper compartment. Only the two pilots had windows.

Of course, having a good crew provided a sense of comfort, and in Sam's opinion he had one of the best. Aware that the tradition and rules relating to fraternization never really covered the situation of five officers and one enlisted man on the same crew, Sam tried to be careful to show proper respect even when off duty. He admired his officers and figured he'd lucked out when he drew Major Robert Harrington as his aircraft commander.

Gunners admired Major Harrington. To him the gunners were people, not second-class citizens. But his lack of seriousness kept the crew low on the wing commander's selection list for temporary promotion.[6] Sam felt it was worth the trade-off. Besides, even for the gunners who wore temporary tech or master stripes, nothing said they couldn't be a staff or tech sergeant tomorrow. All the wing king had to do was knock them down from select to lead.[7]

An anomaly that somehow slipped the stringent SAC selection process, Major Harrington damned sure didn't fit the image. If you put him in a room full of enlisted men and used an outsider to judge who was most likely to be an officer, he would come in dead last. Commissioned through the old OCS program, Major Harrington didn't have a day of college and by his own admission never completed a professional military course. Flippant, boisterous and consistently funny, he stirred up trouble for the hell of it.

Take what he did on a Headquarters SAC check ride. On such a ride an unsatisfactory rating could ground the crew and get the wing commander fired. The evaluator riding in the instructor-pilot's seat, centered aft of the two pilots seats, could be as subjective as he wanted to. Not surprisingly, these evaluators were treated as gods.

But not on this occasion. Halfway through the evaluation Major Harrington toggled his interphone switch and told the crew to "disregard oxygen discipline" after he looked back and saw the evaluator smoking with his mask hanging. At 41,000 feet this should have been an automatic bust. Somehow he got away with it.

A superb pilot, Major Harrington held the reputation as the wing's best in the intense job of refueling behind a KC-135. But he was better knows for his public disrespect for stupid rules. He laughingly growled at Strategic Air Command's insistence on the use of checklists for the most mundane tasks. "If you've got to use a checklist to take a crap you shouldn't be in the damn airplane," he would say.

During non-critical phases of flight he allowed the crew to chatter back and forth on interphone. When passengers were aboard he led the crew in singing the Air Force song, "Off we go into the wild blue yonder" on the steep post-target turns.

Major Harrington would arrange several treatments for the unsuspecting. An epileptic fit on the entrance ladder always went over well with extra passengers, as did the elaborate ritual of setting two alarm clocks just after take-off. After all, the crew needed to be awake for the bomb run.

Sam chuckled every time he thought about the complex skit Major Harrington prepared for the base dentist who was scheduled to fly a training mission with them. The entire briefing room was in on the plot. Wearing a parka to the briefing, Sam didn't take the gunner's chair in the row of six chairs behind the individual aircraft commanders. Instead he took the fourth seat which was normally reserved for the navigator. Major Harrington, with his rank covered by his parka, took the gunner's seat. Nothing odd about the parkas, it was cold enough outside that everyone on the crew wore one. But none of the members of Sam's crew were in their correct positions. The radar navigator, whose job was to establish timing and identify aim points for the bombs, did the pre-mission briefing as the aircraft commander, although his real crew position was on the lower deck alongside the navigator. Since the radar navigator was the oldest person on the crew there was no reason for the dentist to suspect he was not the aircraft commander. The electronic warfare officer looked young enough to pass for a new co-pilot and he did a commendable job of briefing for the co-pilot. At appropriate times staff officers would ask questions, and when the briefing was completed the lieutenant colonel who was the supervisor of flying elaborately signed the clearance paperwork.

Doctor Pemberton, the dentist, was absolutely certain this was the correct line up. He had no reason to think otherwise, not after going through a day of mission study with them. Enthusiastic although slightly anxious about his special indoctrination flight, he knew it would be worth the effort.

During the bus ride to the aircraft, Sam the "navigator" took the time to explain routes and targets. This charade continued through preflight. At the last minute a heated argument developed about who would make the take-off. It was decided to settle this with a series of coin flips. Darned if the electronic warfare officer— whose normal job was to monitor radios and jam enemy signals— and the gunner didn't win.

To Doctor Pemberton this was an obvious put on. At the last minute the real pilots would come forward. Not a question in his mind that the two individuals stumbling through the engine start checklist were the electronic warfare officer and the gunner. When nobody changed positions on taxi out he started to lose confidence. By the time the throttles were shoved forward for take-off they had his full attention. During the ninety-second take-off roll a discussion on exact rotation speed didn't help. By then the frightened dentist's gloved hands were biting into the small folding seat between the pilots. Probably a good thing he didn't have an ejection seat.

To calm him down, the real EW came forward at level-off with an iced pitcher that appeared to be martinis. When the tooth cracker

14

declined, Major Harrington removed the short parka covering his gold oak leafs and revealed the conspiracy. The martinis were only water and the correct people were flying the airplane. Overall, Doctor Pemberton was one suitably impressed and greatly relieved dentist.

Major Harrington accomplished one other small trick on the way home. The dentist, now comfortable with the way the crew accomplished the refueling and bomb run, accepted an offer to sit in the co-pilot's seat. He failed to notice the pilot nonchalantly cranking in so much nose down trim that it took all his strength to hold pressure on the column. After the dentist put both hands on the controls Major Harrington said, "You got it," and released the stick.

The column snapped out of his hands and the airplane nosed steeply over. Sam knew it was coming and it still happened so fast it startled him. "I guess it's a lot more exciting than a root canal when you don't expect it," he thought.

Sam was enjoying his crew and the time off between alert tours, but towards the end of 1964 he began to develop a vague awareness of the conflict in Vietnam. He didn't think it was something that would affect him. Vietnam was too far away and he couldn't see how Strategic Air Command could get involved without taking bombers off alert. In his opinion, that was just not going to happen as long as the Cold War continued.

Unknown to Sam, decisions were being made that would affect the lives and futures of a unique group of men who never numbered over one thousand at any given time. They have largely been ignored when histories of the Vietnam War were written. B-52 tail gunners defended their country with extraordinary dedication and bravery during this long historic period. This was something these ordinary men, many of whom were husbands and fathers and were well into their Air Force careers, never expected or in most cases sought.

Sam would become one of these men, although he didn't know it yet. He was just glad his unit wouldn't be part of the B-52 deployment to Guam. He had recently started a night school course in marketing at Black Hills State College and a long TDY would mess this up. Sam didn't think the war could last long anyway. He thought that just the threat of the two B-52 wings would be enough to bring the Viet Cong to the peace table.

Chapter Two

B-52 crews generally follow the tone set by the aircraft commander. Depending on the luck of the draw some are not much fun to fly with. Gunners unlucky enough to get stuck with a difficult set of officers can expect varying degrees of misery. Short of removing himself from flying status, a gunner doesn't have much say about when he flies or whom he flies with. As much as a gunner might want to, he can't just say, " I don't want to ride with these jerks."

Awakened at four a.m. and told he needed to fill for a gunner on emergency leave, Technical Sergeant Melvin Cunningham splashed his face with water, pulled on a flight suit and left for the base without bothering to shave. He was a great teddy bear of a man with a crop of thick black hair. Approaching thirty-five, he had been in the Air Force for fourteen years and a gunner for over nine.

"Who the hell will notice whether I've shaved or not," he thought. "It's the middle of the damn night. Everybody will have a beard before we get done. God! I hate these Chrome Dome missions. There're just twenty-four hours of going nowhere. All we do is drone east until we reach the coast and turn north. Most of the time I can't even see Greenland or Baffin Island because of the clouds.

"Some of the guys rave about the Northern Lights illuminating the sky with streams of moving fireworks. I could care less, even if they're something normal people never ever get to see. Normal people can go home at five o'clock and have a beer. They damn sure don't have to fly around the tip of the Aleutian chain before they return home twenty-four hours and ten minutes after they took off. Before we land our replacement will have taken off. So what if our bomber is loaded with nuclear weapons."

Arriving at the squat white building situated under the control tower on Mather Air Force Base, California, Melvin walked into base ops and discovered nobody had pre-ordered food for him. Reasonably decent meals like bite-sized steak and fried chicken must be requested the night before. None of the officers had spared a thought for their substitute gunner. On the long and boring Chrome Dome mission food was a distraction and something to look forward to. Melvin wasn't pleased with the four frozen TV-style dinners and the box of crackers he received from the in-flight kitchen.

"TV dinners are a pain in the ass," he thought. With no oven in the tail, the only way he could cook meant holding an electric frying pan in his lap. That became real fun if there was a little turbulence.

Take-off roll occurred at precisely eight a.m. At eight-fifteen Melvin discovered that a failed relay had cut off all electrical power to the tail. He tried resetting circuit breakers and when this failed he got the book out, looking for something he'd missed. Nothing worked. His interphone received power from another source, so at least he could talk to the crew. Nothing else was receiving current, including his cabin lights and radar. This meant he could not use his radarscope to check on the airplane behind him. The only way he could station keep was to reposition his seat, loosen his parachute straps and raise himself up to look out the window to determine if the trailing bomber was in the correct position. He informed the pilot about his dilemma, but his AC was busy trying to determine why the tip gear wouldn't retract. He blew Melvin off with a "Roger, gunner."

Surveying the situation Melvin decided he wasn't in bad shape for now. It was daylight so he didn't need the lights and there was some heat coming from the air conditioning system. He wished he hadn't set it on low, to cool the green house, before take-off. It was going to stay in that position because the modulating valve for controlling the temperature needed electricity to operate.

Melvin would be okay as long as there was plenty of sun coming in the windows. If he had to he could put on some of the heavy clothing he carried in his B-4 bag. The first refueling would be off the coast of Newfoundland and it would still be daylight. The pilot could descend and bring him forward then.

Melvin's substitute aircraft commander seemed totally unconcerned about his plight. When the time came he denied Melvin's request to come forward. "This requires a partial descent and I'm concerned about the extra fuel we're using with the tip gear dragging," he said. "I don't want to drop to 10,000 feet and burn extra gas to climb back up. If it gets worse back there, I'll think about it at the next tanker."

The second refueling, appropriately named "Cold Coffee," was eight hours away. As the sun began to set, it started to get very cold in the small compartment, which was no longer receiving warmth from the windows above it. Even in a parka Melvin shivered. He struggled in the dark to put on long underwear under his flight suit. "This is tougher than trying to fuck in the back seat of a Volkswagen," he thought as he thrashed around in the small compartment.

Hungry and unable to cook without electricity, Melvin remembered the crackers in his food box. Using his flashlight he located the saltines and ate several handfuls before he realized they made him thirsty. Removing the water jug that was stowed near his right shoulder, he tried to pour from it only to discover the water was frozen.

"Shit," he thought, "It's a long way to the next tanker...I'm not sure how much longer before my ass freezes solid like the goddamn water."

The few times Melvin called forward he received essentially the same answer from the co-pilot: "I don't want to wake the boss, he's sleeping on the upper deck."

As he shivered, Melvin shifted around in his seat, attempting to get more comfortable. Using both hands he moved the helmet around on his head even though he knew it wouldn't do much good. "It's always this way on long flights," he thought as he studied the thick frost accumulating on the metal sides of his compartment. "The weight of my brain bucket increases in direct proportion to the length of the mission." There wasn't much he could do except ride it out. He just wished those assholes up front…

At the second refueling the Zeroes up front remained hesitant to descend because of fuel and the weather below them.[8] Melvin explained his seventeen-hour predicament, of no electricity in the tail, using some rather precise language, and the pilot relented. Following a bouncy, almost violent refueling, the bomber descended into a black, nasty-looking towering cloud. Deathly cold, Melvin removed his straps, folded his seat down and waited at the hatch between his pressurized compartment and the 47-section, the large section that contained hydraulic packs, chaff dispensers and electronic components for the gunner's fire control system. He had to wait until the navigator started the timing required when a gunner went forward on a nuclear-loaded bomber.

What he was about to do was a technical violation of the SAC two-man policy, according to which no lone individual was allowed in the vicinity of a nuclear weapon without a partner with equal knowledge of the task being performed. The workaround required the navigator to monitor the situation through a little window in the forward hatch. The book said the gunner should come within sight within five minutes.

When he got the go-ahead, the gunner was supposed to duck under the so-called gunner killer (actually a chaff rack) in the 47-section and proceed down a narrow crawlway to the forward compartment. This was not easy under any circumstances, and was extremely difficult and dangerous to accomplish at altitude. Any altitude above 10,000 feet required the gunner to wear an oxygen mask and carry a portable bottle that depending on how fast he breathed might carry a five-minute supply of oxygen.

Melvin was highly motivated and had his own way of accomplishing the task. Determined to run through the dark fuselage of the bouncing airplane, he scrambled onto the closed bomb bay doors, skipping the crawlway altogether. Passing between the bombs, he used the nose of one of the two nuclear weapons they carried to swing onto the alternator deck. Only later would he think about the small latches that held the doors closed. He didn't have a parachute available during his crawl, not that it would have mattered. They were over the ocean north of Alaska.

He made it in to the front in two minutes. When the navigator opened the hatch, Melvin was almost overwhelmed by the marvelous warmth and the aroma of pot roast cooking.

Careful not to sound like a beggar, Melvin described his inability to cook in the tail or bring any food forward with him. When the EW took the hot dinner out of the oven, Melvin mentioned how great it smelled. "Sorry, it's my last one," said the bored captain.

Finally back on the ground, twenty-four hours and ten minutes after they took off, a sore and very hungry Melvin wanted nothing more than to sack out, but he had other things to deal with. He bolted down two orders of greasy ham and eggs in the base ops cafeteria and went home to get cleaned up before he reported to his squadron commander. He guessed what that would be all about. Mary Ellen, his about to be ex-wife number three, had probably been making up her stories again.

Melvin's problem was that he was attractive to women. Although he wore a perpetual expression of innocence that seemed to say, "I couldn't have done all that," he could have and probably did—at least once. His captivating boyish charm and roguish smile caused single women to forget their virtue and married ones their vows. This had been hard on his wives, although Mary Ellen was hardly innocent herself.

Mary Ellen wasn't going quietly. California was a community property state and with no kids involved this should have meant, just split the stuff down the middle and say, "It's been fun."

But her lawyer Siemans was a work of art. He skipped the part about her running around and convinced the judge that Melvin single-handedly ran up thousands of dollars in debt he should be required to pay. They even fought over the Tupperware. It turned out that two bowls were missing and Melvin agreed to replace them rather than put up with more crap. He felt lucky to get the clothes she hadn't thrown out and was pretty sure that if the government didn't own his flight gear, Mary Ellen would have claimed half of that.

His still not official ex-wife skipped all the nuances in her vicious pursuit to nail him. She went directly to the top and was almost on a first name basis with Melvin's commander. Her regular phone calls to the dour lieutenant colonel always started the same way, "I don't want to get Mel in trouble, but..."

Melvin's bomb squadron held more than a hundred officers and twenty-eight enlisted men. He figured, probably correctly, he was on the top of his commander's shit list. There was not much the squadron gunner (the senior gunner) could do to run interference since anytime a gunner got in trouble an unwritten rule required his aircraft commander to be involved. The four times he had been in front of the commander, Melvin's AC, Captain Hawley, hadn't supported him a lick.

Captain Hawley didn't like being in the commander's office any more than Melvin. Moreover, he remained pissed about a squabble he had had with Melvin over drawing maps for stateside training missions. Every training sortie required the pilot to have two maps, one low level and one high altitude. The low-level map, with its precise turn points and narrow bombing corridors, was prepared by the navigators, but some gunner, probably out of the boredom of fifteen days a month on ground standby, started drawing altitude maps for his pilots. This practice spread until maybe 50 percent of the gunners voluntarily drew maps.

To Melvin it seemed reasonable that the pilot drew his own high-altitude maps. He was the one who used them and he was also the person with ultimate responsibility for the safety of the airplane and crew. Although drawn to a different scale than those used for low-level bombing, errors could still be fatal and in Melvin's eyes this was clearly an aircraft commander's responsibility.

Melvin resisted until Captain Hawley bluntly ordered him to start drawing pilot's maps. His first effort was drawn in dull grease pencil and was extraordinarily sloppy with some of the turn points twenty miles off. This led to some words between them, so the next map was detailed and precise, but drawn entirely in red pencil that was unreadable under subdued cockpit lighting. His aircraft commander never asked Melvin to draw another map, but clearly held a grudge.

Now Melvin was standing in the commander's sparse office as Captain Hawley and the commander discussed Mary Ellen's statement about an alleged shoving incident between her and Melvin. It included a place, date and time that lined up with the middle of an alert tour Melvin had pulled. Anyway you looked at it the alert pad was a controlled twenty-four-hour-a-day environment and access badges were checked on entry and exit.

Melvin listened as Captain Hawley worked up a tortured explanation for the colonel about how Melvin had managed to get downtown. It sounded remotely plausible. Melvin could sneak out of the facility in his flight suit, get to his car, leave the base by passing through the main gate and drive fourteen miles to Mary Ellen's apartment in downtown Modesto. He could shove her in front of no witness and return without anyone noticing his absence.

The frustrated commander could see this was a stretch. As much as he wanted to, he knew he didn't have a strong enough legal case to hang Melvin for this incident.

"I've had it with trying to referee this damn divorce," he growled at Melvin. "You either shut this battle down or I'm going to take a stripe. If I don't have grounds, I'll make up grounds."

Other than an occasional friendly bar fight, Melvin considered himself easy going, but his experience with Captain Hawley totally soured him on officers. "I can't put up with the demeaning crap some of them deliver," he thought. "If anybody wonders why I hate officers they just have to look at my miserable experience with those commissioned assholes."

Only four days later things changed for Melvin because of the Gulf of Tonkin incident in August 1964. The Southeast Asian war started to receive attention from the American public and President Lyndon B. Johnson began steps to substantially expand the effort. This would bring the B-52's into the conflict in June 1965. To this point Strategic Air Command involvement was limited to tanker and reconnaissance support. SAC leadership endorsed the decision to use bombers from their nuclear deterrent force to bring a rapid end to the hostilities.

Melvin was relieved when he heard he was to be deployed to Guam. It came at an ideal time. "If nothing else it's going to make it harder for Mary Ellen to stay on my ass," he thought. "Maybe it'll give the goddamn commander something to do besides gnawing on my butt."

Living downtown made it easy for Staff Sergeant Jim Steadman, a gunner in the same squadron as Melvin, to hang around with his civilian friends and forget the Air Force for a while. People knew Jim as the guy who lived down the street. Like everyone else he washed his car, mowed the lawn and enjoyed going to picnics. Neighbors from his street would get together and talk about their families and sometimes they would pile kids, dogs, sandwiches and coolers of soda into Jim's old Dodge pick-up and go riding around in the deltas surrounding Sacramento.

Jim considered himself an ordinary guy, but of course how ordinary can you be when you fly in the tail of a B-52? Clearly this was not a normal eight-to-five job. Like most B-52 gunners, Jim spent twelve to fifteen days a month residing on base with his crew. His neighbors knew he was gone a lot, but didn't know he regularly lived in an austere partially buried concrete block building located close to the end of a runway. The close proximity to his aircraft allowed his crew to start engines, pull chocks and become airborne within fifteen minutes.

All it took was the proper Emergency War Order codes to become an active participant in World War III. Jim didn't talk about this or the nuclear weapons in the bomb bay. This wasn't exactly something his neighbor who worked for Pepsi-Cola would understand, nor would he understand flying alone in the noisy, dirty and often bumpy tail. His neighbor wouldn't be aware of the risks either. Without a control column or throttles there was not much a gunner could do if the officers up front made a mistake. And a hell of a lot of things could go wrong with the airplane, but as a general rule Jim trusted and respected every crew he'd flown with.

Jim and his wife Elizabeth were looking forward to moving to Turner AFB Georgia when rumors about the deployment to Guam began to circulate. Both of them thought Albany, Georgia, would be a lot better than California. It would get them closer to where they were raised, and their twin girls' grandparents still lived in

Everett Springs, a little town on the southern edge of the Blue Ridge mountains. The girls would be teenagers in a few years. They were good kids, but didn't need to be in California where there was just too much of everything.

Jim was expected it when his orders to Georgia were cancelled. He could count just as well as the wing commander and since his replacement hadn't arrived, without Jim this would put the wing one gunner short when they deployed to support the war in Vietnam. Jim accepted the change without question. He was aware that Vietnam was heating up and he felt an obligation to the oath he took when he entered the service.

"If the military wants me to do it, I'll salute smartly and get it done," he thought. That was how Jim had been raised from childhood. Going back to before the Civil War, most of the males in his family had served in the military on one side or the other. His father and all four uncles volunteered for World War II right after Pearl Harbor. His older brother David earned a Purple Heart and a Bronze Star in Korea.

Although he would never use the word, it was patriotism that had motivated Jim to enlist right out of high school. He considered serving his country the right thing to do and planned to make the military a career. It beat anything available in Everett Springs. Another factor was that his father often expressed regret about getting out of the Army. "If I'd stayed in after the war ended, we'd have been a lot better off and I could be drawing a retirement check now," he would say. "You can't get anywhere cutting logs."

Married at eighteen and a father at nineteen, Jim had eleven years in the Air Force, although he was not quite thirty. At five feet ten inches and 190 pounds he was solid, not fat, and he worked on his fitness with fifty push-ups every morning. A marine would call his frequently barbered light brown crew cut "high and tight" and his round face prompted Elizabeth to call him Charlie Brown, a name she had used for him since seventh grade.

"I can handle this standing on my head," Jim replied when Elizabeth asked if he worried about flying combat for the first time. "This is what I signed up for. I'm not going to like being away for six months, but we've had it good for a long time. When you are in the military you don't pick what you want to do. I'm not going to burn my bra just because they want me to go to war."

"You ain't got a bra, Charlie Brown," smiled Elizabeth, "but I understand and we'll be fine while you're gone. I knew that when you came in the Air Force that there would be some times when you might have to go away. Your job has been good for a long time and we can put up with a little separation."

ANDERSON AIR FORCE BASE, GUAM, 1965

"So much for keeping gunners from the same wing together," Jim thought as Melvin introduced their new roommate, Staff Sergeant Cal McGraw. At six feet and 135 pounds, Cal provided a striking contrast to the six-foot-one-inch Melvin who easily weighed 215 pounds. Cal was thirty-one, but looked older. He wore an olive drab cotton flight suit, the kind issued before Nomex became the standard. Normally these were baggy at best, but on Cal the "small long" suit fit his frame like a zippered laundry bag. His flying boots, while technically black enough to comply with Air Force regulations looked like they had been worked over with a Hershey bar and shellacked. His white neck scarf, while not exactly dirty, was not exactly white either.

Once established in the room Cal kept to himself and didn't enter many of the bull sessions that were common. After he had know Cal for a while Melvin would joke, "He's so quiet, it's like talking to wallpaper."

Cal deployed from Carswell Air Force Base where he was somewhat notorious for an incident involving a pelican. The incident began as two Forth Worth police officers were sitting in their almost new 1965 Ford police special patrol and the dispatcher called.

"Check on the pelican creating a disturbance in Stan's Bar and Grill at 1851 Camp Bowie Drive."

"Say again!"

When they arrived the lawmen found one very pissed off pelican hissing and flapping its wings at anyone who tried to approach it. The floor was littered with broken liquor bottles the pelican had knocked off the back bar during one of its tantrums, and several patrons appeared to be injured.

"That thing must have diarrhea," Cal said to the taller of the two policemen. "I'm amazed that much shit could come out of one bird." He did not volunteer the information that he was the one who had brought the exotic bird into the bar in the first place.

After some discussion about where the formerly white pelican came from and how it got in the bar, the larger of the two cops told Cal, "Sit down and shut your face."

Twice refusing assistance, the two policemen loaded the befouled fowl into the cage in the back of their almost new vehicle.

Cal wasn't arrested and the disturbance probably wouldn't have gotten to his commander without the small article in the Fort Worth *Star Journal*. Probably the thing that saved him was the scramble to put together full up crews for the upcoming deployment.

AIR FORCE SERGEANT BAFFLED BY BIRD

"Staff Sergeant Cal McGraw, a member of the 7th Bomb Wing at Carswell, was unable to explain where he found the pelican he apparently brought to a Fort Worth bar last Tuesday night. A pelican is a large web-footed bird normally only found in warm tropical regions. According to records, no pelican has ever been sighted this far north of the gulf. When asked why he did not attempt to contact the appropriate agencies, the Air Force sergeant said, 'it's only a pelican'."

In the first two months Melvin was on Guam, the operation called Arc Light had not flown a single combat mission. Melvin considered the whole thing a giant goat rope. The entire base was in various degrees of chaos. There wasn't enough room in the shops for the maintenance people and plastic covered pallets of supplies were taking up space on the parking ramp.

Melvin had only flown four training missions. "Other than hanging around or going to an occasional training session there's not much to do except change our damn rooms," he said to Jim. "I know the room swaps were generated because of a decision to bust up the crews and house us enlisted gunners separately from the officers, but why couldn't the bright staff figure out a simpler way to do it?"

"It'll get better when we start flying missions. My theory says we go the night after next," said Jim. "Nothing's on the flying schedule for tomorrow and the pilots are going to briefings. Have you seen any navigators lately? My thought is they're off mission planning somewhere. Look how quiet it is around here. I haven't seen any maintenance people in the chow hall. I'll bet you money they're eating box lunches on the flight line in between loading bombs.

"All the signs are there and unless I miss my guess we are finally going to do what we came for. They will want to bomb at night, so if you work the time zones and look at a midnight drop, you could come up with a pretty good estimate as to what time take-off will be. The staff is just trying to keep it secret."

"What the hell for?" asked Melvin, "Don't gunners have clearances or do they just figure we're mushrooms like the old gag, 'keep us in the dark and feed us shit.' I don't much care. I'm ready to go, anything has got to beat this sitting around. Besides it'll build character for guys like you that have never been divorced and don't know anything about war." *I'll bet you Mary Ellen could kick their asses in a heartbeat.*

When they received orders for their first combat mission, the gunners, along with most of the officers on Guam, were relieved the boredom had finally ended. As a group they were eager to finally go. None of them felt any real sense of danger, and none suspected they would make the headlines.

RAPID CITY, SOUTH DAKOTA, JUNE 1965

Sam picked up the *Rapid City Journal* and looked at the headline: **B-52's COLLIDE ON FIRST MISSION.** He didn't know any of the gunners flying out of Guam and as he scanned the article he thought how normal his life at Ellsworth was. He was pulling alert, going to college at night and flying a few times a month. He had plenty of time to be a husband and father since he could do most of his studying while on alert. Once in a while he found a poker game, but that was no longer his priority. He was still generally oblivious to the Vietnam War, although reading about the B-52's flying out of Guam caused him to think how the situation might eventually affect him.

ANDERSON AIR FORCE BASE, GUAM

Melvin and Jim listened as a usually reticent Cal spoke with animation. "Didn't you hear the radios? Somebody was talking about changing lead and I think Red Two moved up. I don't know where the hell the original Red One went. Anyhow the next thing they were squawking about was timing and at some point I think the dumb-asses decided to lose time by making a 360-degree turn with a whole damn formation of fifteen airplanes. I was in Blue Two and was close enough to observe the fireball when they hit.

"One bomber went by us like a bat out of hell in the other direction and probably missed us by less than fifty feet. They must have run 'em head on. I mean holy shit, it's lucky I'm not a drinking man or I'd be on my second bottle of Jim Beam."

When he finished talking Cal quietly settled back in his normal place, a straight-backed chair next to the door of the room he shared with Jim, Melvin and three other gunners. He then picked up the beer he'd opened before he sat down and began to sip. His little speech about not being a drinking man didn't mean beer. "Beer isn't drinking," he would say, "it's just replacing fluids."

"This could have happened on a training mission," said Jim. "In the long run I don't think it's going to affect us any more than losing an airplane at home. It's always tough on family and friends and nobody knows that better than my wife Elizabeth. She's literally held several wives in her arms after they lost their man. She still prays for Mary Hull. She was with her when they told her her husband bailed out over Colorado. I'm sure you heard the story about how it took thirty-two days to locate his body. He made it to the ground, but froze to death. The others walked out.

"This is one of those things that happen with airplanes. Nobody can blame it on the war. Somebody just got the timing screwed up. I just hope nobody uses it as an excuse to back off. We need to be doing this."

Two days later Melvin watched Jim get ready for a flight that would turn out to be anything but normal. "In case you don't come back we need to split up your stuff before you go," said Melvin. "I want the short-wave radio."

Chapter Three

OVER THE PACIFIC OCEAN

The shutdown was normal, if shutting down an engine in flight was ever normal. A simple blink of a light theoretically indicated an over-temperature situation, in or around the number eight engine. This was not common, but with seven other engines on speed it was no problem. Over 70,000 pounds of thrust was still available. A touch of rudder instantly corrected a slight yaw as the pilot retarded the throttle to flight cut off. Pulling the T-handle on the top of the instrument panel ensured that fuel, hydraulic and electrical power was cut off to the dead engine. Extra rudder pressure was trimmed out with the large wheel between the pilot and co-pilot. It was no different than what they had practiced in the simulator and in truth the shut down did nothing the autopilot couldn't handle.

Response to the unexpected was something SAC B-52 crews continually practiced on peacetime training sorties. However, no matter how many times a simulated emergency was given by an evaluator, it was never the same as the real thing. The first page in the pilot's Emergency Procedures Flight Manual said, STOP-THINK-COLLECT YOUR WITS, and aircraft commanders were trained to keep their cool when things started to go badly wrong with the airplane. Sometimes overreaction could be as bad as underreaction and in almost every case, smooth crew coordination was vital. Short of structural breakup, fire was the emergency the crews feared the most.

With no moon to disturb the blackness of the unseen ocean below, Jim watched the dead engine for the faintest sign of fire. "Probably just a bad detector," he figured. "Any fire and I'd see it."

With no thought of turning back the pilot added just a touch of power to the remaining seven engines. It was three hours since they left the runway at Guam with over three tons of pounds of bombs aboard. Another hour and they would meet up with the tankers just taking off from Kadena Air force Base in an Okinawan rain shower. Jim wondered if his buddy Mike Smith was one of the boom operators. He envied Mike for his three-hour flights. His KC-135 would be back on the ground by the time Jim's bomber came off target.

"Of course except for the refueling Mike rides in a space with no windows," Jim thought. "No, tonight I'd rather be a gunner, Mike can't see the sky from where he sits. It's like a million specks of light sprayed on the blackest of backgrounds. The lack of pollution over this part of the Pacific must explain the brilliance."

Looking up, Jim could see nothing but stars and the single red light on the tail above him. Turning his head, he looked at the three stars in Orion's Belt. He regretted that Orion was the only constellation he knew by name and decided that some day he would learn more. He'd buy a star book and carry it on night flights.

Sitting upright with the full weight of the helmet pressing down on his neck, Jim knew his crewcut would sting before they landed at the end of the twelve-hour mission, and his head would be so wet that if he ran his hand across it salty water would drip down his forehead.

For a moment he thought it would be good to take his helmet off and just wear a headset, but he immediately decided against it. He had vowed never to do that—there were too many tales of cracked heads. He had never been bumped on a night like the present one, but the risk was too high. He didn't need all the scars on his head that he had on his helmet. Besides, if he didn't wear it he wouldn't have his oxygen mask hanging at the side of his face like the regulation called for. They were above 35,000 feet so he supposed he should have it on. "But between me and nobody, who's going to know?" he thought.

Looking down, Jim could see a sprinkling of lights from the Philippines. Since there were not many lights, he knew it had to be one of the outer islands. This meant tanker rendezvous was no more than twenty minutes away. He'd better start getting his junk stowed.

"Gunner, pilot. You awake?" asked Major Anseth, Jim's aircraft commander, in clipped tones acquired over years of commanding large aircraft.

"Roger, sir," said Jim.

"Take another look at the number four pod. I've got a faint glow in the number eight warning light. I think seven has blinked red a couple of times. It's out now, but take a good look. Put a light on it. I don't want a fire out there." Without a pause Major Anseth addressed his co-pilot: "Co-pilot, you fly the airplane, I want to tap the EGT (Exhaust Gas Temperature) gauge."

The pilot suspected something was happening with the dead engine. In the dark Jim saw nothing unusual so he took the Aldis lamp out of its holder and pointed it in the general area of the number four pod on his left side. Turning his head to avoid the effect of the thousand-candle power brightness from this big trouble light, he waited a minute before he looked at the illuminated area. Seventy feet away number seven and eight engines were clearly illuminated in the artificial daylight.

"Nothing, no...Hold it, number eight is shut down, there shouldn't be anything coming from it," he thought. It was faint, but he saw smoke or at least vapor. It was hard to tell exactly, but a stream of mist appeared to be coming from between the tailpipe and cowling.

Whatever was causing it must be somewhere between the engine and cowling. Fuel line? No, fuel was shut off, along with wiring and hydraulics. It had been an hour since number eight was shut down. There was not much to burn on a dead engine. Not after that long anyway. It had to be coming from number seven somehow, but how?

The explanation turned out to be a cracked fuel nozzle on number seven. It was spraying its burning fuel sideways onto the diffuser case instead of aft into the combustion chamber. First there was a pinhole of flame, hot enough to cut through the fire shield separating the two engines. It was so pinpointed it activated a fire detector on number eight, missing its own detector while burning a hole that trapped the heat and flames between the cowling and the sister engines as it worked its way up the strut.

Jim reported the smoke just as Major Anseth saw the fire warning light in the number seven T-handle above his head go steady. Engineers were clever when they put the warning light in the same fist-sized T-handle that was used to shut down the engine. There was no possibility of mistakes. Major Anseth was already pulling the emergency T-handle when he started talking.

"Gunner keep the light on those engines, let me know if you see any flame. Nav, wake the radar and get the EW up. I want everybody buckled in and on oxygen. Co-pilot, squawk emergency seven-seven-zero-zero on the transponder and be ready to get on the rudders with me…I want to keep the power up on one and two until we get out of formation…Gunner, flash your light at number three. If he gets under a half-mile, call me."

Everyone was awake now. Major Anseth was glad he was in the seat now, and not lying on the upper deck alongside the EW.[9] He didn't fully trust his young co-pilot, First Lieutenant Jack Parsons, with the airplane just yet.

"Gunner, flash your light at the aircraft behind us," said Major Anseth, "I don't want it in your turret." He was worried that the aircraft behind them in the three-ship cell might not immediately recognize he had pulled back power and slowed down. The last thing he wanted was a mid-air collision.

"Roger," replied Jim. "Be advised that I can see flame configurations coming from behind the strut. I'm not sure where they're coming from because all I can see is the inboard side."

Major Anseth knew he needed to put priority on getting out of the "one mile cell" formation. He thought the procedures called for taking power off the opposite engines, to stop the yaw, but that didn't make sense. They had one aircraft in front and thirteen behind them. Everybody was at the same altitude with one-mile separation. If he pulled back power his aircraft would get overrun in the dark.

It would be better to keep the remaining engines in military thrust so the airspeed stayed up. He thought he could handle the yaw. When the time came he would let off the rudder pressure and let asymmetrical thrust turn them out of the formation.

"Pilot, this is radar. I've contacted Charlie (wave leader) and told him our problem and that we would probably make a right turn out of cell. Ah, our position is 180 miles from Mactan Airport on the 273-degree radial. When you get a chance I have TACAN (Tactical Air Navigation Radio) frequencies. If you need it I'm standing by to salvo bombs. Do you want a Mayday call?"

"Negative, negative," replied Major Anseth, not daring to repeat the word Mayday. That was something he didn't want to think about yet. "Give me headings to open ocean though, ah...there's islands below us," he said, thinking of how pissed the Philippine government would be to receive thirty-five tons of live bombs. It was not like a nuke. There was no way to guarantee they were safe, not with impact fuses installed. But he knew he'd better consider getting rid of them before landing even if the fire went out.

Jim monitored the fire, occasionally observing a flicker of flame in the kneecap area where the strut merges with the wing. The co-pilot, with a better view, briefed Major Anseth. "Flames are running from the inside cowling and moving up the strut to the top of the wing."

As they left the formation, Jim felt the aircraft bank to the right and then level up. He listened as Major Anseth spoke on the interphone again.

"Co-pilot, let's start pulling back on one and two and see if we can get this beast trimmed up. Your throttles...now do it easy... that's it...now start taking the rudder out. EW, see if you can get me Guam on the HF. If not, get me Kadena, tell them our situation, tell them we are looking at Mactan as an alternate." Without pausing he continued, "Co-pilot, what control do we talk to for Mactan? Look it up...Gunner, what's happening with our engines?"

"This is gunner," said Jim identifying himself, just like he had been taught to do in an emergency to eliminate any possible confusion over who is speaking. "I've got a couple of pretty steady flame configurations coming back from both sides of the strut. It's hard to see from here, but I think I can see a glow above the wing."

"Roger, understand flame configurations, report any change," said Major Anseth, his mind racing. Their best bet would be to get permission to land on Philippine soil. He clicked his interphone switch.

"Radar. Pilot. Whose permission do I need to chug off these bombs? If I remember correctly, it will only be in authorized areas. One off the runway at Guam and the other thirty-some miles off the Vietnam coastline. There are probably no plans for an open ocean drop. Well that can wait, our problem will come on landing."

He did not utter the thought that came to him next: *That is, if we're going to land.*

The fire grew more intense and Jim watched flames streaming back along the underside of the wing. Intermittently he observed fire above the wing, yet he felt strangely secure in the tail. There was comfort in the familiarity of his compartment where he could reach out and touch its cold metal. The panel lights glowed without flickering and nothing around him suggested he could soon be in the water. It was hard to imagine that a little fire not much bigger than campfires he built as a boy could destroy the bulky B-52 that protectively held him safe from the elements.

Bailout would mean leaving the comfortable sixty-degree compartment. The outside air temperature would be forty degrees below, blasted by four hundred mile per hour winds, maybe less if Major Anseth slowed the bomber down, but Jim was not encouraged by the thought of leaving the airplane. Too many things could go wrong, especially at altitude. Unlike the officers up front, he had no ejection seat and his procedures for bailing out were downright thorny if there was any turbulence or the bomber went steeply nose down. He tried to remember the instructions he received in training. In training it all sounded so uncomplicated. Slide the seat forward and pull the yellow turret jettison handle.[10]

Next his checklist said pull the integrated release handle and release the parachute from the seat.[11] Then all he had to do was roll out of the opening left by the jettisoned turret, dragging the survival kit strapped on his butt with him. But it just didn't always work that way. That was why the Air Force installed rope "hand holds" throughout the tail compartment after they lost several gunners. That way the gunner could escape during something other than level flight. He still thought trying to fall up as opposed to down could be a problem.

Major Anseth worked frantically, trying to figure out which valves to close to stop the flow of JP-4 jet fuel into the number four pod. He thought that the fire probably started in number seven engine and somehow penetrated the titanium firewall. It must have bypassed the fire shut-off valves as it worked itself up the strut. The fuel had to be coming from somewhere and that was its most likely source. It also might be plumbing or the tank itself that was feeding the fire.

"Jack, shut off the cross feeds and let's see if we can transfer fuel away from the left outboard tank," Major Anseth said to his co-pilot who managed the fuel controls from his side of the cockpit.

Jim wondered how much aluminum was bubbling away in the structure. If there was magnesium in the strut, there was no way for that to go out once it got started. That stuff would burn under water…

Major Fraizer, the radar navigator, broke in on interphone: "Pilot, I couldn't raise the command post so I've got Looking Glass on the HF, whenever you can talk to them, over."

Looking Glass, Strategic Air Command's airborne command post, was orbiting over Harlan, Iowa. The controller spoke to the stricken aircraft over the Pacific with no more trouble than if he had been in another aircraft in the same formation.

"Understand Gull Two Four, your location is orbiting forty miles DME 290-degree radial Mactan Tacan…six souls…hot guns. Understand…fire on number seven and eight engine uncontained. You have aborted Red Two. If information correct request intentions, over."

Major Fraizer was on top of it again. He'd passed the correct info and even caught the call sign change from the formation call sign of Red Two to Gull Two Four when Red Three assumed their position in the formation.

"Ah, Sky King, Sky King," said Major Anseth, "Gull Two Four is looking at emergency landing at Mactan airport...break...break, we have full bomb load...request permission for open ocean jettison, over."

"Standby, Gull Two Four."

The airborne controller relayed the information to the general officer flying on the Looking Glass mission. Minutes passed while the officer talked to aircraft specialists in the Offutt underground command post. The final decision would be his.

"Gull Two Four, this is Sky King...break, break...negative jettison at this time...repeat, negative jettison, break, break...do not over fly Philippine land mass...break, break. If Gull Two Four can confirm structural break-up imminent further instructions possible, read back over."

"That's just beautiful," thought Major Anseth, feeling his anger rise, "Here I am with a burning airplane strapped to my ass. They want to know if it will break up. Hell, I don't know. If the fuel transfer doesn't put the fire out soon I wouldn't bet on how long we stay in the air. Right now with a full bomb load I can't fly over land to bail out my crew if I wanted to..."

Then turning to the co-pilot, he said, "Jack it's your airplane. I'm going to get on the radio."

"Sky King, Sky King, this is Gull Two Four. Be advised I am declaring a Mayday...I repeat, Mayday...be advised I am looking at dumping bomb load for the purpose of heading nearest land for possible bailout. Over."

With a flick of a switch, Major Anseth was on interphone. "Radar, get on UHF guard...declare a Mayday, talk to Air Rescue...give positions...goddamn it, Jack, stop fiddling with whatever you are doing and fly the friggin' airplane. They did teach you to hand fly, didn't they? Get the roll out and keep your wings level. You pay attention to the airplane, I'll talk on the radios."

With two outboard engines shut down the autopilot couldn't compensate fast enough and the pilots were hand flying the bomber. The tall tail on the D-model B-52 provided plenty of rudder to work with and Major Anseth wasn't concerned about the lack of control effectiveness. He was wondering how this beast would fly with the last forty feet of the wing burnt off.

Then calmly and with no trace of the fleeting anger of a minute ago, Major Anseth spoke. "Crew, this is the pilot. For your information be advised, I am planning to don a chute and water wings and am seriously considering waking the EW."

Jim chuckled. It was the sort of thing that might not be funny on the ground, but with a burning airplane it was absolutely the right thing for Major Anseth to say. It calmed the crew and took advantage of an inside joke about electronic warfare officers in general. Unless there was some sort of missile or fighter threat, there wasn't much for the EW to do in flight. Of course, the same thing could be said for gunners.

Major Anseth continued, "You all know our situation. Right now the machine is flying, but I'm not too sure how long it will stay that way. My intentions are to fly this heading for two more minutes… EW, you get a time…This should put us around a hundred miles from land. If the situation hasn't changed, I'll dump the bomb load, permission or no permission. Then we will try to make land and bail out. Right now I want everybody ready…it could be violent. Let's have a station check on Call.[12] Gunner."

"Roger sir, Gunner's cabin altitude 8,000 feet, oxygen panel checked, zero delay lanyard stowed."

In turn the others reported.

"EW, panel checked."

"Nav, panel checked."

"Radar, panel checked."

"Co-pilot's panel checked, cabin altitude 8,000 feet."

"Pilot's panel checked. Okay guys, that's the way I want you to go if necessary, "said Major Anseth as he leaned over the co-pilot to see what was happening with the fire. He strained, but all he could see was darkness. "Damn, maybe things are changing," he thought.

"Gunner, pilot, what do you see?" asked Major Anseth. "Both lights are out up here and—"

Jim cut in, " Pilot, I think you've just lost seven and eight."

"No shit," said Major Anseth, his temper flaring again. "I shut them down."

Jim's statement was going to take a little rewording if he was to get his point across. He began again, returning his pilot's anger.

"Damn it, pilot, that's not what I'm trying to tell you. I think number seven and eight engine have departed the aircraft. I saw something drop in a trail of sparks and now all you have out there is a stub where the nacelle was. I say again, if you are ready to copy, engine number seven and engine number eight have departed the aircraft."

"What?"

"Yeah, I saw what looked like the rear of both engines drooping and then they were gone. I can't see any fire, but there's a lot of fuel vapor streaming out."

"Come to think about it, I probably felt them go," said Major Anseth. "I thought it was just the co-pilot kicking the pedals around. I should have caught that the need for the big change in trim was not just because of the fuel transfer."

Becoming a tail gunner on a six-engine bomber reminded Jim that flying was more than looking out the window. It had some thrills and they weren't out of the woods yet. Fuel was streaming aft past the tail and there was a danger it could re-ignite.

After an uneasy fifteen minutes the left outboard tank completely drained and the leak stopped. Looking Glass was informed and they were directed to return to Guam. From what Jim could hear on the radio, the battle to dump the bombs was lost. This clearly stupid decision had to have been made by someone higher than their wing commander, back on Anderson.

Jim supposed the rationale was that the aircraft would be light on fuel which would put its landing weight within limits, even considering the bomb load. But he thought it was more likely they needed the bombs or the decision was made by a group of officers sitting in an air-conditioned room.

Jim knew the landing would hold his pilot's attention. Balancing up the airplane by moving fuel from the right outboard to the main body tanks wouldn't be a problem. There was plenty of room since they aborted the refueling. What couldn't be compensated for was a lack of a good go-around capability. At some point the combined forces of gravity and slow airspeed couldn't be rapidly overcome by the thrust of the remaining six engines. He worried there wasn't enough rudder to handle the asymmetrical thrust of full power on four engines on one side versus two engines on the other. This meant in practice that they had one shot. It would be more dangerous with their full bomb load.

The key to success would be airspeed and runway heading. Touch down in the first one-third of Anderson's 12,900-foot runway was critical since there was no way to try again without greatly increasing the risk. Best flare based on a combination of aircraft weight and temperature would be 137 knots. Major Anseth would shoot to be at best flare plus ten knots at twenty feet over the end of the runway. Even with a good airplane this was challenging, requiring extreme concentration and sensitive control and throttle movements.

The process of descending from 35,000 feet began seventy miles out. Three radios were set up, one to air traffic control, one to the command post, and because of the emergency, one on guard. The crew started running checklists to get the airplane ready to land. Last on the list would be gear and flaps, with the flaps coming down about two and one half miles out. During the approach and landing a lot of things had to go right, yet in spite of Jim's anxiety the prospects weren't that bleak. Even with the loss of one-fourth of the power and about eight tons of metal they still had a lot going for them.

When it needed to be, the B-52 was one tough airplane, especially the D-model, which even had back-up systems to back up systems. Other than engines, every system on the airplane was sound, including hydraulics, electronics and instruments. The airbrakes worked so they could slow down on approach and they had what they needed to stop safely including steering, brakes and a drag chute. Putting the broken bird back on Guam was mostly a matter of the necessary flying skill.

"No hill for a hill climber," thought Major Anseth who had about a thousand hours on his contemporaries. "If I had any doubts I would have never brought the bombs back. For that matter, if it was close I'd bail out everyone but myself and the co-pilot."

Major Anseth nailed the airspeed and as he pulled back the throttles to begin the flare he was exactly over the runway threshold.

The touchdown itself was firm, but uneventful. Jim heard the drag chute door open and observed a fully opened and beautiful drag chute. It always felt good to know they were down, but this time he felt a slight thrill when he reported, "Chute out and blossomed."

Normally they would taxi clear of the runway, but because of the damaged bomber they stopped straight ahead and were immediately surrounded by hoards of firemen and maintenance personnel who quickly gathered around the jagged stump that once held number seven and eight engines.

During the emergency the need to perform, along with the fast pace of events, obscured any fear Jim might otherwise have felt. He trusted Major Anseth. They had been together almost three years. Anseth wasn't like some of the other pilots Jim had heard about who suffered from both inexperience and an overestimate of their capabilities. Major Anseth was cool to the point that if they had lost a wing, he'd just say in an unemotional voice, "Crew, for your information, our left wing has fallen off, go ahead and bail out in order."

The crew stood around talking under the shade of the wing until maintenance started to hook up a tow bar to move the airplane off the runway. Then they took the bus and rode to debriefing. The concerns they must have felt about the emergency were typically unspoken. A few jokes were made and the EW complained about getting woken up. The navigator reminded everyone about how the decision to retain the bombs was covered by the old saying among SAC crews that "Sometimes it's better to beg for forgiveness than ask for permission." But typically, no one admitted to any dread about what could have happened and how easy it could have been to have been killed if the airplane had exploded.

Back in the compound, Jim felt some lingering apprehension. Trying to cover it with talk, he'd already told the story twice, refining it as he went along. Using humor to cover his unease, he said to Melvin, "Man, I was so sure I was going to bailout that I drank all the water in the tail. I was actually disappointed when the fire went out. I'd already made up my war stories."

Chapter Four

In 1965, few people in America had any inkling of what lay ahead for their nation in Southeast Asia. President Johnson was only just beginning the build-up of troops there, and most Americans would not have been able to find Vietnam on a map.

If you were young and growing up among the cornfields in Iowa, the thought of a far-off war in a distant corner of the globe did not enter your head. It certainly didn't enter the head of thirteen-year-old Bobby D. Olson, who lived in the small farming town of Kellogg, Iowa, sixty miles east of Des Moines. Bobby was more interested in soccer than war, and he was just starting to notice girls. While the first two B-52 wings were being deployed to Guam, Bobby D's main concern was figuring out how to start his older brother's Harley Davidson. The single cylinder, 125cc three speed was in a shed in the back of house and when his brother left for the summer, he gave Bobby specific instructions not to touch it. Just to be sure he removed the coil. This turned out not to be a serious challenge for Bobby. It did not take him long to discover that the coil out of an old Plymouth belonging to the next door neighbor worked fine, after a little coat hanger engineering.

Bobby would enjoy himself riding that semi-stolen motorcycle around the back roads of rural Jasper County all summer long. He hardly had a care in the world. Vietnam wasn't even something he thought about.

If you discounted one mid-air collision and the loss of two B-52's, Melvin and Cal completed their six-month combat tour uneventfully. Neither wanted to leave Guam and both tried without success to extend.

"It makes a hell of a lot of sense sending us home when we want to stay," Melvin said as the sat in their room in the compound the day before they were to leave. "There's got to be a lot of married guys who would rather skip the war and take care of their families. I didn't leave anything back there except a some ex-wives who just want to screw me over. I know the whole goddamn war is dumber than dog shit, but it's the only war we have and it sure beats the crap out of having to pull alert and fly Chrome Domes."

Cal nodded. "I don't mind flying or even sitting alert, it's just all the SAC bullshit we get. The tigers are always on my ass for one thing or another."

Neither Cal nor Melvin expected to return to Guam. They assumed their part of the Vietnam War was over. At the time no one realized the first deployment was a prelude to seven more years of war.

Jim had a premonition though. He returned from the war in September 1965 and unlike Cal and Melvin he was pleased to get back stateside and see his wife Elizabeth. On his third night back he sat on the bed and told her what he had been thinking.

"I heard today they're going to reinstate our orders to Georgia, but my gut tells me this might not be all good news. I don't think we're going to get out of Vietnam any time soon. SAC is going to keep rotating the bombers and my guess is it's only going to be the D-models. What if Turner is next on the list? I'll do what I've got to do, but can you stand a husband that's only home six months before he goes again?"

"I'm not going to think about it tonight, Charlie Brown," said Elizabeth as she pulled the straps of red nightgown over her shoulders and let it drop to the floor.

By the beginning of 1966 it became fairly obvious to Sam that Ellsworth would be next on the rotation. So far all the B-52's deployed to the Vietnam War were the newer (but maybe less capable) F-models. Now Ellsworth D-models were returning from the Boeing overhaul depot in Wichita, Kansas, painted black and camouflage, a big change from the white bellies designed to reflect the light from a nuclear blast. In addition to paint, the bomb bays were modified to hold a larger bomb load and there were some structural beef-ups to the airframe.

Sam worried the deployment would impact his college plans. Frustrated with slow promotion, his plan was to get a degree and apply for Officer Training School. As far as he was concerned, the tail had too many risks in the long term, and as a poker player he understood odds. If you flew long enough sooner or later you were going to draw a bad hand, even without the war. He wondered if he should get into pilot training; at least that way if he got killed he'd get to do it himself. He had accumulated forty-one semester hours now plus the nine he was currently taking. A deployment could knock those out, and a couple of them were mandatory core courses that would be hard to reschedule.

ANDERSON AIR FORCE BASE, GUAM, MARCH 1966

Sam guessed right about the deployment and by March 1966 he found himself with mixed feelings about being in Guam. He felt excitement about being in a new place, and the war itself provided feelings of adventure. Yet he knew he was going to take a hit on his college courses and he felt bad about leaving Cathy and his boys. She showed some of her German background and took it stoically, but not without reminding him that he'd told her that once he became a gunner there would be no more long separations. He worried about how she would get along in his absence. He knew she never liked his short stretches on the alert pad and this time he would be gone for six months. As Cathy would say, "That's not the way a marriage should work."

As wars go, flying missions out of Guam in the early days of the Vietnam War didn't offer much in the way of true hardship, but it took adjustment to get used to living in such close proximity with so many other people.

The gunners had previously known some of their roommates only casually, if at all, and it required time to learn their habits and idiosyncrasies. It was simpler for officers because they stayed together as crews, and in officer country the pecking order was more clear-cut. The aircraft commander usually set the routine and refereed when necessary. For the gunners there was no routine since they were all on separate crews and sometimes it took a lot of gnashing of teeth before they learned to adapt to each other. In time many would become lifelong friends.

Crew changeover took place in increments. Every day several crews would come in from Ellsworth or Turner AFB in Georgia and every day several crews from the departing unit would leave for home. Maintenance and other support people rotated the same way. For a while there were parts of four bomb wings operating out of Anderson AFB. Sam had been on the first crew deployed and he was advised to opt for a room on the first floor. It was a real pain if you had to drag your bags back and forth from the third floor.

Sam's bottom floor room was in a three-story dormitory located in a two-acre area known as the compound, so named because of the six-foot-high, barbed wire-topped chain link fence surrounding it. At opposing ends of the compound were two gray wooden guard shacks resembling outhouses without a door. At each shack, a bored air policeman checked badges to validate that those who entered were on an authorization list.

The compound also contained a large parking lot filled with motorcycles of various shapes and sizes. Many of these were smuggled in on aircraft by crewmembers returning from R&R in Japan. Someone once said, "You haven't lived until you've watched a hundred drunks on a hundred Hondas trying to get through a four-foot gate."

In addition to the dormitory where the crewmembers lived, the compound contained a rusty yellow one-story concrete block building that held the chow hall, a large crew briefing room and a number of smaller rooms used for mission planning. Above the entrance was a sign badly in need of paint that read.

**Through these doors pass the
best flight crews in the world.**

Below, in grease pencil, someone had written, "I didn't know they let TWA in the compound." This irritated some senior officers, but their attempts to remove it failed. Erasures and threats only generated more colorful addenda.

Fairly self-contained, the compound held a small post office with individual boxes for the crewmembers, who now often called themselves the crew dogs, and a pickup point for laundry. Sam especially liked the fact the second-floor day room of the compound had been converted to a poker parlor that pretty much operated around the clock.

Of the six non-commissioned officers Sam shared the air-conditioned double room with, five were B-52 tail gunners. The sixth worked in the squadron orderly room. Technically he wasn't authorized to live in the compound since it was reserved for crewmembers. But being a bright, not so young staff sergeant, who among other things maintained the housing roster, it made sense to pencil himself into the extra bed rather than live with twelve other smelly GI's in one of the non air-conditioned dormitory rooms set aside for TDY enlisted personnel who were not on an aircrew.

One of Sam's new roommates was Jim. Shortly after Jim returned to California from his first tour, he and Elizabeth packed up and moved to Turner Air Force Base, Georgia. But after that things happened pretty much as Jim expected. Two months after settling in their base house a neighbor told them their new wing would be deployed to Guam.

"It's going to be tough to go again so soon," Jim said to Elizabeth. "When I get back I hope it won't be like the last time when I almost couldn't tell the twins apart. They're growing so fast it scares me that I'm going to miss out on something and the next time I look they'll be married. This is going to make me something of a veteran, but I don't think it's like anything near as bad as what my Dad or brother went through. I just hate to leave you alone."

Like the first time, Elizabeth expressed understanding. "I know you have to do it," she said. "We'll be fine. I'll have the girls write their names on their foreheads with a crayon and I'll wear a red dress so you know me when you get home. Don't worry, we've done it before and can do it again. You just be careful, Charlie Brown."

Melvin had been transferred to the same bomb squadron as Sam so they already knew each other when Melvin started to drag his stuff into the room they would share for the next six months.

"If we're going to get veterans in here," said Sam, "Does that mean I can't hang up my peace symbol?"

"Nah. As long as you don't belch or fart too much we're going to get along," said Melvin. "I'm back in my favorite war so there's not much you can do that will piss me off."

It was obvious the gunners from Glasgow AFB who previously occupied the room knew how to address the crew rest mandated by Strategic Air Command. Combat missions out of Guam averaged nineteen hours from first briefing to debriefing. Five or six gunners assigned to different crews and flying and resting on different shifts could disturb the sleep patterns of the others. To avoid conflict they created an enlightened rule and boldly posted it on a large cardboard poster tacked to the latrine door:

UNDER NO CIRCUMSTANCES WILL PERSONNEL ON CREW REST DISTURB THE PARTIERS

Master Sergeant Tom Vinroot's bed was almost in the center of the room. Close to two rooms actually. A latrine complete with shower split up the space that was smaller than a double garage. Plastic sheeting on the jalousie windows kept the Guam moisture out and the air conditioning in. Wooden lockers old enough to house anti-mildew light in their base blocked off the six beds from what could best be called the common drinking area. Not that there was any ban on drinking in bed. Even fussy Tom, who was starting to become known as "Mother," knew better than to object.

Tom's nickname stemmed from his meticulous manner and the painstaking way he approached everything. Tom worried about everything, from having enough toilet paper on hand to ensuring everyone met the flying schedule. He was the ranking member of the room and had been in the Air Force for twenty-two years. Career-wise he was also the most successful and had filled the squares for another promotion. He was assigned to the top crew in the wing and hoped to make senior master sergeant soon. Combat flying wouldn't hurt and he wanted to share his experience with the youngsters.

He doted on Darrel Anderson, the youngest member of the room. Andy was what some gunners would call an abnormal drinker, almost a total abstainer. Short and slight, he maintained his dirty blond hair in a California style, combed back on the sides with a crewcut on top. He was so youthful looking he could have passed for a high school student even though he was a staff sergeant, albeit a new one. He'd been promoted along with Sam only two months before they deployed to Guam.

Andy, a bachelor, knew enough to avoid Sam's games of skill and chance. This made him fairly unique in the amount of spending money he had. Typically most of the gunners on Guam had a wife and family back in the States to support and this didn't leave them much to fool around with.

Although he'd never admit it publicly, Andy suffered from a fear of the tail. He made his peace with the war by sleeping. Sometimes he would sleep fifteen hours at a stretch followed by a short break and then a couple of good naps. Give him sixty hours between missions and he could get in better than thirty-five hours of solid slumber.

In the first weeks they were on Guam, Andy and Sam formed a partnership and agreed to make the payments on a Datsun station wagon owned by an officer returning to the States. Sam suggested they try renting it out.

Shortly their room was established as the home of HURTS RENT-A-CAR. This very unofficial business met an obvious need for off-base transportation. It thrived instantly and rapidly grew to include another Datsun, a Volkswagen and the pride of the fleet, a Nash Rambler with reclining seats. Although the name HURTS posted on the door pretty much described the condition of the machinery, there never seemed to be a shortage of renters. Usually these were officer crewmembers living in the compound.

It was a simple business really. A battered stenographer's notebook served as a rudimentary reservation system. There were no forms, no drivers' license checks and no green stamps. Most of all, there was no rule on drunk driving. But it hadn't started out that way.

In the beginning, Sam and Andy wouldn't rent to drunks. But after watching for a few weeks it became clear that no matter how sober a driver was when he left, a significant percentage of them came home blind.

More than once Sam found one of the empty cars parked sideways in the parking lot, lights on, key in the ignition and doors open.

Obviously the rule needed revision. The new version said, "Only minor assistance in turning the key is allowed." That was close enough.

To serve outsiders, who could not get in the compound, a sign was posted on the fence about fifteen feet abeam of Andy and Sam's bottom floor room. It displayed an arrow pointing to a pile of rocks. The instructions read, "Pick up a rock and throw it at the closest door." This was the signal for someone in the room to come out and make the transaction.

The other roommates agreed to help out when necessary in exchange for space-available use of the cars. HURTS agreed to pick up common room expenses such as soda for the refrigerator and booze. Mother assumed the responsibility for keeping adequate stock levels on hand.

It wasn't long before Mother picked up better than two cases of beer a day from the Class Six store. On some shopping days he would buy quantities of hard liquor because of the importance of keeping a supply of gin, rum and vodka on hand for HURTS clientele. Customers weren't the only people served. A lot of officers, Sam felt, were inherently cheap anyway and would come by for a free drink or six. Traffic usually picked up after the Officers' Club closed.

In addition to such business enterprises as HURTS, there was of course serious business to attend to.

One afternoon Sam eased into his seat in the briefing room and watched the crews starting to straggle in. He was about ten minutes early so he had time to talk to Scotty Burns, a Turner gunner, who was next to him in the back row.

Sixteen gunners were scheduled for that night's mission. Only fifteen (five three-ship formations) would actually go, since one crew was a planned spare in case of maintenance or other problems before take-off. They would go through the motions including briefing, preflight and engine start. Then they would wait with engines running until they were either launched or released. Usually release came about twenty minutes after the last bomber broke ground and it was too late to catch up with the airborne formation.

"Who's the lieutenant colonel in the khakis who just walked in?" asked Sam. "Is he one of your Brand X guys?"

"Yeah, I think he's assigned to our ADO (assistant director of operations," said Scotty, "but everyone calls him the Hat Colonel."

"What's that all about?" asked Sam.

"Didn't you see him outside the door looking at everyone who came in? When we came over here they put your wing from Ellsworth together with ours from Turner. The new (provisional) wing doesn't need two DO's and two ADO's. I don't think they had a real job for him so he checks hats."

"You've got to be kidding me," said Sam.

"No really, of course it isn't quite that simple or it wouldn't take a lieutenant colonel. He also does haircuts and zippers. I don't know if somebody assigned him the job or whether he took it on himself, but he darned sure is dedicated to ensuring we are properly dressed. Yesterday he caught my navigator coming out of base ops without a hat and my aircraft commander has to reply by endorsement. Like an old British sailor once told me, 'Fight she might, but shine she must'."

Sam liked Scotty, whose Christian name was Peter. He was short, at a tad more than five-four and he weighed over 150 pounds, but the distinctive thing about Scotty wasn't his roundness, it was his brogue. Born in the small town of Forfar on the eastern side of Scotland, he'd kept his accent. He even played the part, in the way he handled the curved stem briar pipe he carried. Scotty made a ritual out of filling its oversized bowl and then carefully tamping the tobacco with his thumb before lighting it.

When Scotty mentioned his wife was complaining about being lonely, Sam thought about how Cathy was handling it. He knew she was busy raising the kids, but six months was a long time to be alone. He was not there if she had to fix the car or take one of the kids to the hospital. But he knew she would make it, just as she always did when he was stuck on the base for days at a stretch. That didn't mean she liked being a single parent.

The mission that night was going to be a Viet Cong control center in an area of South Vietnam called the Iron Triangle. Sam tried to visualize what a Viet Cong control center must look like.

The best he could come up with was a series of thatched huts at the intersection of several primitive trails. There were probably some hammocks strung between the tall trees, a few cooking fires and some sort of canvas tarp protecting a little hospital area. He couldn't decide whether it would have any vehicles. Probably just bicycles. The jungle was probably too dense to handle anything bigger.

When the briefing ended the pilots and navigators stayed back for detailed target study while the gunners and EW's were released. In the stretch before second briefing, the EW would pick up in-flight lunches for the crew and the gunner would haul the officers' bags to the crew bus. These bag drags irritated many gunners since most of the officers lived upstairs. This meant lugging flight gear down two or three flights of stairs before hauling it to the parking lot.

As Sam went to get his crew's bags he thought about a story he had heard about the Great Bag War, which supposedly took place sometime before he arrived on Guam. It probably was not true or at least had been exaggerated, but there were gunners who swore that it really did happen. It seemed that many aircraft transited Anderson and some gunners, tired of loading officers' bags, retaliated by tossing them on baggage carts belonging to C-141's, C-5's and C-130's on their way to various parts of the world. As the story went, it got so bad that an officer would break out into a cold sweat if he thought his gunner was about to touch his bag.

Sam knew a lot of the guys perceived moving bags as demeaning for an NCO. He did not necessarily feel that way, but moving fifteen bags was a pain in the ass. He was glad he had finally made staff sergeant or the system probably would have suggested only airmen do the bag hauling. Before Andy signed in, Sam was the lone airman in the bomb squadron. If he heard the briefing room needed painting, he knew that he might as well get out the drop cloth.

Arriving over the target in the dark meant taking off in the late afternoon. The sun would have all day to heat the "greenhouse" created by the windows surrounding the top of the tail compartment. In theory, maintenance was supposed to cool the tail with a portable air conditioner prior to gunner preflight, but most of the time this didn't get top priority. If the ground crew experienced difficulties getting the airplane ready, a gunner could expect the tail to be a sauna. Hell! Guam was a sauna. It was not uncommon for switches and side panels to be too hot to touch without gloves.

Sam hurried through his interior preflight. He ran a quick check on the oxygen panel and inspected his primary and spare parachute. After a fast look at the straps he pulled on the back of his chute to check the static line reel and glanced around before climbing back out of the tail. In five minutes he returned to the relatively cool shade of the horizontal stabilized. "If I'm sure I've got oxygen and a way to bail out, everything else can wait until engine start," he thought.

During taxi the engines never put out enough bleed air to allow the tail air conditioner pack to operate efficiently, so by the time they rolled on to the runway Sam was soaked. On climb out the air conditioning turned cold and its breeze attacked his sweat with a vengeance. By the time they leveled off at 35,000 feet, Sam felt reasonably dry and comfortable. He checked his fire control system for operation and charged the guns. Since they weren't going to see any fighters there was no reason to take the pin out of the fire safe switch, so he just left it in.

Sam sat back for the long ride, which consisted of one refueling, one bomb run and one landing for a total time of twelve hours and ten minutes. Later, when he thought about the fact that he was getting combat pay for this, he summarized the experience in his head.

"I got up out of a good bed in an air-conditioned room, walked to an air-conditioned chow hall, sat in an air-conditioned briefing room and rode an air-conditioned bus to the airplane. Then I rode to war in an air-conditioned bomber listening to country western music coming from a tape recorder the EW patches into the interphone system.

"On landing I rode on another air-conditioned bus to debriefing and walked across the hall in the same building to eat eggs cooked to order in the air-conditioned chow hall. Tough, anyway you look at it. If I disregard the heat I have to pass through between air-conditioned events, the experience is no different than a training mission. In fact probably easier, without any low level."

Jim's flight was only a little more eventful. He flew the night mission in Black Three, the last ship in the formation, because of a scheduled fire-out of his tail guns. This was something that was done on a rotating basis to test the effectiveness of the fire control system. On each mission, one specific (by tail number) bomber attempted to fire all of its 2,400 rounds of 50-caliber ammunition over open ocean, and the results were scored.

After landing, Jim went directly to Malfunction Junction for debriefing. Under a battered cardboard sign that read Fire Control, a technical sergeant in well-starched fatigues asked him, "Test fire go okay?"

"If you call one gun okay. Number one never did fire and two and four quit after about a hundred rounds," replied Jim.

"How many times did you charge them?" asked the sergeant."

"About twenty-five," replied Jim. "I also banged them through all the limits."[13]

"Did that get anything to start again?"

"Nah. I could have charged one, two and four until they were empty and they still wouldn't have fired."[14]

"At least that would have given you credit for a 100 percent fire-out. Right now we're averaging less than 60 percent," said the sergeant.

"It kind of defeats the purpose of having a gunner," said Jim, who wasn't the only gunner concerned about reliability of the guns. Among gunners there was speculation about icing being the cause of non-firing guns.

Fire-out percentages dropped when the bombers flew out of Guam. The two variables that changed related to high humidity and high altitude. When the aircraft flew out of inland bases they weren't continually soaked by the moisture in the air or the constant Guam rainfall, and fire-out altitudes were 25,000 feet. With the Arc Light missions the fire-outs were accomplished on returning missions where the formation's altitude was 35,000 feet or higher.[15]

Mother thought this theory might be correct and met several times with his counterparts in maintenance to discuss a fix. These badly overworked NCOs were more concerned with systems where a malfunction could cause an aircraft to abort a mission. Whether the guns worked or not, the mission went. Occasionally combat missions were even flown with stow pins in the turret because maintenance ran out of time to make a fix. This meant the guns could not be moved at all.

After completing maintenance debriefing Jim stopped in the parking lot to talk to two gunners he had seen in debriefing. They walked to Gilligan's Island together.

Gilligan's was located in a parking lot outside the guarded compound. It consisted of a semi-round curbed-off grassy area sporting two picnic tables and a lone coconut palm. Lashed to one of the picnic tables was a twelve-foot bamboo pole carrying a flag that had the inscription, Gilligan's Island. No one knew who kept replacing the frequently stolen flag.

Crewmembers met up on the island after debriefing to swap harrowing tales and drink the two ounces of medical alcohol poured into small paper cups from a bottle of Old Methuselah by uniformed medics. Not every returning flyer took the two ounces so the medics were liberal in their distribution of "Old Loudmouth."

For the thirstier crowd the Officers' Club sold beer for ten cents. Flights were flown and heroic deeds were recounted on this figurative island. Some dedicated souls even stayed long enough to drink with the next day's fliers.

Some officers created a small band consisting of three guitars and a drummer, and nights when they weren't flying they would gather in one of the second-floor rooms to sing. That night they gathered on Gilligan's Island and serenaded the returning crews with an original collection of off-color songs.

One of the gunners asked, "I wonder if the Gruesome Foursome is going to play their latest hit. It starts out to the tune of the song 'Honky-Tonk Angels,' and goes, 'My navigator couldn't find the Vietnam coastline.' Then it goes on about how they didn't know God made handicapped navigators. It says about the same for pilots and the rest of the officers. When it gets to gunners, it's not I don't know. It's 'I always knew God made handicapped gunners'."

"That's typical Zero material," said the other gunner in a surly tone. "If we are so goddammed handicapped, how come they let us fly?"

Combat was becoming tedious. Missions were generally uneventful and unless a gunner was a drinker or card player, there wasn't much to do on the usual two days off between missions. Other than the twelve hours mandatory crew rest before flight, gunners were pretty much unencumbered by any other duties on their days off. It was easy to get cynical.

"Is that all you guys do? Bitch?" asked Andy as he walked in and threw his helmet bag on the top of Sam's locker.

"How did the flight go?" asked Mother.

"It was hell, real hell. I almost slept through the bomb run," said Andy in mock seriousness.

"I'd believe that," said Mother, "You could sleep through your funeral."

"No kidding, I almost did sleep through the bomb run. It was smooth as hell and with the seat down, I sacked out all the way from the tanker. When I heard the Ace call 'Coast inbound ten minutes,' I figured I could get a couple of more good z's and the next thing I know the navigator is calling IP." (IP was the initial point for the start of the bomb run where the navigators started the timing and made fine adjustments to target headings.)

"What did your pilot say?"

"Didn't even know, I guess," said Andy. "I forgot about my radar and didn't get it timed out until after we hit the target."[16]

"You didn't have your radar on?" asked Mother as he got up and moved Andy's helmet off Sam's locker and put it on Andy's where it belonged.

"Why in the hell did you have your radar turned off?"

"The noise bothers me and I turned it off so I sleep. Besides what in the hell did I need it for? We were the last dog in a three-ship formation."

Pete Robertson, a loud and sarcastic gunner from another room was listening. His hearing loss from riding behind the eight Pratt and Whitney jet engines on the B-52s probably explained his abnormally loud speech. He was so noted for his consistent profanity that his quieter roommates gave him a nickname that stuck: Hog Jaw.

"See!" he said, pointing at Mother, "A goddamn gunner could sleep through the whole goddamn war. Half the targets are just trees and monkeys anyway. We're part of the biggest toothpick manufacturing effort in history and we're fucking useless, just along for the fucking ride. Ain't nobody going to shoot at our ass."

The reality of war hadn't sunk in. To the gunners on Guam it was just kind of boring, but this would change sooner than they realized.

Chapter Five

ANDERSON AIR FORCE BASE, GUAM, APRIL 1966

Sam's afternoon dragged on. Out of boredom he checked the next day's status in the small room that served as the crew post office. At three in the afternoon missions should have been displayed on the bulletin board. It surprised him to see nothing posted. Missions usually went up not later than 11:30 to give the next day's flyers twenty-four hours notice. Not thinking much about it, he went back to his room.

Mother was talking. "If you guys are hearing about not flying, it's official. They're going to give maintenance an extra day to work on the birds."

Giving maintenance time to work on the aircraft seemed reasonable. Crew chief and technicians alike worked twelve-hour shifts, seven days a week trying to keep up with the constant wear and tear on the bombers, which typically flew every other day. Even twelve hours was an understatement. More like thirteen counting the changeover at the airplane, or in the shop. It didn't leave much time to ride a bus home, eat, do laundry, write letters, sleep and get ready to go to work again. How they lived made it tougher. Twelve to a room identical to the one the gunners lived in, but without the luxury of air conditioning.

Since no missions were posted, every crew was scheduled to go to the personal equipment section early the next day. Jim thought this was probably only a check of masks and helmets. If they were doing it at nine in the morning, he would have the whole day to do something. If a mission came up, the mandatory crew rest clock couldn't start until after the crews were done having their equipment checked.[17]

On a typically hot and muggy Guam morning, two crews at a time were getting fitted for flak vests in the personal equipment section. The procedure went fast. "You look like a medium—try this on," the airman in charge would say. Once size was determined, another airman made an entry next to the crewmember's name and called out briskly, "Next."

By eleven-thirty everyone had been fitted and about a dozen gunners were loitering outside the gate to the compound. Hog Jaw was expounding on flak vests. "I asked the airman what they were for and he said 'to protect vital areas'. I told him that was bullshit— they don't have any pants." He placed both hands over his crotch, which drew a laugh from everyone.

The conversation turned serious as they began speculating among themselves. "How do you get in the seat with a parachute on over a flak vest?" said Jim.

"These things are a real pain in the ass unless you need them," agreed Andy.

"So why would we need them?" asked Hog Jaw. "Is something up?"

No one knew.

Speculation increased as the day wore on and people were beginning to doubt the official reason for the stand-down.

The missions were posted at 2100 hours. The one designated "Rock 111" would take off at 1500 hours the next day. First briefing would be at 1100 hours. Instead of the typical sixteen, thirty-three crews were scheduled—thirty primaries and three spares. The lack of passengers was curious.

Although a basic B-52 crew consisted of six people, extra passengers were common. By using auxiliary seats up to four "strap hangers" could be accommodated. Normally every sortie contained a few staff members and others whose only excuse for being there was the combat pay and tax exemption. But on this obviously unusual mission, not counting the two full colonels who were scheduled with the wave leaders as airborne commanders, every bomber was limited to its basic crew. No one could figure out what was going on. The officers either didn't know or weren't talking. Aircraft commanders when queried just gave the SAC salute—a palms up shrug.

Because everyone was so unsettled, Sam stopped trying to get a poker game started. He also decided to ignore the gossip. He knew it wouldn't do any good and they would find out soon enough what the mission was all about. Besides, he needed to write some letters home. That was a challenge, coming up with something interesting to say to Cathy every day. She was not interested in the missions and even less so with his poker hands. What else was there? There were only so many ways to say, "I love you and the boys."

The conversation continued in the common area until almost three a.m. but no one was hung over. Mother strongly discouraged drinking the night before and everyone sensed something was different about the upcoming mission.

Sam spent a restless night and the squawk box in his room went off with a wake-up call three hours before it was expected. It told them to report to their aircraft commanders within thirty minutes. They were to receive survival radio training at 0800 hours.[18] Technically this call would break crew rest if mission times did not change—and they didn't.

The radio training conducted in the crew briefing room was perfunctory. Other than heavy emphasis on individual personal authenticators—the classified word or series of numbers used to verify that the person using the radio was not the enemy attempting to misdirect the rescue forces—it didn't cover much.

Sam's mind was racing. It didn't take a genius to figure out something big was up. This was just not normal—flak vests, broken crew rest, survival radio training and no passengers.

Then it hit him like a thunderbolt. *We're going to strike North Vietnam.*

This would be a first. No B-52's had ever gone north of the DMZ. Sam felt a rush of excitement tinged with some trepidation. This was the real thing. They were going to strike somewhere in North

Vietnam. If not the heart, at least an area critical to the movement of arms, equipment and supplies to South Vietnam.

First briefing confirmed that Sam's guess was correct. In flat, unemotional language, Major Watson, a staff briefer, presented the strike coordinates and mission timing. The briefed target was Mu Gia Pass, a break in the mountains on the border of North Vietnam and Laos. Located north of the city of Na Phao, its importance was its location. It created a choke point in the Ho Chi Minh Trail.[19]

"As you probably know, KC-135 tankers are here because of a typhoon evacuation from Kadena. They will take off from Guam intermixed with bombers in one-minute increments. Altitudes, except for refueling, will be 35,000 feet and the formation is one-mile cell. En route aircraft will refuel with the accompanying tankers at 29,000 feet in the provisional refueling area Gulf Foxtrot.

"Tankers will break off and return to Kadena. The map you are viewing shows the target and MiG threat areas. The red circles represent SAM rings.[20] Radio silence is paramount. If there are no questions, Captain Fox will brief the weather."

"Holy shit," thought Sam. "I never even heard of those MiG bases he was talking about in North Vietnam. Now I've got to worry about fighters coming from them." He was even more worried about the missiles mentioned in the briefing. "Seeing one of those puppies could get my undivided attention."

The weather briefing concentrated on Typhoon Paula. It had by-passed Okinawa, making the base there a viable alternate landing site. Captain Fox continued, "Cloud cover over the target is broken with projected thunderstorms. Updates will be given at the second briefing."

The pilots and navigators remained behind to accomplish mission study while the gunners and electronic warfare officers were released. During the slightly less than two-hour break before they were due back for the second briefing, tension built. For most it was more excitement than fear.

But not for Andy. The thought of flying over North Vietnam scared him. He thought about going to the flight surgeon and getting put on DNIF (duty not involving flying). He knew he could probably claim a head cold caused by the drastic temperature change between the hot ramp and the coolness of the tail at high altitude. But this malady wasn't related to his real motivation. Andy wasn't sure he understood it himself. He wished he was assigned to G-models where he could ride up front. From what he'd heard, none of the G-models were ever going to get tagged for the war.

Thinking about his girlfriend Rosalie didn't help his funk. He missed running his hands through her long amber hair or teasing her about her freckles. He wanted to be with her. He wondered how married gunners handled the separation from their wives and families. He knew that Melvin had been divorced at least twice and Hog Jaw probably more than that. He needed to propose and settle down with Rosey. Then he could apply for a transfer or even get out of the Air Force, although it would be hard to give up seven years he had towards retirement.

But after thinking about his roommates and Mother, Andy decided it would be to hard too face them if he grounded himself prior to a mission. "What the hell," he thought. "I've been scared in the tail so many times, I might as well be scared again. At least this will be a real mission."

In contrast to the fear Andy kept to himself, Jim and Mother were actually looking forward to going north. "Maybe I'll have something to tell my brother that will match his stories about winter night patrols in Korea," Jim said.

Mother had another reason. "I'm an old man by combat standards and I might never get the chance to do something significant as a gunner. This might be my last chance."

At second briefing the mission parameters were repeated and there was more discussion of the SAM rings and the possible fighter threat.

"MiG cap will be four F-4's from Takli. Radio silence will be in effect from prior to engine start until landing back at Guam.[21] External aircraft navigation lights will be turned off at coast in. Gunners will monitor trailing aircraft on radar and use their handheld light to warn those that come too close."

Weather in the target area was updated and the wing commander gave a bland pep talk to the crews that lasted less than three minutes. If the specifics of the mission were disregarded, it would be easy to think this was just another sortie. When the chaplain gave the short prayer given at every mission briefing, Sam expected to hear the customary words. Usually he hardly listened to them, but this time the words were startlingly different.

A solemn Captain Goodwin, the chaplain, appeared nervous as he began: "Dear Lord, bless these crews as they embark on this particularly dangerous mission. Protect and guide them, especially those who might not return. In Jesus name, amen." After a pause he said, "For those who would like communion, I will stay behind."

From what Sam could see, several more crewmembers than usual took communion, but the only gunner he saw in line was Jim.

When he got on the bus, Sam was still thinking about "those who might not return." The ride to the airplane was quiet, so he guessed the others might be thinking the same thing. He'd heard there were two crewmembers talking about refusing to go, but there was no way to know if this was rumor or fact.

When the crew got to the airplane it was ready. After being briefed by the crew chief, the EW joked, "Where is a broken bomber when we need it?" But in truth, everybody on Sam's crew wanted to go, if for no other reason than they would be able to talk about it later.

Typical engine start and taxi radio calls were dispensed with because of the radio silence requirement. They were accomplished in accordance with a precise timing sheet. At the correct time Sam's crew rolled into a stream of mixed bombers and tankers in a nose-to-tail parade that clogged the taxiways with their slow elephant-like walk. Sam was twenty-third in a stream of thirty bombers. That made him forty-fifth in line by the time they mixed in with the tankers.

Airplanes were already taking off when they finally moved out of their parking spot. "I wonder what the Russian trawler must be thinking now?" Sam thought. Throughout the war a Russian trawler had been sitting three miles off the end of the runway at Anderson Air Force Base, and this ship could sometimes be seen from the island. Maintenance troops joked about it. "If the Russians out there are paying attention they must be rolling on the floor. Our radio calls are so screwed up we should charge them to listen."

Like every mission out of Guam, a refueling was required to give the bombers enough fuel to complete the twelve-hour round trip. This time the formation used the coined term, "Mass Gaggle." This was clearly descriptive. Thirty KC-135 tankers, side by side, lined up across the clear sky with thirty B-52 bombers directly behind them, getting ready to mate. It was impressive and there were contrails as far as Sam could see. He regretted not having a camera to capture the view.

It was dark when they crossed the Vietnam coastline north of Da Nang. Sam heard the navigator call "Feet dry."

"It's time to arm the guns," thought Sam. After ensuring the firing safety pin was in place Sam activated the charging switch and heard the mechanism cycle, indicating that rounds were in the chambers. Just to be sure he cycled them again but did not remove the fire-safe pin. More concerned about the bomber directly behind him than potential MiGs, Sam would not remove this pin casually.

The clouds below were broken and in the gaps Sam could see numerous lights as he watched trails of fire from rockets and mortars shooting skyward in continuous arrays. At night South Vietnam was always lit up, but whether the lights came from cities or military bases Sam didn't know. The ground fire increased as they passed over Khe Sanh heading north and then abruptly ceased as they crossed over the DMZ. By the time they got to the IP the radios were starting to get noisy—so much for radio silence.

Many bombers in the formation were echoing Paris Control, a radar facility north of Da Nang. "MiG warning code yellow...MiG warning code yellow...MiG warning code yellow."

More keyed up than apprehensive, Sam checked his radar and scanned the sky. He saw nothing behind him except the seven trailing aircraft. Installing a green filter on his Aldis light he signaled the aircraft directly behind him. Radar showed it at exactly one mile. Not that he needed radar because for some idiotic reason the bomber still had its wing lights on even though they were now over North Vietnam.

Radios continued to be chaotic and the sky below and to Sam's right was lit up. Sam thought that some of it was probably lightning from the expected thunderstorms, but he also suspected he was seeing anti-aircraft fire. At first he thought it was like watching the movie "Twelve O'clock High" but then he realized it was not the same at all. The movie was in black and white. What he was seeing was in Technicolor.

Sam kept scanning and tried to make sense of the radio calls. Now airplanes somewhere in front of him were saying they were dropping flares and chaff.

In the clutter there were also calls where the voices were screaming "Flak! Flak! Flak!" and some unrecognizable bomber call sign said they were shooting.

"If all that was going on in front of us, what will it be like when we get there?" thought Sam. "No way to call for a re-deal. I'll have to ride it out with the hand I have."

Pumped with adrenaline and almost euphorically alert, Sam constantly checked his radar for MiGs. He saw four unidentified targets on his scope and noted several unusual blips that were dropping rapidly behind.

"What the hell are those," he muttered. "Chaff from the airplanes up ahead?"

It was impossible to tell who was who in all the noise, which included jamming from his electronic warfare officer. Taking his head out of the scope Sam began his visual scan again. Other than the idiot with the wing lights on, he saw nothing.

"Bombs away!" called the radar navigator as the airplane made a steep right turn. It seemed like only minutes before Sam heard the pilot call "feet wet," indicating they had crossed the coast outbound.

In minutes all the radio traffic from the bombers suddenly ceased. Sam checked on the birds behind him. Extending his radar to its full range of 7,500 yards he counted one, two, three, four airplanes. That was all. Sam felt a sinking feeling in his gut. There should have been seven. "Oh shit!" he said out loud. "We've lost at least three bombers and probably more."

He knew that his buddy Andy was somewhere behind him in the formation, but Sam couldn't tell what airplanes were missing. It was a long, silent five and a half hours back to Guam. With Radio silence back in effect, there was no way to learn who was down.

This gave him time to think about a worst-case scenario. If three airplanes behind him were down, what about the twenty-two in front? He did the math in his head. Three out of seven equals almost 43 percent. Forty-three percent of twenty-two was something like nine or ten airplanes. "God!" he thought. "There's no way we could have lost thirteen bombers, is there?"

That was more than twice as many gunners in his room, and as far as he knew every one of them had flown. He thought about Jim, Melvin and Mother. Could they be down along with Andy?

Mechanically completing debriefing, Sam drearily walked to the picnic tables at Gilligan's Island. He dreaded what he would learn there. As he approached, the buzz of conversation seemed lively. He looked around at the familiar faces. He checked and double-checked. Andy, Melvin, Mother, Jim, Ed Dwyer and Grance Thompson from next door, Scotty Burns from upstairs, Jim Merrill, Tom Schrantz, everybody. Even that asshole Hog Jaw was there. They had not lost a single crew.

"What the hell happened?" Sam asked everyone, the relief visible on his face. "We're all safe."

It wasn't until later that Sam and several other gunners sitting in a Guam bar figured it out.

Nening's San Miguel Bar was owned and operated by Mama Nening, who had been a young woman during the Japanese occupation of Guam. Prior to being discovered by two Ellsworth gunners its clientele consisted mostly of local fishermen and a few sailors. Situated on the outskirts of Agana, its resemblance to bars seen in Puerto Rico was the source of its common name, the Rum Shack.

Constructed of scrap materials, palm fronds and old parachute sections, it looked tropical, but flimsy. Its furnishings consisted of mixed, well-used war surplus tables and chairs. A large rusty metal cooler sat behind the bar fronted by several rickety stools. Adopted by the gunners as a hang out, its big attraction was the liberal hours and the way Mama Nening graciously cooked the whole chickens they bought at the base commissary. If a broke gunner needed a beer, Mama would extend credit.

Sitting around a dirty wooden cable spool turned on its side, the gunners drank beer as they came up with an explanation for the mission chaos. For a start, the planning was poor and the majority of the navigators were confused by some of the aiming points. The pre-selected bombing offsets were critical. They used a fixed point that would show up on radar as the basis for computing timing and geometric angles to the target. These were screwed up, which didn't help the confidence level of the lead crews. Nor did the lightning reflecting off the clouds, especially when it was combined with ground fire, even though the ground fire was not reaching their altitude.

"My radar thinks we might have missed the target," one gunner said and two others nodded in agreement. " He also said that formation discipline broke down after coming off the target and all the bombers never did get joined up again. They just lit out for Guam."

It was finally deduced that Paris Control tracked two MiGs lifting off from a North Vietnamese field. They broadcast MiG warnings on the UHF Guard frequency monitored by all aircraft. No enemy fighter got within fifteen miles of the formation, but this warning, repeated by numerous aircraft, saturated the radios. Several friendly fighter pilots skirted or cut through the B-52 formation in their eagerness to chase the MiGs.

To deceive the MiGs, the lead bombers began to drop chaff and then flares to decoy heat-seeking missiles. None of the hyper-charged crews had ever observed flares at night before and someone called them out as flak.

One flak call led to others. Soon a dozen radios on the open guard channel were screaming "Flak! Flak! Flak!" The chaff explained the strange blips Sam observed on his radar. But did one of the gunners actually start shooting? Whatever happened was being kept hush-hush. The gunner wasn't talking. The alcohol-fueled consensus among the group was that he fired two three-second bursts at an F-4C.

Rumors of shooting at friendly aircraft would surface later in the war, including one about two confirmed F-4C's shot down by B-52 gunners. This probably didn't happen, but there is less doubt that in the excitement of the moment several bombers may have come under fire from the guns in the aircraft ahead of them. One B-52 pilot swore he screamed on the radio to the gunner in front of him, "Do I look like a goddamn MiG?"

That night Mama Nening's concern for "her boys" started a tradition. Secretively, and one at a time, she presented each of the gunners in the bar with a tropical sea bean to serve as a good luck charm. No one ever knew where the bean came from or its exact name, although it may have come from Saipan.[22]

Ritually she shined this small irregularly shaped dark brown bean on the side of her nose. When she did this she always explained it was her last one. That night she gave out her last bean six times. Over the years she would give out many more last beans to gunners.

But there were several gunners who never qualified for a bean, including Hog Jaw whom Mama Nening felt was too obnoxious. Mama rule was that she had to like you, and although you could get sloppy drunk, you had to behave yourself. Certain words were prohibited and if you wanted a bean, you couldn't fight.

A formalized ritual would grow up around the "gunner's bean". A gunner must carry his bean at all times and could be challenged for it at any time. If he couldn't produce it he must buy the challenger a drink. Many other rules would evolve over time.

Back in the compound, the Gruesome Foursome was working on a new song. Created around the fact that the Mu Gia Pass raid failed to hit the planned target it began,

> "This is a song sung by a band
> of North Vietnamese field workers:
> We heard a great mighty rumble,
> We heard a great mighty roar,
> Half of Cambodia crumbled away."

Then came the chorus:

> "We knew we were safe in Mu Gia that day."

Chapter Six

The orderly room clerk sharing the gunner's air conditioning confirmed the story about the two officers who refused to go on the North Vietnam bombing mission. One went to the airplane with his crew and at some point hid in the short grass between the parking ramp and the taxiway. Since it was daylight this proved to be somewhat problematic for him. Quickly escorted from the flight line he was replaced by a substitute. The second officer was the electronic warfare officer from one of the lead crews in Sam's wing. He didn't hide, he just said, "I'll preflight the airplane, but I'm not going..."

And he didn't. Someone who saw the former spot (temporary promotion) major a few days later in the BX said, "He had captain bars on his shoulders and he looked pretty downcast and unhappy. I don't know what will happen to him."

Hog Jaw, with his usual grace, said, "All they are going to do is to ask the cowardly sonofabitches to resign. If a fucking gunner refused to go, you can bet he would be parked under Leavenworth. If you're a goddamn officer and you chicken out you get to be a fucking civilian."

After a while, the gossip about the first mission north settled down, only to be replaced by rumors that another mission was being planned. Sam ignored the rumors as much as he could and returned to his old routine of sleeping days and playing poker nights. After an only moderately successful game he went to the mailroom. As soon as he saw the flight schedule he knew the rumor mill about returning to Mu Gia Pass was correct. He hadn't forgotten how botched up it was the first time and he couldn't imagine the next one being any more screwed up, but with mighty SAC, you never knew.

The second mission to North Vietnam began uneventfully. The fifteen bombers rolled as scheduled and the silent refueling was smooth.

The bomber formation maintained radio discipline this time and the only radio chatter on the Guard channel was coming from fighters and gunships working targets in South Vietnam. Sam monitored closely, but other than his navigators accomplishing the bombing checklist on interphone it was disarmingly quiet.

Suddenly the electronic warfare officer called "lock on," in a low-key manner identical to what he would sound like on any training mission. For a second Sam disregarded it until jamming started to bleed over into the interphone system. Looking down to his right he saw both the nose and tail APS-54 lights were red.

"Cripes! The EW just called lock on and now he's jamming. Why in the hell doesn't he say something? If the APS-54 lights are lit it means something is tracking us. If it's an SA-2, where the hell did it come from? We shouldn't be inside of a SAM ring yet—or are we?"

The navigators calmly continued with the bombing checklist and started the countdown to bombs away. Sam's aircraft commander didn't mention the threat, which meant Sam's apprehension and frustration built. He didn't even know what to look for other than a black telephone pole with its tail on fire. Not knowing what direction to look, he scanned the sky behind and below him fruitlessly

The missile scare was still on Sam's mind when the pilot called "feet wet," indicating they were on the way home. It was probably nothing more than ground radar, and if other aircraft in the formation picked up on it, nothing was said. But he guessed that if they kept going north it was just a matter of time until a SAM got a B-52.

Back in his room after this second mission to Mu Gia, Sam was trying to figure out the horrendous noise above him, which sounded like a swarm of moving bees. Something was going on in the compound, but what? Finally he decided the noise must be coming from several motorcycles on the railed walkway surrounding the second floor. Intrigued by how they got there, Sam went outside to look. Six Honda 90's piloted by intoxicated officers were making complete circles of the compound dormitory. This required five ninety-degree turns including a "dog leg" over the Commander's dark office. Their best times were running about one lap every five minutes.

A cheering crowd at Gilligan's Island watched the parade of noisy Hondas, which expanded to eight very fired up and helmetless officers and gentlemen. There was not a gunner in the pack although in truth that might have been because the average gunner couldn't afford a motorcycle. The excitement didn't last long before the sound of sirens could be heard and two blue air police trucks pulled up to the gate closest to Gilligan's.

Three air police sergeants and four airmen, dressed in fatigues and wearing side arms, joined the spectators, but did nothing until a staff car driven by an air police major drove up. Walking through the gate, the small army of military cops proceeded to the second floor and confronted the about-to-be grounded riders. The motorcycles were carefully taken down the stairs and pushed back to the parking lot. That should have been the end of it, but alcohol continued to flow and shortly after the air police left, another motorcycle cranked up.

Badly misjudging his approach, one of the just chastised lieutenants crashed on the stairway, next to the orderly room, on his way back to the second floor. Although not badly injured he had enough Honda rash to generate concern among one of the officers, who was still wearing his chaps from the last sortie. Usually, these were turned in at the personal equipment section upon mission return, but due to the late, 2 a.m. return, all fifteen crews had brought their chaps back to their rooms. Alcohol-befuddled logic, being what it is, drove some unknown officer to fire a flare signifying the injury. Arcing nicely to more than two hundred feet above the compound, it led to a return of the air police.

Ten gunners were congregated outside Sam's room watching the show and Hog Jaw was expounding on the situation.

"Nobody gives a shit what the officers do. As long as they fly the goddamn missions they can get away with anything," he said bitterly. "Everybody thinks gunners are a bunch of drunks and they don't even notice the Zeroes who still behave like they are at a fraternity party."

Sam couldn't help but wonder what the gunners who were so outspoken about officers would say if they knew he was taking college courses to try and get a commission. He didn't mind taking officer's money in a poker game, but he knew they all couldn't be lumped in the same pot.

He thought about his crew and smiled. He realized he'd drawn a good hand even if they didn't exactly fit the SAC image. Yeah, they kidded around some, but they treated him decently and were always deadly professional when necessary. In fact, he'd never seen Major Harrington lose his cool. It might bother him if he had to "sir" lieutenants and captains younger than him by five and even ten years, like some of the older heads had to do. He'd bet Sergeant Vinroot was an NCO when some of the officers riding the motorcycles were still in elementary school.

Meanwhile, back in the States, Cal was struggling. Almost half his salary went to debts and without combat pay it was hard to keep up. Unable to afford an apartment he was forced to get a room in the NCO barracks. It got so he looked forward to alert. This gave him a chance to be around gunners rather than the personnel toads and vehicle maintainers he was forced to live with. Alert offered another advantage for Cal. Booze was forbidden. Regular meals and seven days at a stretch without a drink didn't hurt him.

Life passed in kind of a blur. Cal couldn't think of much about Carswell he liked. He felt about the same about Fort Worth. "If I wanted to be a cowboy I would have stayed in New Mexico," he thought.

When Cal wasn't on alert or flying he spent most of his time in a dingy bar in White Settlement, a Fort Worth suburb. Mostly Cal stuck to beer. With hard liquor, things tended to get a little crazy.

He hadn't forgotten the encounter with the Fort Worth police over the Pelican. Jim Beam was his downfall that time just like the day he fell off the stolen horse. After a few drinks it seemed simple to climb the fence and go for a ride. After all the horse was running loose. How was he to know the owner would get upset and call the police? At least this didn't lead to an article in the Fort Worth *Star Telegram.*

Cal was sitting quietly in the library of the alert facility glancing at the newspaper. The wing gunner, dressed in starched khakis, walked in and said:

"How long would it take you to get packed if I was going to send you to Guam as a replacement for a gunner that has to return?"

"Would fifteen minutes be too long?" responded an elated Cal. "You're not messing with me are you? I don't own anything I can't pack in a B-4 bag. If you need somebody, I'm your man. In the meantime, you got any shoes you want polished? You put me on this I'll kiss your ass and give you twenty-four hours to draw a crowd."

News of Cal's impending arrival soon reached Melvin. They were not close buddies but they had known each other from the first time they were on Guam. The squadron clerk sharing the room reluctantly agreed to moved out to make room for Cal. He'd been a good source of information, but Melvin suspected that information went both ways. He told his roommates:

"It's better to have someone who doesn't work with the commander on a daily basis even if that someone is Cal McGraw. Just keep in mind that he probably holds some sort of record for getting in trouble."

Cal's seventeen-hour flight to Guam was broken by an unplanned stop at Travis. So when you counted ground time and the hours spent packing up his barracks room, he'd been awake for more than thirty-four hours without a drink. So when Cal first arrived, he was not up to much conversation with his new roommates. Rudely stuffing the four still packed bags containing everything he owned in the last empty locker, he quickly slam-dunked six beers and flopped onto the only open bed. He proceeded to sleep for fifteen hours without so much as a trip to the latrine.

Upon waking, Cal pawed around in his locker until he came up with a tan Samsonite suitcase containing an unopened quart of vodka. He began to drink seriously enough to cause his demise and in two and a half hours he was dead to the world. He remained in this passed out state until Melvin, just coming back from a mission, stirred up a pitcher of "gunner's punch".

This orange concoction was normally made in no less than two-gallon lots. The formula consisted of one half-gallon vodka, one half-gallon gin, one pint 151 proof rum and two quart cans of orange juice concentrate. This was shaken with ice and properly served in a stolen aircraft coffee jug. The strong orange juice concentrate masked the flavor of booze.

Socially correct gunners placed a bottle of vodka alongside the gunner's punch in case some unsuspecting officer wanted to mix a screwdriver. This would create spectacular side effects and the projectile nature of the orange barf it generated was scientifically interesting. The mixture Melvin made faithfully followed the original formula in proportion, except he substituted 180-proof grain alcohol for the rum.

Suffering from a severe internal fire from his previous indulgence, Cal got out of bed and sat in the chair nearest to the refrigerator. Wearing nothing but his jockey shorts he started to drink the deadly mixture. Shortly he arose unsteadily and moved to his bed mumbling "dirty gremlin bastards" several times. Total day: fifteen minutes. Total booze consumed: about three full water glasses. Total coherent words: less than nine. That had to be some sort of record. Hell! Cal had several records.

The day after Cal obliterated himself on gunner's punch, Jim took his place. Without clearing it with anyone, he quietly took the seat reserved for Sgt. McGraw in the briefing room.

The aircraft commander glanced back once and pretending not to see, quickly turned away. On the way out to the aircraft none of the five officers on the bus indicated curiosity about Jim being there. Obviously, they knew Cal and didn't want to ask too many questions. Better to be blind than explain the substitution. No one even changed the forms to credit Jim for the mission.

While Cal was just arriving in Guam, others were about to leave. Mother was the first to go home and he did this in one straight seventeen-hour shot on a B-52. He returned to his old routine quickly. On his first Saturday back at Ellsworth he went through the same ritual he always performed every Saturday before he went off to war. This involved getting up before the rest of the family, making coffee and preparing pancake batter from scratch. Then, after making a pitcher of orange juice, he would sit down and read the paper until the others awoke.

On his first Monday back at the base, Mother was the first one in the gray flat-roofed building containing the "Standboard" office. As a member of an evaluation crew his job was to check the knowledge and performance of the wing's gunners.[23]

Mother knew there was a lot of work to do. Crew evaluation stopped during the six-month deployment and crews didn't get to practice a lot of things such as low-level flight or emergency procedures.[24] Time alone without any over-the-shoulder evaluation suggested the gunners would be sloppy, but after spending six months as an ordinary crew dog it was going to be harder for Mother to bust people he had become familiar with as individuals. He was determined to do it, however, because he honestly believed that doing it by the numbers was important.

Sam wasn't lucky enough to return home by bomber. For him the KC-135 ride took over twenty-five hours, counting the stop in Hawaii to refuel. He wasn't enthusiastic about having to go by tanker, and the seventy passengers riding in canvas troop seats were cattle-car loaded. Even taking a piss involved tramping over more than a dozen people. Still, going home meant living in a real house—not six guys to a room. Sam's reunion with his family was happy and tearful as they mingled with the crowd who met the tanker. There was even music.

He felt grubby from the long ride so before they landed, he'd shaved, brushed his teeth and cleaned up as much as he could in the small latrine behind the KC-135 cockpit. It took a long time for his bags and boxes to be unloaded, but he was home and would shortly be able to take a shower. Sam knew exactly who to share this with.

Andy was the third of the roommates to leave and like Mother, he returned on a bomber. He wished Rosalie would be there to greet him, but things had been tense when he left and she hadn't been good about writing. They hadn't known each other that long and weren't married so she had no real obligation to meet him.

He envied guys like Sam and Jim who had families waiting. Although hopeful, he expected there would be nobody to meet him when they landed. It was awkward watching the officers joyfully hug and kiss their wives and children in front of the bomber. While they unloaded their flying gear and the boxes of goodies from Guam and Okinawa, Andy dragged his four battered bags to the nearest hanger and caught a ride to the NCO barracks.

The transition between tours was difficult for some gunners. Most were obviously elated when they came home to family and friends, but a few found it hard to get back into a routine. The reality of pulling alert and flying training missions again seemed like just going through the motions, and the Soviet threat no longer provided the motivation it once did.

Jim was eager to finally be home. He'd spent twelve of his last eighteen months flying missions out of Guam. His break between tours was only a few days over six months. That just wasn't long enough. During that time he had moved Elizabeth and the girls from California to Georgia, taking thirty days leave en route. He had barely settled everyone in the new house before he went back to the war for another six months.

Adjusting to being home again was harder than Jim expected. He found himself pacing around and banging his hands for no reason that he could ascertain. He lived in a spotlessly and nicely decorated base house where the beds were made and the dishes washed. He could frequently smell the pleasant aroma of bread baking in the oven, yet it was almost like he didn't belong.

It felt unusual to be using his old push mower on the lawn, waxing the car, or dressing up for church. He was uncomfortable at the PTA meeting Elizabeth took him to. She was on a first-name basis with tens of people and he didn't know a soul. Elizabeth had changed too. It was subtle, but she was more forceful with the girls and tended to take the lead in decisions about things she would have deferred to Jim in the past. "What do I expect?" he thought. "She's been running the show."

Elizabeth sensed his unease and with a sly smile said, "You need a beer, Charlie Brown."

Cal worked out an agreement to stay and Melvin was the last man from the room to return. Back in Rapid City, where he'd only been stationed for two months before he went to Guam with the wing, he hunted around until he found an apartment complex he liked. It was similar to the one he lived in when he was married to Mary Ellen, but the people seemed to be friendlier. He bought some used furniture and settled in after purchasing a used stereo wall with fifty LP's, including some of the great blues singers like Muddy Waters. Two hanging lamps and a Chinese screen added to the atmosphere. By turning down the lights Melvin hoped to create the proper mood.

He missed the camaraderie and the easy life on Guam. There was somebody to cook your meals and do your laundry, and nobody got on your ass if you had a beer when you were off duty.

Melvin wanted to get back to life as a war dog. After a little research he learned that the base in Oklahoma was next in the rotation. He was able to change stations and get assigned from Ellsworth to Clinton Sherman Air Force on a crew that would depart for Guam two weeks after his arrival.

ANDERSON AIR FORCE BASE, GUAM

Shortly after landing back on Guam, Melvin had a unique experience. He was standing with his new pilot and co-pilot when the co-pilot, Lieutenant Butterbrook, turned to him and said; "Sergeant Cunningham, please inform our aircraft commander that I'm going to the BX."

Captain Palm, who was less than two feet away, waited for Melvin to relay this and then said, "Sergeant Cunningham, remind the lieutenant he needs to be back by noon."

"That's just great," thought Melvin. "A pilot and a co-pilot who won't talk to each other except in the airplane."

Some of the animosity between them obviously related to the eighteen-inch thick bamboo pole Captain Palm carried like a swagger stick even when he was not in uniform. When asked about it by fellow officers he would reply without a smile, "It's to beat my co-pilot."

Melvin knew this was exactly correct. Captain Palm, who was short anyway, had trouble reaching across the eight throttles so he would thwack his co-pilot across his helmet to get his attention.

Melvin thought Lieutenant Butterbrook was 230 pounds of solid dumb. He couldn't keep up with what was happening on the airplane and often didn't respond to radio or interphone calls. A smack would bring his mind back. Then he would sulk about the insult of getting hit. Finally the lieutenant totally quit speaking to his pilot on the ground.

Melvin could see that getting respect from the new officers was going to be a joke. In spite of the fact that he was several years older than any officer on his crew, he knew for a certainty there was a long gap between his officer crewmembers and himself, the only enlisted "swine" on the crew. Even Melvin's forty-one combat missions carried no weight.

It wasn't as if his officers were any beauties. His aircraft commander, Captain Wesley Palm, was a graduate of the Naval Academy who transferred to the Air Force upon graduation. He was plainly obsessed with himself. Totally humorless and fanatical about making all the decisions, he was not concerned with either the skill or the careers of the members of his crew. At a recent briefing he'd told them to think of themselves as his sexual advisors: "If I want your fucking advice, I'll ask for it."

In truth, Capt. Palm didn't have much to work with. His crew had been assembled only three weeks before they deployed to Guam. For any less arrogant pilot it would have been cause for concern. The navigator, First Lieutenant James E Sullivan III, became famous when his first rubber check arrived in the squadron before he did. In the Air Force, particularly Strategic Air Command, personal financial responsibility was mandated. Merchants quickly learned that if they forwarded bad checks to the individual's commander, the commander would almost always ensure they collected. When the offender was an officer, response was generally immediate.

The EW, First Lieutenant Terry Greenwood, made his name when as a brand new officer he drove his Corvette through a Holiday Inn parking lot in excess of a hundred miles per hour. The Corvette went to a base storage lot.

Reduced to a bicycle, he rode this off the high board at the Officers' Club swimming pool. The bicycle joined the Corvette in the storage lot.

The crew's radar navigator, a full-blooded Cherokee Indian named Pat Sams, was involved in an ongoing scandal with a full colonel's wife. This probably led to his recent pass-over for major.

Melvin's new co-pilot, the aforementioned First Lieutenant Edward Butterbrook, was a classic. He washed back twice in undergraduate pilot training and only survived initial B-52 training at Castle because of the critical need for co-pilots created by the Vietnam War. At Ellsworth it became fairly obvious he had what could be euphemistically called some shortfalls in his flying skills. His first aircraft commander tried several remedies, including routinely shouting at him. When that had no effect, in frustration he turned him over to the director of operations (DO) who scheduled several extra flights with himself as the instructor so that he could personally shout at Lt. Butterbrook.

In spite of some world-class, high-volume ass-chewing this was unsuccessful. If anything, the lieutenant's flying skills deteriorated further. This led to him being considered for grounding by a Flight Evaluation Board just as the unit received orders for deployment to Guam.

But the board was cancelled and so Lieutenant Butterbrook was assigned to fill a shortage on Captain Palm's new crew. People suspected the wing king had a "gutful" of Captain Palm's arrogance and hand-picked the officers to go on his crew.

He probably did that for the whole crew, including Melvin. Melvin's reputation had preceded him and he certainly was not on anybody's popularity list.

On their first solo mission as a numbered crew, Melvin thought, "Jesus, these children could get us killed, the way they coordinate." Two flights later, Melvin decided their first training mission had been a high point in the way they worked together as an aircrew.

One day, shortly before daybreak, Melvin was returning to his room after a particularly annoying flight. A gunner named Norm Lake walked up to him and said, "Your guy Cal just took a piss in the parking lot right in front of the crews coming back."

"That's his problem," said Melvin sharply. "He's not my guy. Just because we share a room doesn't mean I'm his keeper. He's spent a lot of time over here. I figure the humidity makes him a little thirsty. It's so damn hot a guy's got to have liquids. Cal just oversaturates himself once in a while.

"Speaking of hot," he continued, "I nearly passed out sitting on the runway yesterday. By the time we took off it must have been 150 degrees in the green house. Before we got airborne I was dizzy. To top it off, we were in chop all the way from the Philippines. Then the pilot eats my ass when we land because my idiot co-pilot overran number one on the way home. I wasn't watching and the first thing I know, this B-52, bigger than life, is off our left wing. At first I thought it was Blue Three overrunning us, then I noticed I had an extra airplane behind us.

"My ace, who usually never sleeps, had some sort of bug. He was off interphone in the bunk. I tried the co-pilot, but he must have been sound asleep. So I got the EW to go check on him. The idiot co-pilot pulls the throttles back until we're where we belong in the formation. It was no big deal, except my pilot got royally pissed off because I didn't wake him."

"Why didn't he eat the co-pilot's ass?" asked Norm.

"Probably figured it wasn't worth it," said Melvin. "He says I know better, the co-pilot might not. I shouldn't have to baby sit dumb-dumb, he's a lieutenant and I'm just a stupid sergeant. Like I said, it was no big deal."

"No big deal! You could have collided," said Norm.

"No, I mean no big deal not to wake the pilot. Once the idiot co-pilot saw where we were, he got it straightened out. Besides the EW had to almost walk on the ace's face to go forward, why the hell didn't he wake him, he's a goddamn officer."

"What was the gunner in number one doing?" asked Norm. He should have caught the overrun." [25]

"Must have had his head up and locked. I suppose Captain Palm will track him down and read him the full seven acts. If I ever get a chance I'm going to break it off in that dumb-assed co-pilot. He just stood there like a mute when I was getting reamed for his screw-up."

Chapter Seven

KOZA OKINAWA, MARCH 1967

Before he left, Melvin couldn't resist telling his roommates with exaggerated seriousness, "I have an important announcement to make. I am going to Okinawa for the express purpose of rest and relaxation. While I am on R&R I will be visiting both art galleries and some of the museums."

If war has any good points, one of them has to be R&R. The idea of allowing combat crewmembers a one-week break after they had flown a certain number of missions was originated to reduce chronic stress and fatigue. The reality was that in seven days some crewmembers became so relaxed and rested it took five or six missions before they fully recovered. This rest trip often caused a strange metamorphosis in what was normally a sane and responsible man. When he arrived at his R&R destination he was astounded people could behave like they did. But shortly he became just like them. Not everyone turned into a lunatic, however, and many crewmembers just took the well-trodden tourist route.

Melvin's first stop was Air-start Alley, a small passageway between Gate Two and Maromi Streets. Named for its illicit comparison between compressors used to start airplanes and some of the more exotic pleasures waiting to be purchased in doorways, its star attraction was Gloria with the Velvet Throat. The alley with its bars and bar girls made it at a point of interest on Melvin's itinerary.

In the Texas Bar, Melvin was met by a friendly Japanese bar girl who asked him his name. When he replied, she asked incredulously, "You Melvin from Guam?" When he replied in the affirmative she continued, "I know you, I no know your face, but I know your name, you clazzy."

Behind her two other girls were giggling and snickering between themselves. This was Melvin's third R&R in Okinawa and the girls remembered him best for sponsoring a "titty" contest. His reputation was firmly established when he located a male sailor who placed third. Before the week was over Melvin would add to his fame.

Satchko, one of the girls who giggled when he introduced himself, poured drinks for the table. Pointing at an undistinguished-looking man in his thirties she said, "Fellow at bar is officer. Officer GI want short time, I no be at your table, I do, I like short time, bang-bang-bang, five dollah."

His mischievous mind working overtime, Melvin thought about the Marine standing by the next table who was lugging a movie camera with two large battery-powered strobes. Having been in the back where the girls lived and sometimes worked, Melvin remembered the sliding walls dividing the cubicles. Instructing Satchko, he waited until she went to the back with the officer and then marshaled his forces. Everyone, including the bar girls, took their positions.

Trying to stifle their laughter, they waited for Satchko's prearranged signal. Hearing a solid kick, they slid back the wall separating them from Satchko and her naked partner. Blinded by the floodlights, the more than mildly startled officer did not yet know he was facing seven people, but he clearly understood Melvin's booming voice, "We're from Stars and Stripes doing an article on R&R."

At breakfast the next morning in one of the more rickety eating establishments in Koza, Melvin met a master sergeant. The rather plain-looking NCO in garish civilian clothes sat down and introduced himself as John.

"If you're not stationed in the Pacific, what are you doing over here?" asked Melvin.

"I'm a chaplain's assistant and we're over here on a pastoral visit. My boss is a priest who attends to the spiritual needs of the families of the men who are over here flying combat missions. My normal job is youth groups and working with young airmen."

"You sure this ain't just a shopping trip," asked Melvin.

"Oh no," said the master sergeant. "If you've got some time I can show you how we are doing the Lord's work. I think today we are visiting an orphanage and then I'm going to assist the Father while he listens to confessions. You're invited to come with me if you would like."

"I'm sure he's going to find people with plenty to confess, but no thanks, preacher. I've got a busy day. Maybe I'll see you around if I happen to come by the chapel."

Later, Melvin visited a Koza barbershop. His face was covered with warm scented mud following a procedure that began with steaming hot towels and a little Japanese girl shaving him with a straight razor as she seemingly cut each hair individually. It reminded him of the "Hotsie Baths" he enjoyed whenever he went to White Beach.[26]

Coming out of the shop, Melvin met the master sergeant, whom he tagged Preacher, in front of China Pete's. Preacher's arms were loaded with packages and without enticement he followed Melvin into a small dim bar. The jukebox was playing loud Japanese music with a female singing words something akin to "She ain't got no yo-yo." A cute black-haired oriental named Tamicho hugged Melvin.

"Buy me drink skivvy GI," she said.

Like most of the nessia girls in the bars, she was young, and her faint Asian beauty was enhanced with large fake eyelashes and judicious use of cosmetics.

Melvin explained to Preacher that he was okay with buying bar girls drinks, but they must drink the real stuff—no Saigon tea allowed. After three Orions, the local beer, Tamicho started to tease Preacher. Calling him by his first name, she asked, "John, why you no sit with girl, you too old?"

Copying her abbreviated English, Preacher replied, "I straight arrow, friends call me last of straight arrows."

"You no straight arrow, John, you cherry boy. No like Melvin, he butterfly boy. Butterfly boy no good. Play testo-testo, all girls on street. You cherry boy, I do for love."

Melvin interrupted her. "And five dollars for the room. You probably need to get out of here before you start behaving like an officer."

Preacher ignored the advice and kept matching Tammy, drink for drink. It wasn't long before he left the table and went into one of the back rooms with her.

"Just the type of example to set for the young troops," thought Melvin as he sipped his beer. "I'll bet his confession is going to be interesting."

Soon after Preacher disappeared, Melvin went back out on the street and ran into his radar navigator. They drank until the bars closed. This was an exception to Melvin's policy on drinking with officers. He liked Capt. Sams who shared his distaste for Capt. Palm, their aircraft commander.

With two days left on the R&R an early start seemed appropriate so they agreed to meet again, this time at eight a.m. in the Texas bar. Captain Sams arrived fifteen minutes late with Lieutenant Butterbrook alongside him. Melvin was not overjoyed to see his oversized co-pilot, but "what the heck," he thought, "maybe he'll buy a round."

Seated at the bar, a maintenance NCO named Jack, whom Melvin knew from Guam, turned and greeted them as they walked in.

"It's amazing who you meet when you only frequent high-class establishments," Jack said. "You sure got some ugly friends. That one looks like he's grain fed and his partner looks like Geronimo."

Soon a serious chug-a-lug contest was underway. First, Jack would race Lieutenant Butterbrook in downing a can of beer. Then Captain Sams would challenge the lieutenant, followed by Melvin, who was no slouch in this brand of competition. With a ratio of three to one it didn't take long to get the big and oblivious co-pilot sloppy drunk.

"I think it's time to get out and explore the countryside," Melvin said. "A couple of Marines told me about a place called Kin Village. They said it had some pretty remarkable temples."

Actually, Kin village, located just outside the gate of the Camp Hanson in Okinawa, held a series of bars. Because at the time most of the Marines stationed there were deployed to Vietnam, it was reputed to have a significant number of underemployed bar girls.

The four GI's stuffed themselves into a little yellow Nissan and told the Sukoshi (little) cab driver their destination. With "blubber boy" in the center of the back seat it was a tight fit. The taxi driver's unhappiness might have been because of the early morning hour, although more likely it was due to what Blubber Boy produced on the trip. Within ten minutes of setting out, Lieutenant Butterbrook unloaded what looked like two gallons of barf on the front of his shirt and down into his lap. There was nothing to do but continue, and when they got to Kin Village the driver pulled up to the first corner and waved them out with an "Ugh," and a shake of his head to show his disgust.

Now a new problem developed. Nothing seemed to be open and it was questionable how long they could hold the limp co-pilot upright. Even for three of them he was heavy and for obvious reasons nobody wanted to put their arm around him. Taking him by the wrists, they began to drag the lieutenant down the dusty street. It was broad daylight and several Japanese, dressed in traditional clothing, watched as they passed the closed shops. Finding an open bar, two blocks from where the disgusted cab driver deposited them, Melvin talked to the male oriental stocking the cooler behind the bamboo bar.

"Okay," said the man, "put Stinko in back room, girls not come back until later."

Stripping Lieutenant Butterbrook down to his jockey shorts, they manhandled him onto the bed, which was much too small for his large body. Taking everything but his jockey shorts, socks and shoes they set out to find a laundry for his vomit-soaked clothing.

Locating a Mamasan who said, "Can do easy—three hours," they set out to occupy themselves for the afternoon. Options in the little village were limited to two restaurants and about twenty bars. They chose the latter and forgot about the semi-naked lieutenant.

It would be twelve hours before they remembered him, and during this time Melvin would get into what he called a small fight with a Marine who didn't like his long hair.

Kin Village is a Marine town, but most of the grunts stationed at Camp Hanson were in Vietnam. To the few who remained behind, Melvin stood out. His long bushy hair violated even the loose Air Force standards.

In the evening, three Marines accosted him on the dark street. "What's a commie, hippie bastard like you doing in our town?" asked a tall redhead in civilian clothes. Almost as tall as Melvin, but twenty pounds lighter, the Marine started to poke and push while his two buddies watched and laughed. Melvin slowly waved his open hands in front of the irate Marine.

"Hey man! I don't want any trouble," Melvin said. He looked nervous as he continued to move his hands in front of the increasingly pushy jarhead who was now spitting in his face and poking him in the chest with a finger while violently questioning his loyalty and ancestry.

The cocky redhead jabbing Melvin was put off by the timid gestures of his victim. He didn't realize he was facing an experienced bar fighter with the confidence off a big man who delighted in opportunities to hone his fighting skills. This turned out to be a major mistake in judgment. Melvin knew what it was like to taste blood and considered taking on three Marines by himself just a fair fight. Still waving his hands, Melvin began to unbutton his antagonist's Levi jacket. Once unfastened, he used both hands to leisurely spread it back, exposing the front of the jarhead's shirt. Then in a quiet voice that sounded like it belonged in a doctor's office, Melvin said, "Hey man! This is going to hurt a little bit."

He threw a single punch to the chest. Following a sound resembling two bulls colliding, Melvin winked at the two awestruck Marines still standing. Looking down at the one he'd dropped Melvin said, "Hey man! I told you it was going to hurt a little bit."

Lieutenant Butterbrook, now wide awake and sober, had no idea where he was or how he got there. Badly needing to urinate, he looked around and saw he was in a small room with the walls covered in bamboo sheets. In one corner was a small earthenware jug used for drinking water. Out of ignorance and desperation he relieved himself in it. Confused and searching for his clothes, he could hear country and western music radiating through the thin walls. At intervals dark-haired Oriental girls would peer in and giggle.

The stream of giggling bar girls, fascinated by the size of the huge and almost naked co-pilot, increased as the word spread to their professional colleagues in other establishments. Covering himself with a sheet pulled up to his neck, Lieutenant Butterbrook waited anxiously. He had no idea of what he should do.

It was after midnight when Melvin remembered his co-pilot. He was still with the three Marines. They had become pals after they learned Melvin was a B-52 gunner. All three Marines were veterans of ground combat and had heard and felt the effect of the B-52 Arc Light strikes on Viet Cong positions close to them. They loved it when the bombers pounded the enemy.

Melvin explained to them the small problem involving the lieutenant. "How are we going to retrieve Stinko's clothes?" he said. "Everything in Kin Village, except the bars, closed long ago."

One of the Marines suggested they get the Shore patrol to help them. The Marine and Navy cops woke a Mamasan who ran the laundry, and ten dollars later she displayed an open tooth smile as they left with the stranded officer's clothes.

Melvin expected Lieutenant Butterbrook to be pissed off, and he was surprised when he was greeted like a long lost brother. "I guess a little time apart does that," he said as he handed the grateful officer his clothes.

Back on Guam, Melvin's life once again revolved around the flying schedule. In comparison to Okinawa, it was pretty routine. His latest mission count was now one hundred and eight.

ELLSWORTH AIR FORCE BASE, SOUTH DAKOTA, JULY 1967

Mother, Sam and Andy were all readjusting in their different ways to life back in the States. It wasn't long before the headlines in the *Rapid City Journal* caught the attention of everyone on base, and took the returnees back to the conflict they had just left.

TWO B-52 BOMBERS COLLIDE OVER VIETNAM

Dianne Vinroot was shopping when she saw the headlines in a newspaper rack outside the Base Exchange. She knew it couldn't involve Tom because she had just left him at home, although it still caused a little shudder as she thought about it. "That little rat Tom must have known about it and he didn't say a word. He was working on base all morning. He must have heard something. Probably didn't want to worry me, but I'm still worried about him. He's been at this too long and he needs to retire before I read about him in the newspaper."

In fact Mother (a name Dianne was not even aware of) received only preliminary details on the collision. Once again it involved a lead change, just like the first mid-air collision in 1965. He correctly deduced it was related to the three-ship Vee formation where the bombers merged into close proximity to consolidate the impact of bombs on target. He guessed that somebody blew the coordination and they came together. Gunners were supposed to watch spacing, but there was not much a gunner could do to prevent the airplanes from smacking each other when they were so close. He wondered if the fact that there was a major general flying on the lead bird caused somebody to get stupid.

The call signs of the two aircraft involved in the collision were Red One and Red One of the gunners was from March Air Force Base, California.[27]

When the two aircraft collided it was immediately apparent to him what had happened. His pilot gave him an order to bail out, but he never heard it, nor did he need to. The tremendous explosion and heat were all that he needed to know that it was time to get out.

When the bombers hit, his first reaction was to reach out with his right hand and grab a strap to pull himself forward, but when he did this the heat was so intense that the skin on his right arm peeled off. He reached for the turret jettison handle with his left hand and the skin began to peel off his left arm. He felt like he was sitting in a tin can in a bonfire and he was glad to see the turret go. As he came tumbling out of the aircraft at 32,000 feet he started to spin rapidly, and he extended his arms to stop the spinning. Once he stabilized he noticed he couldn't see the ground because of the cloud cover. This was a big concern to him because he knew they had just started the bomb run and he really didn't want to land in the middle of a group of enemy soldiers that only a few minutes before they were planning to drop bombs on.

At about 14,000 feet the parachute began to open automatically and he pulled the seat pack release to deploy the life raft and survival kit that was attached to him. He then started to pass through the cloud cover and could see he was going to land in the South China Sea. This was a wonderful sight because he knew that American forces controlled the sea and someone would be out to pick him up soon. He pulled on his riser release as his feet hit the water; the parachute released from him and he started to bob up and down in the water as he tried to get into his life raft. It was at this point he began to feel the burning sensation of the salt water on his freshly burned arms. He finally got into the life raft and tried to see if anyone else was near him. The sea was pretty rough with swells of about ten feet and he never did see any of the other survivors while in the water. In approximately thirty minutes an F-4C flew over the top of him and rocked its wings to let him know help was on the way. For the next two and a half hours he sat in his raft throwing out dye markers and watching the sky for a helicopter. When he was picked up at 10:30 July 7, 1967, he was taken to the Army hospital at Vung Tao, South Vietnam.

It wasn't long before another bomber made the newspapers, although not the headlines this time. Apparently a B-52 coming off target had trapped fuel that was unusable due to inoperative boost pumps. The pilot elected to land at Da Nang Air Force Base in South Vietnam. The aircraft landed heavy and was unable to stop on the runway. It slid into a minefield protecting the outer perimeter of the base. The gunner was the only survivor.

CLINTON SHERMAN AIR FORCE BASE, OKLAHOMA

After his second tour of duty on Guam, Melvin returned to the States and moved in to a small, one-bedroom apartment outside of Clinton Sherman Air Force Base in a town with the unique name of Burns Flats. There he did pretty much whatever he pleased when he wasn't flying or pulling alert. Although not a neat freak like Mother, he fixed his place up so it looked decent. Lieutenant Greenwood, who lived in the same complex, helped him paint and once in a while they went out together. Melvin wasn't sure how he liked running with a young officer, but since neither of them held any specific prejudices against women with loose morals they sometimes chased broads together. Even though he liked the somewhat wild lieutenant, this didn't change his overall distaste for officers. And nor did it change his opinion of being in the States. He kept seeing stories about the war protesters and always provided his standard response when somebody questioned him about the Vietnam War: "It's not a very good war—but it's the only one we have."

Melvin resubmitted his formal volunteer statement to return to flying Arc Light missions and this time he was accepted for transfer to the Columbus Air Force Base, Ohio, the unit scheduled next on the deployment list.

CARSWELL AIR FORCE BASE, TEXAS

When it was Cal's turn to reluctantly return from Guam, he had a mere ten bucks in his pocket. Back at Carswell he had little option but to check into the NCO barracks. Tired, hungry and desperately needing a beer, he got one of the maintenance guys to take him to the Office Bar just outside the west gate.

It was three days before he finally got a room, and when he checked in he was still wearing the flying suit he had on when he left Guam. The disgusted airman handed him note telling him he was scheduled to go on alert in the morning. Miraculously, he still had his bags and as he dragged them to the second floor he felt even sicker, knowing he no longer had the ten dollars.

After Cal cleaned himself up and rested for a few hours he managed to get to the alert pad on time. Other than the fact that he got to sleep regularly, it was no more fun than he remembered it. He needed to get back to the war before something happened to end his career. In Guam he didn't need a car, but back in Fort Worth he was worried about getting a ticket for drunk driving. He couldn't risk another one and he really tried to stay away from the bottle. But as a gunner he had days off at a time and his barracks was a major drag. All the other NCO's in it worked normal shifts and he had nothing in common with them. He could only hang around so long without getting bored stiff. He didn't even have any friends, so the only way to get to town was to drive, and sometimes things happened.

When he heard March Air Force Base was deploying and needed two gunners, he was first on the list of volunteers.

ELLSWORTH AIR FORCE BASE, SOUTH DAKOTA

Mother was thinking. It was nothing he could put his finger on except the process of elimination. The war was showing no signs of letting up and if you counted the units flying D-models, it was going to be their turn again soon.

He was eligible to retire, now might be a good time to pull the plug. He liked what he was doing but it drove Diane crazy. She worried every time he went flying and the last separation was rough for her. His problem was that he thought it was wrong to take the money and then bug out because of the war. Maybe if he stuck around, he could get promoted.

Meanwhile, Andy was discovering that he didn't know how to deal with his wife's emotions. Despite Rosalie's failure to meet him when he returned from Guam, and his feelings that they might be on the outs, she seemed delighted to see him when they finally got together. So delighted, in fact, that she became pregnant.

Probably more motivated by her pregnancy than any desire to be a gunner's wife, she nonetheless agreed to marry Andy. Sam was Andy's best man at the wedding, which was held in a small Catholic church. Although Sam missed the practice because he was flying, he didn't screw up. During the short reception he watched as Rosalie hovered over Andy. Whenever Andy started talking to one of the gunners, she would take his arm and move him away. When they started to leave, Andy made the mistake of hanging back, wanting to talk with his brother. A testy Rosalie said, "Get in the car now."

Back in their apartment, Andy told Rosalie about his plans to transfer to G-models where he could ride forward. This generated an argument about moving. She didn't want to leave her mother. He tried to tell her that as long as he stayed in the D's he might have to go back to Vietnam. She ignored this. "It won't be fair if you went back again," she said. "What about us? It's bad enough when you spend days on alert. How could we handle it if you were gone for six months?"

Andy tried to explain that he could avoid going back to the war if he changed airplane models, but Rosalie didn't grasp the concept. Her belief was that he didn't have to leave home unless he wanted to. Obviously, if he loved them he wouldn't go. She responded bitterly when Andy attempted point out that he was in the military and he didn't get a vote. Her attitude bothered Andy. If she was so unrealistic this early in their marriage it didn't augur well for their future.

As for Sam, he began to forget the war. At first it had been hard not to think about it, and in an unexplainable way he sometimes missed the company of his roommates. But life was pleasant being a husband and father again. His oldest boy Nick was now in Cub Scouts and they worked together building pine wood racers. Starting with a kit furnished by the Scouts, they shaved and sanded a block of wood into a replica of an Indy car. Then melting fishing sinkers they poured the molten lead into a hole carved in the bottom and filed away the excess.

A kitchen scale determined when exact maximum weight was achieved and then they began work on the undercarriage. With a power drill and toothpaste they polished the small nails used to connect the wheels to the body and carefully aligned them fore and aft. It worked, and after liberally applying powdered graphite before every run down the steep plywood ramp they proudly received a second place trophy. "Not bad for the first time out," said Sam, who was enjoying himself. Some days it was like he'd never gone to war.

But he suspected things were going too well. He was comfortable at home and working hard on his college courses. This semester he was taking economics, accounting and introduction to music. This last subject was a classic no-brainer. For about half the class they would listen to classics and the instructor would say things like, "Listen to this passage, you can hear the sonata allegro." Sam heard nothing that made sense to him, but it didn't matter. The test came out of the book so he just memorized the names of the composers and a few things about them. Since there was no assigned homework, it looked like an easy A.

"I need to remember life runs like a poker game," he thought. "You think you've got it made and some clown draws an inside straight on the last card. With my luck, something will come along that screws my plans up. I just hope it isn't this Tet business. All I need is another trip to the war."

Before the Tet Offensive was launched in January 1968, the prevailing view among most B-52 crewmembers was that the United States was rapidly winning the war. Now they weren't so sure. No one was yet concerned about failure to achieve ultimate victory, albeit much slower than had been hoped. It was hard to see a quick end to the bomber deployments.

Weeks of rumors prepared Sam for the official announcement of the deployment. The wing would return to Guam for another six months. Actually it would only be 179 days, like the first time. That way no one got credit for a combat tour and in some obscure way this made the Air Force system look better. To Sam, this was a big rip-off. It was outrageous to think that some pointy-headed bureaucrats in the government had actually developed a system that misled the public about the number of troops in Vietnam by not counting those who were there for less than six months. Sam knew that if he ever got his commission his records would not show a Vietnam return date. So with his enlisted time he'd be number one on the list of second lieutenants eligible.

As Sam packed he couldn't help thinking about how long he would be gone again. No question missing his family would be the hardest thing, but he was extremely frustrated with the break in his college work. He wondered if there was a way to take a correspondence course or something. He also wondered about what it was going to be like flying what was called the "carousel," where crews changed bases every thirty days. This was a big change and if they were going to drag their bags around once a month it made sense to cut back what he was bringing with him.

WESTOVER AIRFORCE BASE, MASSACHUSETTS, SPRING 1968

Turner Air Force was closing and Jim and Elizabeth received orders to Westover just in time to line up with the wing departure for Southeast Asia. They stoically prepared themselves for another separation. It was going to be hard for both of them as Elizabeth would again be a single parent and Jim would miss his family and all of the things they did together. Anyway he looked at it, it was going to be tough to be a war dog again.

"You're my hero Charlie Brown," said Elizabeth. "If you can do it, I can too. The twins know you didn't ask for this war. It's something we can't control so just be careful. I don't want to lose my big, round-headed man. We'll still love you when you get back."

ELLSWORTH AIR FORCE BASE, SOUTH DAKOTA, SPRING 1968

Rosalie took it hard when she heard the news that the wing was deploying. She did not understand the military. Andy tried to pacify her by telling her that when his enlistment was up he would get out of the Air Force and go to work for the telephone company. He meant it too. It was what he wanted to do. He never liked riding in the tail and he liked combat flying even less. But that didn't please Rosalie either. Although she hated the fact that he was being sent to Vietnam, she didn't want him to get out of the Air Force. All she could see was the steady paycheck and the $1,200 bonus he'd get for another four-year commitment. She stuck to her position even when Andy explained that if he reenlisted, he might have to do the war yet again. She couldn't see how illogical her position was. She was whining big-time that their daughter Kathleen needed her father, but at the same time she did not want Andy to get out of the Air Force.

Her position didn't make sense and Andy wanted to just throw up his arms. Marriage had been a major change for him and he was struggling to adapt to it. Less than a year ago he'd been a bachelor with plenty of money. Now he was driving a car with a baby bottle in the ashtray and trying to keep up with the bills. Rosalie didn't want to move into a base house so his rent down town was almost twice his housing allowance. Right after the wedding she started buying things for the house and their credit card debts were getting high. He couldn't seem to explain the to need to cut back on things and he wondered how Rosalie would do when he was gone. He wondered if she understood that he needed some money to live on.

Like Andy, Mother was getting some grief from his wife. He had elected not to retire and he convinced the wing gunner he needed to return to the war ahead of the rest of the unit. He knew many things had changed and he wanted to be able to update the gunners on the carousel. While there he would try to sort out billeting issues and make as many advance arrangements for his gunners as possible. Diane tried to talk him out of it.

"I don't see why you need to go or why you are so eager to go early," she said. "You know how hard on me it was when you were gone for six months. I'm too used to you doing all the worrying and I don't do well by myself. What if something happens? You've got four kids you need to think about. If you would get over your remorse about missing out on World War II and Korea you could retire tomorrow."

"Oh, nothing's going to happen," Mother replied. "I've been doing this too long to let something hurt me. I'm just going to be a staff guy anyway. The kids will be fine. They're not children anymore. It's hard to believe that Tommy our baby is almost fifteen. He's got a level head and in the big scheme of things six months isn't that long."

Diane suspected Mother was trying to put on a good front for her. She knew he was too much of a worry wart and fuss budget to be so cavalier about leaving home and going back to the war. He was faking it because inside of him he felt a responsibility to what he often dryly called God, Country, Duty and Strategic Air Command.

ANDERSON AIR FORCE BASE, GUAM, FALL 1968

Before their units were programmed to return home, Melvin and Cal campaigned to continue flying Arc Light missions. With no families to worry about they had nothing pulling them to the States. Melvin looked at life on Guam as just one big party while Cal considered it a financial gain. The mess hall was free and he would receive per-diem and combat pay. That was almost an extra one hundred dollars a month. Cal knew that if he could stay off the bottle he'd do better in the war than at home. This time he'd really made up his mind. If they allowed him to stay he would volunteer for every flight he could get. He was convinced that if he was able to keep flying he could stay away from booze.

It was logical for SAC to approve their request to extend. If nothing else it would mean two other gunners could stay home, and why should the Command send a non-volunteer when they didn't have to? Of course, as Melvin would say, "There is no discernible evidence that the staff weenies in the Omaha Puzzle Palace called SAC Headquarters are heavy into logic. After all, the facts might confuse them, so I'll probably get screwed again." But this time, Melvin was wrong. Common sense applied, and he and Cal both received extensions.

When Mother arrived to join them, he moved into a double room similar to the one he stayed in on his first tour, except this one was better decorated, with half-gallon whiskey bottles tied to the overhead pipes. There must have been fifty of them and it was clear Jim Beam was the drink of choice. Mother shared his new quarters with Cal, Andy and three other gunners he only knew casually. He was disappointed to learn Melvin was in another room and he tried to get this changed without success. When he and Melvin first met he'd been ready to dislike Melvin because he'd been warned by one of the wing gunners that Melvin's easy-going demeanor was deceptive. He knew Melvin had a small reputation as a bar fighter and rumor had it that he would punch someone and then say with a grin, "Nothing personal, just recreation." But as Mother got to know Melvin, his view changed, and he began to appreciate Melvin's irreverence and apparent total lack of worry.

Cal was another story. On the last tour Mother worried about him constantly. Sometimes, in spite of his best intentions, Cal would take a single drink and deteriorate rapidly into an alcoholic fog with no guarantee he'd stop drinking in time to make a flight. Mother tried to counsel him but didn't have much success in getting him to religiously watch his flying schedule. It looked like it was going to be more of the same this time around.

When Andy came in after a mission, Mother asked him, "Have you seen Cal? I've only seen him for a minute in the last two days and his bed's untouched. He's scheduled to fly tonight and I'm getting frantic."

"Nope," replied Andy "maybe the birds ate him."

" I don't know, I think he's on Gilligan's Island. I saw him yesterday. He came in here to get something out of his bag and left again. I suspect he was thirsty and needed to get something out of his private stock. Would you go see if you can find him."

Cal was sitting on a picnic table with four beers in front of him when Andy walked up from across the dark and mostly empty parking lot. There was irritation in Andy's voice when he said to no one in particular, "Mother sent me out for Sergeant McGraw. He said he'd better be in the Christian Science Reading Room or he was going to have his ass. "

Cal looked scrawny. His prematurely gray hair needed cutting and he had at least two days of white stubble. He told Andy he wanted to finish his beers, but with every minute it was getting closer to first

94

briefing. Before that he would need to shave shower, pack his B-4 bag and suit up. Not a whole lot of time to waste on sleeping, let alone sobering up.

Andy had to drag Cal back to the room. It had really pissed him off when Mother sent him to retrieve Cal and he was in no mood to put up with much crap.

Cal was in civilian clothes and didn't have his identification badge, but the bored-looking airman second class, who had been watching the party on Gilligan's Island, knew they were gunners, and since they never gave him shit like some of the tight-assed officers, he waved them through.

Entering the room, Andy, who was still irate, said to Mother, "I've got your favorite drunk and he's walking under his own power. I don't know why you don't just turn his butt in. He makes us all look worse than we are. Besides, I'm tired of his sorry ass.

"I don't know if you know this, but he pissed on the floor the other night. We ought to make the turd sleep on the lawn. At least then he wouldn't barf in our shower. It's just a matter of time until the sonofabitch does something we can't cover up. I damn sure ain't going to fly his flights. This shit scares me as much as anybody, but I don't stay in a drunken stupor."

Mother disregarded Andy's uncommon outburst. He told Cal to get cleaned up and dressed in a flight suit. "If you've got any time left you can sleep in the chair by the door. But not until you got your stuff together and are ready to go. You also need about ten gallons of coffee."

"I'm good, the only thing I need is one small beer," said Cal lighting a cigarette."

Back in Iowa, Bobby D. Olson remained oblivious to the war, despite the fact there were now nearly a half million troops in Vietnam and that the war was the central issue of the presidential election of 1968. As far as Bobby was concerned, the war was something the adults talked about. He was fifteen now and had his driver's license. He was looking at a Pontiac Tempest four cylinder and wondered how it would run if he put a V-8 in it. He continued to play soccer and think about sex.

Chapter Eight

ANDERSON AIR FORCE BASE, GUAM, MARCH 1969

The game was Texas "Hold 'Em" and it was time for Sam to get out. Suckered in by a pair of tens in the hole, he stuck around for the fifth up card. Clearly a dumb mistake. There were too many people still in the pot and with three hearts showing, somebody was going to have a flush. Even if he hit the third ten, the odds said he shouldn't have stayed in for the last up card. He knew better and he kicked himself when the dealer rolled another heart. Four of the five up cards were now hearts and he didn't have a single red card in the hole. Not exactly a sterling hand and there was nothing to do except run. If he'd been smart he'd have done it before the last card.

Sam studied Harvey, a captain from one of the wings who was sitting directly across the table from him. He hoped Harvey had the winning hand. If I couldn't take the pot himself, his choice was Harvey. Harvey needed at least an occasional jackpot. He was a consistent contributor and Sam didn't want him to lose interest.

He wondered what it would be like playing in a pot limit game with six Harveys. Guys who bet garbage and checked "barn burners." It was like taking candy from a baby's mouth. Clearly good clean fun and he wouldn't feel any guilt, not if they were officers anyway.

Sam could write a book, some of his competition was so predictable. Most of the officers he played against thought they were better than they were. Some who regularly played on the alert pad

96

back home got pretty good at poker, but Guam had a new brand of fish. The officer who last played in college now had over a thousand dollars in advance per-diem that made him believe he was Amarillo Slim.

Their limited experience consisted mostly of straight draw with some five or seven card stud thrown in. This didn't prepare them for constantly changing odds created by Dealer's Choice. Seven Card High/Low, Low Chicago, Eat at the Y and Fiery Cross, were just some of the games usually played with the joker wild for aces, straights and flushes.

Sam still marveled about how Major Harrington had accomplished the set-up the time his crew played the joke on the base dentist. "Poker is the same way," he thought. "Use smoke and mirrors to set up a pattern and then do the unexpected."

In this session, despite his mistake Sam added almost eighty bucks to the more than four hundred dollars he'd made since arriving on Guam less than two weeks ago. If he could keep it going it would allow him to send every cent of his Air Force pay home and keep building his college fund.

He was living in the same room he'd been in the first time. The HURTS fleet, under its third or fourth set of owners, continued in operation and the battered Kelvinator sitting in the corner technically still belonged to him. He'd won it when his three fours outranked the two pairs held by a badly outclassed navigator. He had left it in the room when he rotated. In a strange way, coming back to it was almost like coming home.

Generally when Sam wasn't flying he played poker. He would sleep during the day and play nights. Some of the gunners nicknamed him Sundown, because when the sun went down he got up, but to his officers he was still Sam. He liked and respected his new crew who were temporarily living on the third floor directly above his room. They rigged up a rope and bucket and by swinging the rope they could make the bucket bang on the door of his first floor room. This meant beer was needed and a prompt reply was expected. Since Sam virtually lived in the second-floor day room poker game they expected to be re-supplied by whoever was awake in the room.

One day, tired of the non-stop music in his room, Sam went to see Melvin who lived two doors down. It was raining buckets, but he stayed under the second-floor walkway and tried his best to avoid the huge drops blowing sideways. When he walked in Melvin was packing a wooden crate custom made in Okinawa. With its rope handles it looked like it belonged in a mortuary, and Sam decided he needed to get one if they were going to start flying the carousel.[28] It was big enough to hold everything he needed to haul on the airplane when they moved and it could be padlocked. That alone probably made it worthwhile to get one.

"Where did you get the funny-looking box?" Sam asked.

"Some Papasan on Gate Two Street made it for me," said Melvin. "He did a lot better job than my Okinawa tailor who measured and fitted me for a suit in a bar. The damn thing fits fine when I'm slumped over, but when I straighten up it's a mess."

U-TAPAO AIR FORCE BASE, THAILAND

Melvin was listening as the medic in a white uniform briefed the incoming crews on venereal disease. "There are thousands of whores in Thailand and all but one of them has some sort of VD," he said. Of course the first thing Melvin asked was, "What's her name?"

Thailand was going to be different. Throughout the war Guam didn't really have an established group of bar girls. Melvin took a serious count once and by stretching it he could come up with about five. Not much was left to work with after the three girls monopolized by Zeroes were discounted. He considered this a serious deficiency and knew it was related to both the Chamorro culture and the Catholic Church. Okinawa was great but still offered nothing like what Thailand had in its virtually unlimited supply of attractive Telocks and Puntangs. The main difference was that a Telock lived in a small but clean bungalow, and if a GI was willing to help with the rent, he could establish a steady relationship during his time in Thailand. Puntangs specialized in what was called a "short time" and worked out of one of the many Thai hotels dedicated to this purpose.

The carousel changed living conditions dramatically. Aircraft were continually rotated back to Guam for heavy maintenance and as the bombers moved, so did the crews.

Instead of staying together as a wing, crews were spread out in Guam, Okinawa and Thailand. People were mixed in with other units and there wasn't the closeness of flying with people you knew from pulling alert at home. Commanders were provisional and every move meant changing commanders along with accommodations.

In Okinawa the gunners moved into a dormitory previously used by permanent party airmen. The rooms were smaller, and it was two to a room, with the latrine down the hall. In Thailand the entire crew shared a trailer on the main road coming in from the gate. This made sense from a scheduling standpoint.

The crew that flew together now lived together. The downside was the bunk beds and the small single bathroom. Without even a writing table, there was not much space for six men and getting ready to fly required patience.

Flying out of U-Tapao Thailand, missions averaged only an hour and a half from take-off to target. This was a new experience for Andy.

"Everything happens faster," he thought. "I like this. Not as much time to worry and the short missions sure are a hell of a lot less boring."

As usual it was hot and humid when Andy took off on a flight, but on this occasion he would experience more excitement than he wanted. They were bombing in Laos just over the border from South Vietnam. Entry involved a hook over the Khe Sanh area and because the trailing aircraft had a radar problem Andy conducted a "Bonus Deal".[29] "One thousand yards on center line," he called, indicating the trailing aircraft was in the correct position to drop its load.

The Bonus Deal bomb run Andy was conducting evolved out of the need for a capability to direct a bomber to the target when a malfunction in its bomb navigation system prevented it from aiming and dropping on its own. This innovative concept was based on the gunner using his radar in the tail to monitor and position the trailing aircraft. By using the UHF radio he would report if the aircraft was right or left of center along with the distance between the two bombers. A typical radio call might be "two thousand yards, right of centerline." Based on this, adjustments were made. By positioning the aircraft requiring the Bonus Deal directly behind the lead aircraft, a timing delay before release was all that was required to put the bombs on target, assuming the lead aircraft was on target.

Andy loosened his straps and pressed his face against the window, watching the bombs dropped behind him and waiting for them to hit. Then suddenly he saw what looked like rockets firing off to his right. "Lock on! Lock on!" screamed the EW.

"What the hell?" thought Andy instantly. "There shouldn't be any SAM's here."

He could see three black telephone poles, with their tails on fire, rising toward the formation. "Break right!" Andy shouted at the pilot, "tell the formation to break right…"

Andy felt abnormal G-forces as the aircraft swung into a steep sixty-degree bank. If he'd had time to think about it he would have realized he'd never seen a bomber banked over this far, but he was too busy watching the angle of the SAM's. They seemed to be turning with the bomber and were closing the gap rapidly. All three B-52's in the cell were hard over when the missiles passed, trailing brilliant white light the consistency of a camera flash. The miss was less than a quarter-mile.

The missile launch and its closeness was something Andy hadn't expected, and it sent shudders through his body as he thought about it. For once he was actually glad he was in the tail so the others couldn't see him shaking. He'd been okay when it happened but not now. It damn sure got his attention. As it turned out, it got a lot of other people's attention too. No surface-to-air missiles were known to be in the area and even before Andy's crew got out of the extended debriefing, message traffic was going out to several headquarters.

Andy's crew was celebrating, if that is the right word, their escape from the three SAM's when they were told they had four hours before departure for MAC-V Headquarters in Saigon, where they would undergo more debriefing. As far as Andy knew, this was the first time entire crews had been called to Saigon for interrogation. Obviously, somebody was concerned about where the unexpected missiles came from.

The short flight carried eighteen crewmembers from the three bombers in the affected cell, along with various "strap hangers" from the wing staff. The total of twenty-eight people included Chief Master Sergeant Paul Baxter, the wing gunner, one of the few gunners not assigned to a specific crew. Andy had known Paul for more than five years and he considered him a professional. His uniforms were sharp and his military bearing was obvious without being overbearing. He was easy to talk to and could be counted on to carry the gunners' message. He was not like some staff members who sat in their ivory towers. Andy knew Chief Baxter flew missions on a regular basis. If nothing else that made him different.

SAIGON, SOUTH VIETNAM

It was three a.m. when they landed at Tan Son Nhut. The tropical smell, not much different from Guam, was the first thing that hit Andy when he got off the KC-135. When he climbed on the blue Air Force bus he looked at the iron bars and heavy screen over the windows and decided this was to block thrown hand grenades or small bombs from entering the bus proper. Traveling through the tree-lined streets of Saigon he was awed by the old French city's exotic beauty.

There was not that much traffic that early in the morning, only a few cabs and small motorcycles. If he discounted the numerous olive drab military vehicles, he got no sense of being in a war zone. Everything seemed peaceful.

As they pulled up to the large cream MAC-V headquarters building, Andy's opinion changed. The first thing he noticed was all the sand bags surrounding the hootches and outlying structures.

Escorted into a briefing room the crews began to tell their story to an intense but friendly Air Force colonel dressed in crisply starched fatigues. Discussions were casual and in no particular order. It was obvious the colonel and the rest of his staff sitting in the chairs along the sides of the room were trying to pin down the precise location of the launch pad. The obvious question was whether it was in Laos or just inside the border of South Vietnam.

It was also obvious that the MAC-V staff viewed this as some sort of intelligence failure, with ominous implications for future B-52 missions. Talk of movable or portable surface-to-air missiles launching from unpredicted locations did not add to Andy's comfort level.

When they broke off into smaller groups, the electronic warfare officers and the gunners were shuttled into a separate smaller conference room where they sat around a large table and tried to answer the staff's questions. Mostly it was just a case of retelling the same stories they covered in the big room. When Andy was questioned, he said, "At first I thought they were rockets and then it became clear they were SAMs. I called evasive maneuvers. The pilot banked hard and they missed us by maybe a quarter mile. We were awful close to the explosion, but I'm not a good judge of distances."

A lieutenant colonel waving a pointer in his left hand asked, "Did you see where they might have came from?"

"Not really," replied Andy.

Even when he viewed maps tracing the bombers route, Andy couldn't pinpoint the launch site in relation to any specific landmarks. Considering he was almost seven miles above the ground, and the fact that the missiles came in at an angle, he guessed he was ten or twelve miles from the area where the SA-2 was fired. This was not much help to the folks who were asking the questions. It was not much help to Andy either, knowing that he and his crew were increasingly likely to get shot at over areas previously considered safe.

At least they got taken to lunch at a fairly luxurious hotel and Andy got to experience the sights, smells and colors of downtown Saigon and see the broad array of flags in front of MAC-V headquarters. He wondered how they could have that many allies and not have won the war long ago.

KADENA AIR FORCE BASE, OKINAWA

As Sam moved around the carousel, he landed at Kadena Air Force Base and was bunked up with Cal in a small two-man barracks room. More like a college dormitory than a barracks, it contained two day rooms where one could shoot pool or watch Armed Forces television. Like U-Tapao, it offered the luxury of house girls who, for ten dollars a month, cleaned the room, shined shoes and washed clothes. Sam joked, "You can walk in, throw your clothes in the air and the house girl will catch them before they land. By the time you got out of the shower they are laundered, pressed and hung up in the closet."

Sam didn't spend much time in the room and when he wasn't flying he still worked at being an itinerant poker player. Unlike Guam, there was no set game where players came and went almost continuously around the clock. Here at Kadena they were more sporadic and the pickings were slimmer. More and more the officers were excluding enlisted men from their games and it just wasn't as easy to take the money from sergeants and airmen. Not that they were any more competition, it was just that Sam didn't have the same killer instinct with people he knew could be taking food from their families. Once he tried playing with a group of Marines, but they cured him fast. "Any time you see two full houses, one three's over sixes and the other sixes over three's, you've got to be a little suspicious."

Cal, in spite of his good intentions, was back on the suds and spent almost no time in his room. He pretty much lived in the downstairs day room, which held a small snack bar that served as his chow hall and bar when he wasn't flying. This was officiated over by a wrinkled, white-haired Okinawan Papasan who, at least by his appearance, couldn't be under eighty-five.

Since missions were shorter out of Okinawa than Guam, crews flew every other day. This put Cal on an odd-even schedule. Sober on even days, drunk on odd days. Sometimes this got reversed and Cal would get loaded on even days. The Papasan, who worked from eight in the morning until midnight (and apparently seven days a week), would reach into the cooler behind the rattan bar and deliver beer to Cal, who was nestled in an overstuffed chair in front of the constantly playing black and white television. Besides beer and soda pop, various munchies such as pretzels and potato chips were available.

This limited selection provided what Cal without humor called a seven-course meal—a six-pack and a Slim Jim. Unfortunately a lot of days he skipped the Slim Jim. Already thin, he was looking more and more like a scarecrow. Even on flying days when he tried to stay away from alcohol he didn't eat much, and it was taking its toll. Down to 130 pounds on his small frame, Cal's hangovers were a constant reminder of how close he was living to the edge.

Almost every day brought an example of how the booze was overtaking him. Sam was in Blue Two when he heard lead call, "Blue Two, this is Blue One, take over our position… Ah, our fire control is ah…inop…Ah, you'll understand why, over."

When they passed number one to take over the cell, Sam could see the guns drooping and knew it related to Cal. He thought about their earlier briefing. Sam was standing next to Cal when the room was called to attention for a visiting general officer. As everyone started to stand up, Cal began to slump to the floor. Sam caught him and held him up, but wondered how many others could smell the booze. Sam understood what was meant by "fire control inop."

Things were better when Mother was around to work with Cal. He took the time to counsel Cal about his drinking and he followed through to see that Cal was ready to fly. Sometimes they got into some of the very basic things, like shining boots and getting patches sewn on the new flight suits Mother gently forced Cal to get. Mostly the two just talked, and there would be long periods when Cal stayed off the bottle. He'd been pretty good until Mother's airplane went down. Sam still remembered the day vividly. He was lying in his bed when Ted DeBoar, one of the orderly room clerks, stuck his head in the door and asked, "You guy's hear we lost a jet?"

"No, who?" questioned Sam.

"I don't know, I just heard the commander talking about it."

"How about the people? Where?" cut in Sam.

"I don't know any more than I told you. All I heard was that one of our birds went down at U-Tapao and there was a fire…don't know the tail number or the crew or anything," said Airman DeBoar.

Just then John Cunningham, a gunner from Fairchild Air Force Base in Washington, walked in asking, "You guy's know anything about the airplane?"

"We just heard one was down," said Sam, who remembered Mother was flying. "Ted, have you got a roster from last night's mission?"

"It's on my desk, I'll get it," said Ted as he walked out, almost knocking down Mel Hay, another gunner from Westover who was coming in.

Cal had a frightened look in his eyes got up and started to put a flight suit on. He asked Sam, "Who was the gunner? It wasn't Sergeant Vinroot was it?"

"Hell, I don't even know if he was flying," lied Sam.

What followed was a series of people coming and going, asking questions and receiving no good answers, going somewhere else and receiving several more no good answers. Ted DeBoar returned with a crew roster and it showed Mother was on one of the six B-52's flying out of Okinawa. Finally somebody asked, "Has anybody talked to one of the pilots?"

This seemed like a good idea so Sam left to find his AC. When he returned he was immediately besieged with questions from the off-duty gunners congregated in the small room he shared with Cal.

"My ace says he's been to the command post and either they don't know or aren't talking. The story he got is that somebody was trying to make an emergency landing at U-Tapao and slid off the end and there was a fire," said Sam.

"Was this before or after the bomb run?" asked one of the concerned gunners. "Were there bombs on board?"

"My pilot thinks they aborted the bomb run, but he doesn't know for sure. He says the first airplane is due back in less than an hour and we probably won't know any more until then," said Sam.

"Why in the hell don't they tell us who it is?" piped up Cal. They got radios and they damn sure know by now what crew it is. I'll bet they got the officers over in the briefing room right now and are telling them what happened."

Cal was close to the truth. It would actually be another fifteen minutes before several pilots were told what the command post knew.

Lieutenant Colonel Ken Parsons, the head controller, was briefing. "Amber One had turned from the IP to the target inbound when they called Red Lead saying they were experiencing electrical problems and were aborting the bomb run and were going to return to Kadena. We theorize they must have lost all radios shortly after

this call and elected to divert to their primary alternate of U-Tapao."
He paused and then continued. "From information we have, they
made one low approach and then on the second attempt touched
down long. The pilot, realizing he was too fast, attempted to turn
onto the apron. The aircraft struck a concrete bunker and the fire and
explosion that followed resulted in the loss of all crew personnel."
The lieutenant colonel, who looked tired, stopped and then started
again. "This information is not official, so don't release it to anybody
outside this room."

The crew that crashed was S-01 and the gunner was Senior
Master Sergeant Tom Vinroot. Cal acted as if he were a bereaved
son or brother. He didn't drink until after the memorial service held
in the base chapel. The six funerals would be in various stateside
locations for each of the crewmembers on the ill-fated bomber.

Cal wished he could have gone to Sergeant Vinroot's hometown
of Hollton, Kansas, to tell his family and friends what a great man
they had lost in this stupid war.

Cal stayed sober out of respect for Mother until after the military
ceremony honoring the downed crew. That was when he began to hit
the booze again and the odd-day, even-day schedule restarted with
a vengeance. He spent most of a seven-day R&R in the day room,
only leaving to go to the bathroom. Sam checked on him a couple of
times and both times he was curled up and sleeping (passed out?) in
the overstuffed chair that served as his habitat. Several gunners that
shared the barracks became concerned about his odor, which was
hard not to notice, and decided to take him to his room. Regrettably
he had fouled himself, and even more regrettably, not knowing any
better, the good Samaritans tossed him into Sam's bed.

After this incident, Sam attempted to check Cal's flying schedule
and make sure he got to the briefings on time. The hanging guns
proved this was inadequate, although on early morning flights Cal
was usually okay because the Papasan stopped serving in time to let
him get reasonably sober.

Andy had troubles too. He was sending Rosalie almost his entire
paycheck, but it was never enough. Every letter he received included
a plea for more money, and he just didn't have it. The money he kept
back for himself didn't go very far and twice he'd had to borrow

from Sam just to make it until payday. He'd tried to explain this in his letters to no avail. Rosalie's responses were sharply critical about how selfish he was and how little he cared for little Kathleen.

Melvin was the one who was doing okay. He was the first to complete the circle on the carousel. Sixty days of virtually constant partying almost made the twelve-hour missions look good again. Okinawa was bad enough, but least they only flew every other day. Thailand was a killer. The three-hour flights were too short to get any rest and with only one day down out of every seven, it was getting harder and harder to recover from the night before. On occasion Melvin partied right up until show time, swearing he would hit the sack as soon as he got out of debriefing. Then someone would suggest going out for just one beer and the next thing he knew it was daylight. Like he often said, "War is hell, but it's the only war we have so I better enjoy it."

Sam was going on steady enough. He learned he'd completed a hundred missions. It wasn't something he closely tracked and he probably wouldn't have known it except that one of the clerks who maintained flight records mentioned it. It meant he was close to nine hundred hours of combat time. Statistics alone said this was pushing the odds. "You can only play cards so long before you get a bad hand," he thought. He'd read somewhere that a gunner was killed every twenty thousand hours of flying time. That was in peacetime and he wondered what the hell it was in war. Even if you discounted the risk of surface-to-air missiles you had to consider how tired the crews were getting and the strain on the aircraft.

Just a look at the aircraft 781 Forms used to keep a record of aircraft malfunctions told a story, with their pages and pages of delayed discrepancies. By themselves, none of these deferred repairs were anything to be overly worried about. The B-52 was a solid bird with plenty of redundancy built in, but just because one or two small hydraulic leaks were okay, did it mean ten were still fine? How about the secondary structure? Obviously a few small cracks in the sheet metal were no big deal. What about fifty? A few missions ago, Sam watched a triangular four by six-foot piece of aluminum on the vertical fin peel back in the slipstream. When he reported this to the pilot, the response was, "Let me know when it departs."

107

If the rumors were true, Mother's crash was caused by an electrical problem. At least that was what began the sequence. Did God make that happen or was something repaired incorrectly or missed on inspection?

"Probably missed on inspection," thought Sam, who was aware of how badly stretched maintenance was. It was common for the mechanics to run out of time to do everything. Every day was a new ball game and maintenance had to come up with whatever number of airplanes that were fragged.

Refueling and loading bombs took hours, and something often had to give. Critical repairs could not be ignored and this did not always leave time for required inspections. Sam wondered if aircraft washes sometimes got signed off simply because it rained, in spite of the fact that this would involving missing an opportunity to look over the outside structure

Like maintenance, the crews were dragging. When the missions came every three days there was time for the men to recover and get their minds right for the next go. When they did it every day for six days in a row they tended to become brain dead even when the days were fairly short. The routine didn't help and after a while one day became just like the one before and when a crew needed to respond to an emergency there was no water left in the well. Even though Mother's crew was more experienced and disciplined than most, Sam couldn't help but think of the fatigue factor. He asked himself, "Could they have handled the emergency if they were fresh?

"And what about the airplanes? When we started flying the D-models over here in 1966 their airframe hours were relatively low because of the years they spent sitting on ground alert. I'd guess a typical aircraft only flew five or six times a month. This went up dramatically when we started to fly Arc Light. I think it's starting to take a toll. Parts are becoming more scarce and there just isn't enough time between flights to accomplish every repair. Not when you look at how constantly overworked maintenance people are. Vietnamization hasn't slowed anything down and anybody who thinks it is working is sucking canal water."

In 1969, when President Nixon announced a policy of Vietnamization to draw down the number of American troops and increase the size of the South Vietnamese forces, it had no noticeable effect on the SAC mission, and bomber deployments continued as usual. That year would mark the fourth anniversary of Arc Light and it was starting to get tedious for both the crews and airplanes. Many of the involved units were beginning or had completed their second rotation and a few crews had been there for the third time as part of the constant rotation of crews between stateside bases.

Chapter Nine

ANDERSON AIR FORCE BASE, GUAM

After completing his round on the carousel, Sam was back on Guam. But things weren't the same. It frustrated him getting turned back from officers' poker games because of his enlisted status.

It didn't make sense to him that some days his money was good and some days it wasn't. Whenever there was a shortage of players he was still welcome, but when they could come up with enough Zeroes he become a second-class citizen again. If fraternization was the issue then why was it okay to share bedrooms with officers like they did when they first got to Thailand? He thought Hog Jaw was right when he said, "It's kind of hard to maintain the distance when everybody's snoring and farting in the same room."

Sam understood the issues. All it would take was one complaint from some enlisted man about losing money to an officer. Then the system would forget about the war and make an example. Some days he thought the most important thing was having a good haircut and wearing your hat. It was strange living in a war with streetlights and sidewalks where a gunner could get a letter of reprimand if he threw a beer can on the lawn after a North Vietnam mission."[30]

When Sam went to the mailroom to send a letter to Cathy, he discovered a form letter from the college placing him on academic probation for three incomplete courses.

He was surprised. He thought he had this worked out. He knew he was past the cut-off date for withdrawal when he learned of the deployment, but he talked to his instructors and wrote a letter enclosing his military orders. That should have fixed it. Now he wondered what it would do to his grade point average. He was starting to have doubts. He was already twenty-eight and the cut-off for commissioning was thirty.

Even without the TDY, his schedules were too erratic. He had already been dinged for missing classes. He did his homework and did well on the tests so why in the hell should he get a drop in his grade because he missed three nights? "Man and his Music" was one of the most useless classes he'd ever taken. During the semester he couldn't make a number of classes due to flights and the damn instructor wrote a note on his report card that said, "You did A work, I just didn't feel I could give an A to a man who missed four classes."

Sam was still frustrated when he got to the first briefing. "I guess pissing and moaning won't do me much good," he thought. "I just need to put on my poker face and knuckle down." There were some things he couldn't change, like getting ready to roll down the runway for another twelve-hour mission. More and more he hated these long hauls, particularly after having seen how much easier the shorter flights out of Kadena and U-Tapao were.

With a full 72,000-pound bomb load, the rolling take-off in the heavy B-52D was always dramatic.[31] In Guam it was even more so. The 11,000-foot prevailing runway at Anderson contained several dips and had a slight uphill gradient in the take-off direction. Rumor had it that if all else failed you could drop off the four-hundred-foot cliff at Patti Point and gain enough airspeed to fly.

As the bomber pulled onto the runway, Sam closely watched both tip gears to ensure the strut was outboard and that they were rolling and not dragging. No call out was required, but Sam usually gave a courtesy report by saying simply, "Flaps down, airbrakes down, tip gear rolling."

Unless he saw something strange, like the time he watched an outboard flap start to disintegrate, he would not distract the pilots by speaking again until climb out. At sixty-five knots the pilot said,

"Seventy knots" and when the airplane hit the exact number he said, "Now!" The navigator started a stopwatch and began the countdown to S1 (the point at which the airplane can no longer stop on the remaining runway). The navigator counted down the seconds, "Coming up on S1 in three, two, one, now."

Sam heard his aircraft commander say, "We've got a goer!" and that meant they were committed to the take-off. As often as he'd heard this it still gave Sam a thrill in the way that three Kings on the draw did. Nothing said he couldn't end up in a ball of flame, but he was in the game.

Sam heard the co-pilot say, "Coming up on up stick," but he never heard him say, "NOW!"

He should have felt the lumbering aircraft start to lift off the runway, but nothing happened. A thousand feet of runway rapidly passed by and they were still not airborne. Sam wasn't flying when they went by the ten thousand-foot marker and he knew the folks 150 feet in front of him weren't flying either. Suddenly he heard the pilot say, "Oh, shit!"

Sam felt the nose lift and then slam back onto the runway. He had no way of knowing that at normal "up stick" point the airplane was fifteen knots below the 148 knots it needed to fly. It was eating up runway at an alarming rate and the pilot could see what looked like a giant erector set coming up rapidly.

The aircraft commander knew these were the approach lights for the opposite runway and unless he could make something happen fast the heavy wooden posts with steel angle iron bracing would rip the belly out of the speeding bomber.

In frustration that was compounded by a complete lack of any better options, the pilot repeatedly slammed the control column forward and then pulled it back as far as it would go. The airplane began leap like a porpoise with each bounce and although it was ten knots below flying speed it cleared the posts by inches and wallowed over the cliff.

For a second Sam thought about bailing out, but he immediately thought better of it. That might work for the three officers in the upward ejection seats, but it darn sure would be messy for the navigators whose seats fire downward.[32] And if he tried, he'd probably kill his ass. The book said the minimum bailout altitude for a gunner was five hundred feet and even then it didn't make any promises. They were well below that now.

The airplane felt like it would drop at any minute. They were flying in ground effect, less than fifty feet above the ocean, and Sam could see the small waves clearly. But the bomber slowly gained enough air speed and soon it was able to climb and join the formation.

"I'm only halfway through this damn tour and if there was ever any excitement to it, this is not the kind I want," Sam thought. He was tired of the whole thing. He was tired of bag drags and tired of ever-changing roommates. The guys he was with now seemed to fuss more the ones he was with the first time.

Sam was now living in a house trailer. To make room for more officers the gunners had been moved out of the compound. Now, six continually rotating gunners shared a three-bedroom mobile home complete with a kitchen and two bathrooms. Because people changed so often, and many of the gunners weren't from the same wing, they really never got used to each other.

Without a designated "mother" to referee between the gunners in crew rest and those not scheduled to fly—who felt it was okay to drink breakfast—a new set of frustrations erupted. Some days Sam felt more down than others. It was nothing he couldn't deal with, but the cycles seemed to get lower.

As he watched things change he decided that the lack of routine caused by moving every month made people edgy. He didn't really feel close to a lot of the gunners he bunked with. It was not like living with the same guys for six months. Now it seemed like everything was temporary and people just didn't adjust to each other. Little things like toothpaste on the sink created irritations, and crew rest was a constant source of strife between the drinkers and those who didn't want to be continually awakened by loud parities. Even the goddamn air conditioner setting pissed some people off.

That amazed Sam when he thought about it. There they were in a war and folks were fighting over temperature settings. Of course if he looked around it was hard to get a sense of being at war. They still went from their air-conditioned quarters to their air-conditioned mess hall and rode an air-conditioned bus out to their air-conditioned airplane. What made it more unreal was that on both Guam and Okinawa there were permanent party troops living in base housing.

On trips to the BX, gunners saw wives and children oblivious to the fact that among them were TDY crewmembers regularly flying long and sometimes risky combat missions. Dinner at the NCO club was an artificial reminder that people still led normal lives. Nicely dressed wives shared candle-lit tables with their husbands, and the glassware sparkled against the white tablecloths. Eating there could be an uncomfortable experience for a gunner. Most of them held valid club cards and it was supposed to be their club too, but in truth they didn't really fit in. Flight suits, while technically permitted, looked out of place, and most gunners' civilian wardrobes were limited by how much they could stuff in one of the bags they dragged from place to place. It was not hard for gunners to get the impression they didn't belong.

One of the many things that bothered Sam was that nobody seemed to be looking out for Cal any more. It had been fairly simple for Sam to watch Cal when they shared a room in Okinawa. When they were in Thailand and lived with their crews he depended on Cal's officers to discourage his drinking.

They had been good about this and made it a point to keep booze out of the trailer. At the same time, if Cal just sat around he got bored and there were too many places he could get a drink. The crew oversight and Sam's nagging generally worked in Thailand, but back on Guam it was harder, and Sam couldn't shake the possibility somebody was trying to sabotage Cal.

"It pisses me off," he thought. It wasn't like Cal's roommates know or cared that he had difficulty handling his booze. On a daily basis he was never more than a few steps away from any number of alcoholic beverages. Sam thought this was more manageable when Cal had people in the same room looking out for him. He couldn't prove it, but he knew to a certainty someone was feeding Cal drinks, knowing full well he had more than a minor drinking difficulty.

Two nights later Sam watched Hog Jaw offer Cal a beer, knowing Cal was scheduled to fly. Cal didn't take it, maybe because he really was trying not to screw up and miss another flight. Or maybe it was because Sam was watching. Sam didn't say anything, but he sure thought it. Cal didn't need some sorry bastard trying to stir his shit. Hog Jaw knew damn well Cal had a drinking problem. He thought it was funny to get him drunk.

Sam didn't like Hog Jaw much anyway and if he had known that the loud, foul-mouthed gunner was about to be responsible for Cal getting his foot broken he would have been more royally pissed than he already was.

It happened at a picnic on the bluff overlooking Tumon Bay. The party was an informal get together between maintenance people and gunners, and it was beginning to die down.

Lacking the necessary depth in experienced drinkers due to an impending mission and heavy attrition among the amateurs, there were only about a half dozen people left. Someone brought a Honda 90 and Cal was slouched on the running motorcycle when Hog Jaw, rabblerousing as usual, suggested, "Cal why don't you go out and crash for us."

Cal's lubricated mind took this as a challenge. Not wanting a dare to go unaccepted for too long, he shifted into gear, released the hand clutch and proceeded to misjudge the amount of power. This sent him straight over the bank and out of sight out into the jungle.

Ordinarily this would be no cause for alarm, but when Cal didn't reappear, one of the fire control troops who still had some semblance of sobriety about him, went down to see if Cal was okay. Cal was lying with the handlebars of the Honda on his head and his left foot bent awkwardly behind him.

Assisted by Sam, Cal limped back to his trailer. He sobered up and was contrite, but Sam was worried. "That dammed thing is broken," he told Cal, pointing to Cal's foot. "It's swollen up like a basketball and your toes are all blue. You need to go to the hospital."

"No way," said Cal, "I'm not going to have somebody else fly my missions. It's the only thing I do that amounts to anything. If they ground my ass, I'd be more hopeless than I am now. No way."

"You're going to look a little silly without a shoe on one foot. There is no physical way that thing will fit in your boot."

"I'll get a bigger boot then," said Cal decisively.

It turned out that Hog Jaw not only had a big mouth, he had big feet too—thirteen triple E. Sam wasn't sure Cal could stand the pain of putting one of Hog Jaw's boots on. Given the size of his foot it looked like he was trying to stuff two tons of fertilizer into a one-ton truck. But Cal toughed it out and managed to get the boot on. However, he looked a little unbalanced when you compared his size nine right boot to the oversized left one.

"Now if I can just keep Calvin off of self-prescribed pain medication," thought Sam.

When Cal reported for his next flight, he was decidedly lopsided. His crew accepted this without comment. The prevailing opinion among all of Cal's officers was that it was better not to ask the question unless you could stand the answer.

Andy was not on the same schedule as Cal so he missed most of the medical saga, but he wondered how Cal's foot was going to get better without medical intervention.

On Andy's next sortie he was about halfway down the runway on take-off roll when he watched as the number three engine disintegrated. A pie-shaped piece of metal had separated from the turbine wheel. This caused a catastrophic failure that riddled the flap and the lower wing surface with hot metal. From the tail it looked like sparklers going off and for a few seconds he could see a short-lived fire between the airplane and the extended inboard flap. Andy couldn't observe much with the flaps down and he knew he would not be able to see how much damage had been done until landing. At least there seemed to be no more flames.

There was clearly something to be said for eight engines, Andy thought as he listened to the co-pilot who said, "I felt the throttle kick back and watched the gauge spin down. I looked out on my side and couldn't see anything so I didn't tell the pilot until we were airborne. Not much we could have done anyway."

The crew would continue the mission although Andy was hoping the lost engine might be a reason for an early landing.

"It was a dumb-assed thing to re-enlist," he thought. Now he couldn't get out for another four years and by that time he would be sucked in by the twenty-year retirement program. He reflected on how strange it seemed that Rosalie was the one who talked him into staying, she was the one who had to have the re-enlistment bonus, and now all she did was bitch about him being away from home and how she didn't have enough money.

Even with flying and combat pay he couldn't keep her happy. Before he left he tried to get her to move on base because it would be cheaper and at least there she could hang around with wives who were in the same boat. But no, she wanted to stay downtown where her sister and mother lived. They were about as much help as an empty gas tank. They had no understanding of the military and their approach to her problems made it tougher. "Why doesn't he just tell them he's not going to do it," seemed to be only suggestion they offered.

Rosalie's letters were depressing and Andy worried about his daughter. Among other things he wasn't sure if Rosalie wasn't running around. He knew that sort of thing happened and he'd heard tales of what went on when the unit was deployed. In fact a couple of officers divorced their wives when they got back the last time and if the stories were true the wives were blatantly less than faithful. Andy couldn't put his finger on anything but his last phone call made him suspicious. Several times he used the WATS line set up by the command post and hadn't got an answer. The last time he got a baby sitter on the phone and if he figured the time zones correctly it was three a.m. Rosalie's time.

Melvin of course had no worries about wives. He had got rid of his. He finally caught up with Jim in debriefing. This was the first time they had met up since they both joined the carousel two months ago. "It's funny how you can go this long without crossing paths with someone you know," Melvin thought.

The two talked for a while and then Melvin challenged Jim for his bean, knowing he would probably lose a drink.[33] As expected, Jim produced his bean and then tried to smoothly con Melvin into handing him his.

This was forbidden by the rules. If you hand your bean to another gunner he can keep it. The correct way was to set it down and then let the other gunner pick it up and examine it if he wanted to. Obviously it was illegal to challenge another gunner while you held his bean and you were honor bound to give it back the same way you got it.

The bean ritual required gunners to carry their bean at all times. If challenged they had to produce it anywhere, anytime. This included the shower, where the first indication of a challenge was usually a hand sticking through the curtain. This could be hard to respond to because of the "Bob Herring rule" which prohibited defacing the bean.

This rule came about when Bob tried drilling a hole in his bean and wearing it on a chain around his neck. This was verbally voted down as unfair as the conventions became more formal. Jim was the one who produced the first typewritten copy of the "Rules for the Gunner's Bean."

More than anyone, Jim worked at keeping the bean ritual intact. "Too many people don't follow the rules and some guys have even lost theirs. That's wrong," he thought. "Pretty soon some Zero will be making challenges."

Jim made it his duty to keep up with Mama Nening even when he wasn't on Guam. He wrote her letters and sent her small gifts. As far as he was concerned she was part of his family and a couple of times he had Elizabeth send pictures of his twin daughters to her.

Mama Nening was a tradition for the gunners and for many of them the Rum Shack was like Mecca. Some gunners landing on Guam were known to actually drag their bags with them and visit Mama before they cleared through billeting. Jim enjoyed watching new gunners hint to Mama that they needed a bean. If they got one it was always her last. As always she rubbed it on the shine of her nose and explained it was for luck.

Melvin and Jim didn't run in the same crowd, but the shared experience of combat was something they had in common. They were pleased to see each other. They commiserated about what a shitty deal the loss of Mother Vinroot was and then they talked about Cal.

"Did you know he'd got more missions than anyone over here," asked Jim. "It's got to be more than 250, no wonder he drinks. It's hard to believe anybody in any war could get as many missions as we're starting to pile up. What the hell was it in World War II? Something like twenty-five or fifty?"

"Yeah, but they didn't fly every day like we do when we are in Thailand," said Melvin. "I got twenty-six missions in thirty-one days. You should have seen my bar bill."

"Yeah, but you're single and like being a war hero. I just want to get home," said Jim. "I've got a wife and twin girls who miss their daddy."

Chapter Ten

With the officers getting skittish it was harder for Sam to find action, so he felt good to be in a game again. He was sitting with five officers from a crew he'd never met before. They'd just arrived on Guam, on their first combat tour, with their pockets full of the eight dollars a day advance per-diem they'd received in a lump sum before deploying.

The crew was cocky when they set the limit at two dollars with five dollars on the last card, probably thinking it would intimidate Sam. This made for some pots of over one hundred dollars. Part of Sam's strategy was to study the players and learn their patterns. That night it wasn't too tough. All these guys did was bet and raise. It wasn't long before it became obvious they were taking turns trying to bluff him out.

Sam knew that in straight poker, even if it was pot limit, or no limit, a lot of the bluff related to the size of your balls and the depth of your pockets. Not so with the seven card high/low games they were playing. An aggressive early bluff might run off some of the weak sisters, but with four cards to draw, Sam knew it was unlikely anybody had a lock with three or four cards to go. Besides, in two winner games, like this one, a bluff is unlikely to take both sides of the pot.

Sam watched his front door and played for position. At some point the opposition became so snake-bit that Sam could pick his direction without much fear of competition. After ten hours he computed he'd won over fifty dollars an hour. His competition didn't look happy when he said he had to go and it broke his heart to leave. But he was standby for the morning launch, although it was not with his usual crew. Sam was just a spare in case some gunner dropped out. He wouldn't have to suit up unless he was notified he was going. Normal odds said he would skate, but it turned out some crew from McCoy had come over without their gunner.

Sam never liked flying as a spare. There was no way to know how good the crew was or how they'd treat him. When he left the trailer for first briefing it was raining drops the size of a nickel. "Nowhere but Guam," he thought, and he was soaked before he got to the briefing room.

It turned out he knew the crew he was flying with. They were the same officers from the previous night's game. Except now they were in flight suits and taking their seats for first briefing.

He wondered if he had mentioned he was an enlisted gunner. They darn sure never asked; maybe they let him in the game based on wrong assumptions. Well they wouldn't get much sympathy from him. As far as he was concerned, it was a gunner's job to take their money.

Then a somewhat frightening thought crossed Sam's mind. He was dead tired from his night extravaganza, but at least he had got a pretty solid afternoon nap in before it. He remembered somebody in the game saying that they spent the day getting initial mission certified, which meant their asses had to be dragging. He wondered if the pilots had ever made a take-off on Guam's wavy runway. All he had to do was accomplish some simple checklist items, but those boys had serious work to do.

After Sam started his preflight, he switched on the air conditioner and got a stream of fog from the over-saturated system. This made him think about the heavy rain that was still coming down. No doubt it was a full-blown monsoon. Even the command post was concerned enough to increase separation between the bombers.

When the aircraft turned on the runway for a rolling take-off Sam could barely see the tip gear and he couldn't see the wing tips at all. Everything was normal up to decision speed when he heard the co-pilot flying the airplane say, "I've just lost the center line."

This left no way for the pilot to visually reference runway alignment and it would have been easy to drift off to the side. Which was exactly what happened. In the process of getting into the air, the number one engine ingested a runway marker light, which kicked up when the right tip gear smacked it. The crew never mentioned the incident and continued to press on to the refueling over the Philippines. Unable to handle the turbulence, the pilot didn't get all the required fuel so on the way home Anderson launched the strip alert tanker to give them extra JP-4. The second refueling wasn't much better than the first and Sam's temporary crew chased the tanker all over the Pacific before finally getting a good hook-up. All it took was fourteen and a half hours from take-off to landing.

U-TAPAO AIR FORCE BASE, THAILAND, NOVEMBER, 1969

Jim was in a great mood. He'd finally made technical sergeant. It had been a long time coming. As a staff sergeant with over seven years in grade, he had been frustrated by the slow promotion cycles for gunners. It was not like the officers, where second lieutenants made first lieutenant in eighteen months and captain eighteen months later. He'd started out in aircraft maintenance and some of those guys there had two stripes more than he did. SAC took the temporary spot promotions away shortly after the D-models started flying Arc Light, so he couldn't even count on that possibility. When the spots went, Hog Jaw, never one to turn down a chance to be sarcastic, claimed that the loss of spots was part of a penalty clause SAC established for flying combat rather than just sitting on alert.

The officers took it the worst and there was one former spot lieutenant colonel Jim knew who went around with no rank on his flight suit rather than put his major leaves back on.

For a long time there was little Jim could do to improve his promotion chances. He never went without a sharp uniform and Elizabeth even pressed his flight suit. Respectful of officers, he did what he was asked and always aced his evaluations. There was not much more to be judged on that Jim could control and he had almost given up hope of getting a promotion. Then the system changed.[34] An exam was established, for which he studied with uncommon focus.

He knew he'd done well on the test, yet he couldn't help feeling ecstatic when he was finally notified of his promotion. When he was in basic training he set a goal for himself to retire from the Air Force as a master sergeant. "Now all I have to do is earn one more stripe and survive the war," he thought as he attended the promotion party.

He tried to call Elizabeth on the special "Autovon" line set up for crewmembers to call home, to tell her the news, but he wasn't able to get through. Calls were limited to five minutes once every two weeks. An attempt counted the same as a connection. But the failure to get through to Elizabeth did not dampen Jim's spirits, and nor did the fact that he had to leave the promotion party early to get ready to fly another of the almost daily missions out of Thailand.

The target was in an area of the MeKong Delta called the Iron Triangle. From the air it looked extraordinarily serene and peaceful, with the MeKong River and its tributaries snaking through a carpet of green. A few sandbars could be observed along bends in the river, but there was nothing to show this was the home of the Viet Cong's ninth division.

Not a hint of life could be seen from 35,000 feet. The cloudless sky, broken only by contrails, was absolutely beautiful and it was hard to grasp a sense of combat. Pulling the turret disable switch mounted on a column between his legs, Jim used his optics to track the falling bombs without moving the guns. Downward visibility in the tail was limited and the optics with their slight magnification provided a better view of the bombs striking the target. Usually this resulted in nothing more than a string of red fireballs as the bombs exploded along the aircraft track. Beyond that there was nothing to indicate that they had hit anything specific.

But this time Jim noticed something quite different. There was a huge and rapidly growing mushroom-shaped cloud of gray smoke rising above 20, 000 feet. It continued to grow and was still visible when they went "feet wet".

Clearly the bombs had struck something significant, and for the first time since he began flying combat Jim saw something more than just bombs exploding.

After the mission had been completed, the intelligence officer who debriefed Jim had already talked to the navigators and now wanted to know what Jim saw. He explained the best he could, but he was not sure of the exact altitude of the top of the smoke cloud. Whatever they hit it must have been big, and the Captain who was questioning Jim said he was "pretty sure it was some sort of ammo dump."

KOZA, OKINAWA

The smell of wet concrete came from the narrow passageway where Melvin shared a wooden box with Tomicko, one of the girls he knew. Whatever merchandise this box once held was unknown, the perpetual Okinawan rainfall had long ago stripped its labels away, and time and moisture had painted it a dull gray.

Tomicko was now a street whore, one step above the lowest hotel girl. Four bucks if she could get it, highest bid if she couldn't. Mostly the bids were not high and on this night just before payday there were no bidders. Still Tomicko was a special whore to Melvin. He had never slept with her, but he had known her a long time. She hadn't always been a whore. When he first met her she worked at the Texas Bar as a top of the line Nissa girl, talking Marines on R&R into buying her glasses of colored tea. She used a line that seldom varied from girl to girl, "Buy me drink, dozo." Dozo meant please, and the request was usually accompanied by promises of pleasure after the bar closed. Nissa drinks ran from a low of one dollar to a high of two, and it was not abnormal for a barmaid to drink six or more of these an hour.

Tomicko feared and resented the fact that the bar girls took away money that wouldn't make it to the alley where she worked. She was still more or less a free agent, but she knew her role was just an intermediate step. She owed a Mamasan money and it was only a matter of time before she would have to move to one of the hotels to pay her debt.

The explanation for this was that she lived under a dismal system with several tiers. In Okinawa most of the girls of the night began their careers when they were recruited by a bar owner, or a Mamasan. This might involve paying the expenses involved in moving her from one of the fishing villages on an outlying island to Naha or Koza. She would then sell drinks on a commission system intentionally designed to get her deeper in debt. Her only escape was to sell herself on the street where more money could be made, but this was not very profitable after she paid for the room, and it was usually only temporary. If she remained in debt she could be forced to work it off by selling herself out of a hotel and letting the Mamasan keep most of the money. In reality, only a lucky few managed to snag a GI who would support her. Even this was mostly temporary and generally ended when the GI's tour ended.

"You been on BC Street tonight?" Tomicko asked Melvin.

Melvin nodded yes.

"Many girls on street?"

"Only a few girls, all number ten."

She appreciated the fact that Melvin had rated all of her competition as number ten on a ten-point attractiveness scale where one was the finest. But not really believing him she asked, "Why you all time nice to street girl? All time buy girls in alley ice cream. All time buy cigarettes. GI no have to be nice to street girl."

Whenever Melvin was in Okinawa he went to the dark alley and shared his cigarettes with the girls who plied their trade there. From a little store on Gate Two Street he would buy what passed for popsicles and bring them to the working girls. Some nights he passed around dozens of these flavored ice bars. Melvin wasn't sure why he did this. It was probably because he felt a special comradeship for the whores. Like him, they had no real control over their lives and could be traded at will, just like he had been when he was shipped to Captain Palm's crew.

Melvin enjoyed the streets of Koza with its numerous Americanized bars with names like Club Seven and New York Bar. He liked the lights and the flashing multi-colored neon signs advertising "Floor Show, Floor Show," and enjoyed watching the girls who danced in them. It was the energy of the place that attracted him, from booming music to the drunks filling the streets.

At three a.m. the bars were technically closed, yet a lot still went on. At this time of night a lot of people on the streets were Marines just back from combat and they often wandered around like zombies. Just watching them trying to see how fast they could spend their money was interesting. So was learning that the term "drunken sailor" wasn't an idle phrase.

Still in the alley, Tomicko asked, "Why you no get girl?" as she sipped on a bottle of orange soda Melvin purchased for her.

"Not tonight, I'm going to go see Mama Guru," Melvin said patting Tomicko on the head as he walked away.

Compared to Mama Nening's Rum Shack, the Wolf Club had some not so subtle differences. Mama Guru, the Japanese Mamasan who ran it, weighed slightly over three hundred pounds, and when Melvin walked in she threw her oversized arms around him and gave him an extraordinary sloppy kiss directly on the lips. This was her trademark and even straight arrow gunners came by just to get the bragging rights that went with a patented Mama Guru kiss.

Mama Guru's Wolf Club would have made a USO club blush. It employed bar girls like an accordion works—the staff of Thai beauties expanded and contracted depending on the number of customers. If he wanted to, Melvin could have taken one of these scantily clad girls to the back. Mama Guru would have provided credit if needed. Pretty much everything went, although fighting was discouraged. Not forbidden, mind you, just discouraged. Mama Guru was notorious for giving some loudmouth a pretty solid smack herself.

At two a.m. that night there was not much going on and as Melvin sat alone at the bar he thought, "Jesus, I'm forty years old with three ex-wives. I've got to quit running so hard or I'll kill myself before the war or some stupid pilot does."

ANDERSON AIR FORCE BASE, GUAM

Cal was hobbling big time, but hadn't missed a mission since his accident. When Sam suggested he ground himself, he replied, "The missions are all I have, without them I'd be lost." Taking the large boot off for the first time brought tears to his eyes, but it was nothing compared to getting it back on. Even Hog Jaw cringed as he watched a gaunt Cal struggle to get his swollen foot back into the oversized boot. As a last resort Cal tried putting it on without a sock. He soaked his foot and the tall combat boot in soapy water, but still had to endure nauseating pain before he finally got it back on. Cal swore he'd never take that boot off again until his foot was better.

This meant he could not take his flight suit off to shower because of the simple reason it wouldn't come off over the boot. Not that Cal was a stranger to sleeping in his flight suit. It was just that after a certain amount of time the flight suit would get kind of gross—even for Cal. The solution was fairly easy. Cal would just shower fully dressed and drip-dry. From then on he looked no worse than normal, except maybe for his asymmetrical footwear.

There were a lot of potential complications concerning Cal's untreated foot and some gunners were genuinely concerned about his refusal to see a doctor. The exception was Hog Jaw, who irreverently suggested setting up a pool on which toe would fall off first.

Andy was too concerned about his own fears to worry much about Cal. He worried he was going to die in the tail and every time he flew he became more frightened. But he didn't enjoy the idea of going home to face Rosalie either. Her letters kept getting more caustic and although he'd almost begged her to send him a picture of Kathleen, she never did. She constantly whined about money and him being away from home. It got so he didn't even want to check his mail. Not that it mattered much. In the last week he'd only gotten one letter, which made it two for the month.

As Sam neared the end of his six-month tour he faced the tough decision about whether to re-enlist or not. His hitch would be up a month after he got back to the States. If he planned to re-up it would be better to do it early, before he left the combat zone. That way his bonus would be tax-free.

If he did re-enlist it would be for four more years. That meant he would have twelve years in before he could get out if he wanted to. By that time he would be hooked and he didn't want to spend his life in the tail and keep leaving home for six months at a shot.

Cathy told him she'd like to sleep with an officer and he'd kind of like that to be him. It all came down to the odds of getting commissioned. If he could keep knocking out end of course exams he would be eligible for Bootstrap in less than six months.[35] That would allow him to attend college full-time and complete his degree.

He eventually decided to re-enlist. Thanks to the "Gunner's Beau Rae God"[36] he discovered how to receive transferable college credits through the United States Air Force Institute.

127

He'd never heard of this program until one day he was casually talking in the education office and the civilians briefed him. He could kiss that education officer. By reading the book the night before testing he had passed six in less than a month. By the time he went home all he would need would be nine core courses to achieve the necessary ninety hours. He could knock those out in one semester. With a degree he thought his chances of getting into Officer Training School (OTS) were pretty solid. But it was kind of like going all in on a poker hand. When you raise your hand you don't get a second chance.

Sam's aircraft commander read him the re-enlistment oath in front of the aircraft with the rest of the crew present. A photo was taken and then they all boarded the bomber for another combat mission. It was Sam's 144th.

The six months seemed to last forever. Finally, Sam would be flying home on one of the B-52's. " A straight seventeen-hour shot sure beats the heck out of a tanker loaded like a cattle car that has to stop in Hawaii for gas," he thought.

The night before departure Sam went to the maintenance area to check on the loading of the crew's "goodies". When he walked up Charlie Ramp he saw the airplane bathed in lights and surrounded by maintenance people. The left main gear was on jacks and a wheel was off. The souvenirs and junk going back with them was in a pile the size of a small shed next to the left wing.

"There is no way all of this is going to fit in the airplane, even with the wooden racks they are installing in the bomb bay," thought Sam.

People went nuts in Thailand buying brass candlesticks, alabaster statues, porcelain elephants, oil paintings and other treasures. Sam's crew was no exception. His navigator bought a Papasan chair that must have been four feet high. Obviously the mound of stuff belonged to several crews, not just Sam's. Sam wondered how many staff officers were in the import business.

He figured the only way the ground crew was going to get everything loaded in the bomber was by packing the 47-section so full that it would require a crash axe to go forward.

Maintenance was too busy trying to get the airplane in commission to worry about cargo. A tired crew chief showed Sam the aircraft forms. There were six open Red X (grounding) discrepancies they were working on. These either had to be fixed or downgraded by a maintenance officer. Sam was pretty sure he'd like the brake leak and spoilers fixed.

If it was up to him, he'd accept the other write-ups for an on-time trip home. "Hell," he thought, "one of them is just a navigation system computer. It can't be that hard to hit North America, although I suppose it would be nice to find the tanker."

It didn't startle Sam anymore to see the number of delayed discrepancies on the airplanes. These were items maintenance determined were not critical to safe flight and they were putting off fixing them until time was available. In the States there might be five or six of these delayed discrepancies on a typical airplane. Sam's crew would be dragging fifty-one deferred maintenance actions home with them.

Literally pages and pages of malfunctions had not been repaired. The crews weren't alone in being tired. The bombers were beat to death and they looked it. Their paint was peeling, they were just dirty, inside and out, and the salty air coated them with a white film. In even worse shape than the airplanes were the maintainers.

These GI's were ground down by the never-ending series of launches. They hid their fatigue, but it showed in their eyes and by the way they walked. If you looked at their hands you saw they were covered with cuts, scars and various scratch marks. Black and blue fingernails were common, as was sunburn from working outside in the hot tropical sun. But this did not stop them from performing their magic one more time. Sam's bomber rolled as scheduled and the long trip home was without incident. Cathy and his boys were waiting on the ramp as the airplane taxied into the parking spot.

ELLSWORTH AIR FORCE BASE, SOUTH DAKOTA

Not counting the one off the book mission Sam flew to cover for Cal, he had credit for 147 missions when he returned to the mainland. He had already received four Air Medals, and was now to be awarded his firth. The previous medals had been presented without much formality, but this one was about to be bestowed in a more elaborate ceremony. Twenty-eight other members of the bomb wing were also to receive Air Medals.

The presentation was held in the base theatre. There were well over a hundred wives, children and staff members sitting in attendance. All the medal recipients, in full dress blue uniforms, marched onto the stage and formed a line. After the flag was posted and the National Anthem played, they were called forward individually to salute the wing commander and stand at attention as the citation was read. As the lowest ranking member of the group of mostly officers, Sam was the last to be called.

As they posed for pictures, Sam could see something like pride in his boys' eyes although at nine and ten, they were still too young to really understand what an Air Medal meant. On the way home, Cathy talked about how impressed she was.

"You know," she said, "I was always so busy with the house and the things that go with trying to be a good single mother while you were away, I never appreciated what you must have been going through. You really have flown a lot of missions. I never even considered how scared you must have been sometimes. When I think that you might have been killed, it makes me want to cry. I hope it's over now.

"It's too late now, but I wonder if you should have re-enlisted. I know you've got your mind set on going to college and becoming an officer, but I'm not sure I trust the Air Force. What says the wing won't go back before you can get into school? Don't you get too old at some point? Did we do the right thing?"

"Let's not worry about that now," Sam replied. "Anyway you look at it it's a long way off before the wing goes again. Probably at least a year before we have to worry about it. Hopefully, I'll be in school long before then. Besides, a lot of things could change. The war can't go on much longer."

TURNER AIR FORCE BASE, GEORGIA

Jim's wife Elizabeth, a practicing Catholic, kept a candle burning on the small nightstand in their bedroom while he was gone. Jim didn't know about this and probably wouldn't have understood its religious significance, but he would have liked the thought. Jim had seen a lot in his years as a gunner and knew the risks involved with flying in the tail. His approach to the candle would have been, "I'm willing to try anything. It sure can't hurt."

When he returned home Jim's mission count was 208. Maybe now he wouldn't feel so overshadowed by the combat experience of his father and brother. But once again he found it hard to make the transition to what should have been a normal life.

After being without Elizabeth for so long he was uncomfortable being home again. During the six months he was away on his third tour she had gone back to her own routines and got in the habit of making all the decisions. She had to guide and discipline their two young teenagers while Jim was gone.

The twins, Susan and Sharon, were fourteen now and while they were great kids they had their own lives. They were loving, but more distant, and always went to their Mom for permission to do something. Jim sensed he was upsetting their patterns and didn't know how to adapt. It would just take time, he guessed.

ELSWORTH AIR FORCE BASE, SOUTH DAKOTA

Andy's first few days back started out all right, but then became disheartening. The first conflict arose over unpaid bills. There were overdue notices from both the phone and electric company. The Penney's bill, although not late, exceeded eight hundred dollars. In frustration Andy said more harshly than he intended, "What did you do with the money I sent you? It darn sure hasn't gone for cleaning supplies."

On the positive side, Kathleen was starting to walk. Andy had missed her first steps and that disappointed him, but she was making up for that fast with her smiles and hugs. On his second night back she even might have said Dada, maybe not exactly, but close enough for Andy. He had been a bachelor for a long time and it was something very special to have a little daughter.

Things got worse when after five days home Andy went back on alert. Rosalie screamed and cried. She called him a son of a bitch, as if he could do something about the schedule. He tried to tell her they could talk on the phone and she could come out and visit every night. It would have been easy for her to bring Kathleen out and meet him in the parking lot. She replied, "If you want to see your daughter, you can come home like normal husbands. What kind of father are you anyway?"

CLINTON SHERMAN AIR FORCE BASE, OKLAHOMA

Melvin settled into a different apartment complex in Burns Flat after he got his furniture out of storage. This time he was going to avoid any entanglements. He'd had live-ins before and it always started out well and then they tried to change him. Pretty soon they didn't like his smoking or his hours or something else.

"One sweetheart decided he shouldn't have a beer while he was watching TV. "Christ!" Melvin said. "I picked you up in a bar.""

Melvin didn't want a permanent roommate, although he did not object to an overnight guest. He treasured his freedom and figured that for a war dog gunner, his life was decent, although it would be even better if he could get back to flying combat.

"One thing about me going back to the war," he would think, "is that it won't involve putting up with a lot of tears. I don't know how the gunners with wives and kids do it. What kind of family life is that anyway?"

COLUMBUS AIR FORCE BASE, OHIO

By the time Cal's extension ran out his foot was fully healed, in spite of some dire predictions about what would happen if he did not see a medic. He tried to transfer into one of the replacement wings without success. He reluctantly returned to Ohio, but it wasn't like coming home. With the exception of things like chow and checking in with his squadron he spent most of his time in the NCO barracks.

This got old fast, so Cal rented an unfurnished motel room over the phone. He had never heard of an unfurnished motel room, but the price was right. It wasn't until he saw it that he realized it wasn't exactly a room, but a small cabin in a decrepit motor court built in the 1930's.

Obviously not lived in for years, its only apparent virtue was its cheapness. Living downtown required a car to get back and forth to the base and Cal managed to locate and purchase a derelict 1959 Ford four-door. This black Bondo special was painted with spray cans that only partially masked the underlying yellow color. Overall, it went with the room.

A gunner named Jerry Parker whom Cal casually knew stopped by with his wife Nancy. She was appalled the first time she saw his place, with its one lamp, mattress on the floor and cardboard box technology. She convinced her husband to help fix it up. Cal realized that she was one of those women who when she set her mind on something got it done. She was a better handyman than both of the men. When she got on a campaign to rehabilitate "Poor Calvin's quarters," he didn't argue.

The first thing they did was clean, plaster and paint. Cal resisted at first and then joined in, drafted by Nancy's enthusiasm. It was amazing how much dirt and grime had accumulated and twice they went to the hardware store for more supplies. There was only so much they could do with the bathroom until Nancy came up with a way to patch and re-grout the tile. Once they painted the room it didn't look that bad. The sink and commode were greatly improved with the help of cleanser and elbow grease.

By asking around Nancy came up with an easy chair and a bed frame for nothing. In a secondhand store she located a small table and two chairs for twelve dollars. They looked good after she sanded and painted them. She also created a passable end table by covering a cardboard barrel with draped orange burlap. Six cement blocks and two stained boards made a decent-looking set of bookshelves. Blue drapes, pictures, an old shower curtain and a faded bedspread. all of which Nancy brought from home, finished the decor. In the middle of a slum, Cal had a palace.

To be complete he needed a pillow and sheets, and Nancy offered to furnish these. She went home and got them along with a two-burner hot plate she said Cal could have. He started to thank her and then looked like he was going to cry so Nancy hugged him and kissed him on the forehead. She said, "Cal, this was fun and we don't need any thanks, you're a gunner and my husband's friend, that makes you my friend. Some days we're all just trying to survive." And then with a smile she said, "Just don't bring your sea gull in here."

After Jerry and Nancy left, Cal thought for a long time. He knew he was hard on friends. He used to have a lot of them before he started drinking so hard. He did a lot of embarrassing things when he got on the bottle. Like the pelican in the bar—even Nancy knew about that although he couldn't imagine where she had heard the story. That story caused him a lot of grief. People still razzed him about being a bird molester. "Hey!" they would say, "was that a boy or a girl pelican you got caught sleeping with?"

News from the war was not good. SAC airplanes continued to be lost. Two maintenance people deployed from Sam's wing died along with many others when a fully loaded KC-135 crashed and broke in half landing on Midway Island. The rumor was that problems in the way it was loaded might have contributed to the accident.

The contrast between life overseas and life at home was stark. Nobody really got used to the transition. Gunners and officers alike generally shared a common feeling of aggravation about their lack of control over their lives. For those with families the frustration over unplanned separations was a constant source of anxiety.

"Sam's wife Cathy summed it up when she said to him, "I'm not going to let this get me down, but it's getting so I don't want to hang around with any of the wives I know. The ones from your squadron are all doom and gloom and the ones from our neighborhood are so cheerful I can't stand it.

"I'm glad we live downtown, but you're gone so much I feel out of place talking to wives with husbands who lead a normal life and come home every night. I've had as much 'poor Cathy' as I need. I wouldn't trade you for anything. I just don't want anything to happen to you. This war business frightens me and I know our boys are starting to realize something could happen to you."

"Don't worry," replied Sam. "I don't see any way I'm going back. I'm too close to getting into college full time."

"Where are the boys?"

"They're at the ball game, if you've got any bright ideas, college boy, " replied Cathy.

Sam knew this was a subtle invitation to join Cathy in the bedroom. This wasn't the time to think about the war.

Chapter Eleven

Andy heard that Jim transferred from Turner to become an instructor in a new school at Castle Air Force Base that would transition some G and H B-52 crews into the D.[37] Since early 1966 only the older D-models had been flying Arc Light mission because the newer G- and H-model B52's had not been modified for the large bomb loads the D's could carry. The idea to share the load with some of the crewmembers assigned to aircraft that did not deploy was well received by those crews that had carried the brunt of the load. If more crews learned to fly the D then some individuals would not have to go off to war as often. Andy was pleased to hear about Jim's new assignment and thought, "Good for him. This keeps him in the States and I can't think of anybody who would make a better teacher. Maybe with the G-model gunners moving to the D's I'll have a chance to get out of the continuing cycle of going back to the war."

He knew that he needed to get assigned to a G-model unit. They didn't deploy and this meant he wouldn't have to be terrorized as he had been every time he launched on a combat mission. With 152 missions and over twelve hundred combat hours he had had enough. Even with his promotion to tech sergeant on the same cycle as Sam there was no way he wanted to go back to flying combat.

Interestingly, the promotion caused Andy trouble the first time he wore his full dress blue uniform. Still extremely youthful looking, he continued to wear his hair California-style. Bartenders regularly expressed disbelief even after he showed his ID card. Now, even though he wore five stripes and four rows of ribbons, including his fifth Air Medal that he received at the same ceremony as Sam, a grizzled staff sergeant was gnawing on him in the parking lot outside of the base cleaners.

"Where did you get those medals, sonny?"

"Bought them in the BX for eleven cents apiece. Why do you care?"

Trying to tell the red-faced sergeant he was twenty-eight with ten years in the Air Force just drew a snort. When he tried to walk away the NCO grabbed him by the shoulder and turned him around.

Andy surprised himself with the fierceness of his action. Breaking the grip, Andy planted his feet and looked up at his harasser with fire in his eyes.

"Look asshole. I was flying combat while you were sitting on the ground somewhere playing with yourself. You ever touch me again and you can unbutton your collar to take a piss. Now get the fuck out of my way, junior."

The sergeant realized that Andy spoke like a true NCO and decided it might be a good time to be somewhere else.

Dealing with an arrogant sergeant was one thing; dealing with Rosalie was another. Their marriage hit bottom. The final straw came when he told her about his getting a set of orders to Ramey Air Force Base, Puerto Rico. He explained he would be assigned to a G-model unit that had never gone Arc Light. "Things would have to get pretty bad before they send me," he explained, "because among other things the G didn't have the enlarged bomb bays of the D and its electronic counter-measure systems are not as powerful."

But this cut no ice with Rosalie. After trying at length to explain things to her, Andy decided that she either didn't understand his concern about going back to the war or was living in a dream world. It was probably both.

Rosalie stayed in a continual snit. "You bastard," she sneered. "How can you go away to some tropical island and just leave me? What about your daughter—doesn't Kathleen mean anything to you? You've been gone enough." She started to cry and then screamed,

"If you don't tell the Air Force to go to hell, I don't care if I ever see you again."

Andy's attempts at reason with her failed miserably and whenever he brought the subject up Rosalie would say, "You can leave anytime you want. I hope you don't come back." It was obvious Andy was going PCS (Permanent Change of Station) by himself and although he wouldn't admit it he had mixed emotions about the impending move. Rosalie may have been a mistake and he was more than ready to get away from her constant bitching. At the same time he couldn't bear thinking about life without his daughter. He had already missed too much of her growing up. What kind of life would she have alone with her mother?

The number of short, two-month augmentation tours was increasing since this allowed SAC to add to the size of the bomber force supporting the war without the visibility of unit deployments. However, this resulted in less time off between nuclear standby and reduced the number of airplanes actually sitting on alert from eight to six.

Individuals were also being deployed to replace crewmembers returning early for various reasons such as medical and family emergencies, and even with a war on officers continued to get sent to Professional Service School. So far Sam had missed getting tasked to go as a replacement and he owed that to gunners like Cal and Melvin who continually volunteered to go back to the war and when they got there offered to extend.

Sam got a new pilot, his third since Major Harrington. Against his wishes Major Harrington had been assigned as an instructor in safety school in Texas. Sam wondered about that. There was no doubt Harrington would make a superb teacher although there might be some question how well he was received by the schoolhouse staff.

Sam's new AC, Captain Ralph Allen, arrived directly from Castle where he completed upgrade training from co-pilot to aircraft commander. Not only was he low time, with less than 1,500 hours total in the B-52, he'd never spent a day in combat. With the raggedy-assed state of the tired bombers Sam wondered how well he would do in an emergency.[38]

An old head like Major Harrington could work with multiple deficiencies and a noisy air conditioner didn't distract him from keeping the priorities straight. There was no way to know the impact of the new guy. Both his radar navigator and his EW transferred to staff jobs, taking a lot of experience with them. Sam knew that a younger crew might be just as good as an old one, but he wondered what the statistics would show.

Although he had never actually sat down and computed the odds, he tried to figure out how many B-52's had been lost to accidents involving Arc Light missions. It seemed like the number was ten, maybe more. He asked himself, "How many individual BUFFS[39] (Big Ugly Fat Fellows or something like that) have been flying combat? A couple of hundred if that many? If you consider this on a per sortie basis the losses have been miniscule. What does that mean when you bounce it against a hundred missions?"

In the accident reports Sam read, the common denominator was almost always pilot or crew error. Usually some significant problem with the aircraft, such as loss of airspeed indication, started the sequence and everything went downhill from there. No question a loss of airspeed indication was a major problem, particularly on take-off or climb-out, but Sam remembered how smoothly Major Harrington had handled a complete loss of instrument panel lighting that occurred during a night take-off.

It was hard to see how the situation could have been much worse. It was after midnight on a very dark Pacific night and the clouds were down to about five hundred feet. Sam heard the decision speed call about the same time that all the lights in the tail went out. All four alternators had tripped off the line and because of problems in two relays there was no back-up power available.

"Crew, we've just lost all the lights up here," said Major Harrington calmly, "Nav, you stay on the timing...tell me when you think I should rotate...this may get a little tricky without being able to read the air speed gauges."

"Rog...your ah...ten seconds... five, four, three, two...up-stick, now!"

"Pilot, this is co-…it looks like we are going into the clouds."

"Roger, I'll keep flying the airplane…see if you can get a flashlight on the side panel and re-set the alternators."

Anytime the pilot couldn't read the airspeed indicators on a large airplane like the B-52 climbing out in weather, the most likely outcome was a stall, followed by ground impact. Airspeed was extremely critical and seat of the pants didn't work. Yet other than the co-pilot asking, "Pilot, have you seen the flashlight?" the crew's action and coordination was perfect. What could have been a disaster turned into what Major Harrington called "just another chance to excel." Like poker, it wasn't always the hand you were dealt, it was how well you played your cards. "I hope the new guy understands this," thought Sam.

U-TAPAO AIR FORCE BASE THAILAND

Cal avoided being assigned to a crew and instead flew as a spare. When he wasn't tasked for a mission it wasn't hard to talk somebody into letting him fly for them. Sometimes this meant Cal could get in two sorties on the same day. The more he flew, the less temptation he had to drink. He just wanted to stay overseas and keep flying. It was something to do and it beat lying in a puddle of barf.

Cal didn't track it, but he guessed he was close to three hundred missions. For the first time in his life he was being noticed in a good way. A gunner who was on his first tour actually told him, "I've heard about you and wanted to get to U-Tapao just to meet the war dog of song and legend. Let me buy you a drink." Cal felt good when he could answer, "Can't, I'm scheduled to fly."

Cal didn't object to not being assigned to a specific crew and didn't mind being bounced from crew to crew. His willingness to fly with the crew *du jour* went over well with the commanders. Why rotate in somebody who didn't want to be there from the States. The beauty of flying with a different crew every time was that if he ran across a bunch of assholes, Cal knew he wasn't stuck with them. Even his feelings about officers, which had always been so negative, were undergoing subtle changes.

As the war continued the age and experience of the officer force was going down as the old heads got promoted and moved on. Many of the new pilots were younger and not nearly as blinded by rank as those they replaced. Twenty-six-year-old aircraft commanders with less than four years in the service were becoming common. A lot of them wouldn't have joined the military if it hadn't been for the draft. Once the novelty wore off, they were just as bored with the war as most of the gunners.

ELLSWORTH AIR FORCE BASE, SOUTH DAKOTA

Sam became more relaxed. His young pilot hadn't done anything stupid and school was going well. He was getting close to the magic ninety hours he needed for Bootstrap and even with a nine-hour course load, he was usually able to get most of his homework accomplished while on alert. This meant that his time at home could be spent with Cathy and the boys. One of the things about pulling days at a stretch on alert was that it often meant several days off at a time. This allowed them to make a couple of trips back to Minnesota to visit the kids' grandparents and it also gave them time to do things together. It was great to have the time to be a true husband and father. Sam loved taking the family for rides and they enjoyed at least a weekly movie. Because his boys were getting older, Cathy had successfully got him to join a Lutheran Church. Her argument was that as a father Sam needed to set the example and that his boys had reached the age where they watched what he did.

Sam's obsession with poker gave way to family and the need to spend his time hitting the books. If you disregarded some penny-ante stuff on alert he hadn't been in a serious game in months. He pretty much stopped worrying about the unit deploying back to the war and even if it did go again, he would be in college full time.

The results from Sam's Officer Qualification Exams showed nothing below the 85th percentile and he'd scored in the 97th percentile on the pilot portion. He sent copies of his transcripts to the University of Omaha and expected a tentative acceptance (subject to successful completion of the three courses he was now taking) within the next couple of weeks.

The approval came back sooner than expected and a friendly civilian in the base education office helped him complete the blocks in his application for the Bootstrap Commissioning Program. This would allow him a full year to complete his degree and then attend OTS. Several officers, including his old Aircraft Commander Major (now Lieutenant Colonel) Harrington, provided glowing recommendations and Sam was optimistic when he went to his director of operations to get one of the final signatures. With any luck he'd receive his commission in the fall of 1971.

This was important, so rather than wear a baggy flight suit Sam got dressed in his full blue uniform. It was only the second time he'd actually worn his tech stripes and he'd taken care to see that all his ribbons and brass were installed correctly. With a close haircut and shined shoes, he wanted to make a good impression.

After sitting in an outer office for almost one and a half hours, Sam got in to see the DO. He was a thin-faced lieutenant colonel with fairly narrow eyes. Sam guessed that his appearance, as well as his reputation for being perpetually grumpy, explained why he was called "the coyote" behind his back.

"What the hell are you after Sergeant Jackson?" he asked. "You're so dressed up you look like you are going to parade."

"Sir, I need you to sign my application for Bootstrap."

"You're on Capt. Allen's crew and I just signed your orders. It means you're not going to school any time soon. One of the other wings had to bring a crew back on short notice and we got tapped to provide the replacement. I nominated your crew since your AC's fully checked out and he's never been Arc Light. It's logical for him to be at the top of my list. You guys go Monday morning so you probably need to hustle if you have anything you need to do."

This was the last thing Sam wanted to hear. He thought of the old poker saying, "If it wasn't for bad luck, I wouldn't have any luck at all." How was he going to tell Cathy?

Cathy took the news better than Sam expected and he loved her even more for that. "It's not the news I wanted to hear," she said, "But we've done it before and we can do it again. Two months isn't forever. I'll just have to wait a little longer to sleep with a second lieutenant."

Sam tried to work out a deal with the college teaching the night courses on base, but this meant contacting his instructors by phone.

141

The problem was that the instructors from the campus were not available on the base except on the nights they taught.

Two of his three professors were adjunct faculty members and did not have offices at the school, which was two hours south in the town of Spearfish. Not only was it a hassle to find their phone numbers, but one of them, the accounting instructor, could not be located. When Sam boarded the KC-135 tanker for Guam he still had not contacted the accounting instructor. Nothing had really been worked out with the others, but Cathy agreed to keep trying.

"At best I'm going to going to lose credit for the course work I'm enrolled in," Sam told Cathy. "In the worst case I'll receive three grades of drop fail. The cards aren't falling right and unless something changes my luck, this hand is going to turn into a bust."

ANDERSON AIR FORCE BASE, GUAM

B-52's had been flying combat missions for over five years without a single close encounter with a MiG. Sam was listening as two gunners from Westover Air Force Base expounded on this. The tall one, who had an illegal rusty mustache that looked like it belonged to Yosemite Sam, said, "I wish we'd get some MiGs once in a while. This just riding along is a bunch of crap. I don't give a shit if they shoot us up. At least I'd get a chance to do something besides look out the damn window."

"Rave on, hero," said the short one who was wearing a floppy Australian bush hat.

"Nah, really. Everybody else on the airplane can say they did something. The pilots fly. The navigator navigates. The radar drops bombs. Even the EW listens to a few signals. What the hell do gunners do? The answer is nothing. The reason we're on everybody's shit list is because all we can say is that we rode there and back. Big fucking deal."

"You don't need to get your ass shot down just to prove something."

"I don't think I'd get shot down and if a gunner ever did get a MiG he would turn into something better than a human tip gear indicator. How long have we been doing this and the only thing we've shot at is the damn ocean—or each other."

"I still think a MiG would rip you a new asshole, particularly if it's a 21."

Both of the debaters needed shaves and were wearing flight suits that looked like they'd slept in them—they probably had, since both had come off the same night mission. Sam knew the reference to shooting at each other held some truth. He remembered the first raid to Mu Gia Pass when a gunner shot at something that later was determined not to be a MiG. Sam listened as the two gunners continued to go at each other.

"Don't think so, his gunnery problem is the same as mine and our fire control system is better," said the gunner with the big mustache. "At least we don't have to point the whole goddamn airplane to hit something. Look at the electronics we have to help us. We don't exactly sit out in the slipstream tracking a fighter by guess. We've got radar and computers and all that garbage—"

"Yeah, you're right, garbage. The latest our engineers can design, all hooked to four ten-cent guns that were obsolete twenty years ago. This ain't like the boys in the B-17's with guns sticking out all over."

"We don't need guns sticking out the nose and every side. We don't even need top and belly gunner. In those days fighters could attack from any direction. Now the only good pass a fighter has is from the tail. And that's where we are in the goddamn tail. If a tail gunner could do it then with a hell of a lot less going for them, why not now?"

"Closure rate. A Messerschmitt might have been able to close at two hundred miles per hour tops. What the hell can the MiG-21 do it at what, five hundred knots?"

The argument continued as Sam went to shave and shower. Tonight's mission would be five hours shorter because they would land at U-Tapeo after coming off the target. That meant he had to pack all his stuff again and drag it to the airplane, then unpack and get settled in all over again. Life was a bag drag and the adventure never stopped.

On his way out of the room, Sam stopped to listen again to the ongoing argument.

"No buts," said the gunner in the bush hat. "What it boils down to is the gunner is useless because there aren't any fighters and even if there were, he'd still be useless because his guns wouldn't work. Now! Let's take the unlikely event that a gunner does get a fighter. We'll even take the unlikely assumption that the guns work. The only fighter he is going to see is a MiG-21 and their closure rate is too fast to shoot them down. So, he is still useless."

"Ah…the guns ain't that bad, besides if that's true, why does SAC with all its wisdom still have gunners on the B-52?"[40]

"That's like asking why naval officers still wear swords—it's a damn tradition. All the colonels and generals who set up SAC looked at the last war they fought in and decided they needed gunners. If they had any foresight they could accomplish the same thing with baggage handlers. Give every aircraft commander a rear-view mirror and an enlisted aide and save a lot of flying pay."

U-TAPAO AIR FORCE BASE, THAILAND

Sam's mission count was 172, which by his estimate totaled close to 1,500 combat hours. Two months in the air, two trips to Mu Gia , eleven other missions to parts of southern North Vietnam; everything else over the south. He'd seen exactly zero MiGs.

Excitement, if you called getting locked onto by enemy radar exciting, didn't total more than a few dozen hours, even if you counted the in-flight emergencies. The rest was just uncomfortable and monotonous. Take-off, refuel, bomb, land, eat, sleep and repeat. In between, write letters and when he could, find a game, play poker.

Unlike Sam, Cal didn't keep track of his missions. He wouldn't have known exactly when he hit three hundred if other people hadn't been watching. The wing commander was going to make a big deal of Cal's three hundredth. Arrangements were made for a photographer and a reporter from the Stars and Stripes to record the event.

Cal would be the first B-52 gunner to reach this impressive milestone and it was clearly worthy of recognition. But decorations weren't something Cal thought about and if he had known about what was being planned he might have done something differently.

He was not into awards and so far none of his fifteen Air Medals had been presented publicly. The closest to an award ceremony he experienced was when an orderly room clerk tossed him a small blue box down the hallway saying, "Congratulations on your medal."

Colonel John Milton led the rent-a-crowd, which was made up mostly of staff members rousted from their offices and several senior gunners who, considering the recipient, probably had mixed emotions about being there. With a bottle of champagne in one hand and a Distinguished Flying Cross in the other, Colonel Milton led the group as they followed the yellow B-4 stand being pushed up to the tail of the parked bomber.

The forty or so people on the ground observed Cal's white helmet in the windows of the tail compartment as the airplane taxied in. Then it disappeared from sight

After a time that appeared excessive the tail compartment entrance door swung open and a large green bag dropped onto the stand below with a soft thump. Many moments passed and then a wretched-looking gunner rolled out of the compartment and landed on the bag with a pronounced thud. Whether he was drunk or just badly hung over and dizzy was a subject of much debate among the five senior gunners present. Cal was extremely slow in getting up. Befuddled by the attention he didn't know how to react as he tried to rise and salute the colonel from the stand. But when he stood up, he found that the stand was jacked up too close to the underside of the tail compartment and there was no room to fully rise unless he put his head in the entrance way to the tail compartment.

When Cal finally struggled off the stand, the wing king wordlessly pinned the medal on the front of Cal's flight suit as a captain read the citation and several flash bulbs went off. The colonel then turned and left without returning Cal's sloppy salute. A chief master sergeant commented, "If that's an example of an all-American war hero, I sure don't want to see it publicized in the Stars and Stripes."

Melvin computed he'd flown 282 missions and he still remembered the first one on April 15, 1965. It was the day the two aircraft collided on the first B-52 mission of the Vietnam War. If he had taken the time and effort to count it, his records would show he'd been overseas for 645 days. Not that Melvin minded. With three ex-wives still on his case, he needed to stay overseas just to keep them off his back. The war was an ideal hideout and to him it was just a big party in many ways. Booze was cheap and all the women he could want were available in Okinawa and Thailand. He was probably the only gunner who would say this, but the food wasn't bad either. "Sure beats the crap out of what my exes fed me when they took the time to cook," he would say.

A conversation between Melvin and Sam as they sat on a wooden picnic table drove home how long the war had gone on. "Hey, you're a college boy. What was the length of World War Two?" Melvin asked. "It seems like we've been at this thing forever. I flew my first mission in '65 and it's 1970 now. That's something like five years, ain't it?"

"A little less but close," responded Sam. "As far as World War Two goes, it probably started around 1939, but for the United States it obviously started on December 7th, 1941. I think it ended in 1945. It seems like maybe August of '45. Do the math…one month in '41 then, '42, '43, '44…that's three years and a month. Let's see… August is the eighth month. How about three years, nine months? So SAC has been at this longer than the U.S. was in World War Two."

Melvin started to say something when a chief on the senior staff stuck his head in the door and asked, "You guys want to know what the report says about the last airplane that crashed taking off from Guam?"

"I already know," said Melvin, "the fucking wing fell off."

"That's not what the report says," replied the chief. "It gives the cause as undetermined. I've got the final right here. It says the airplane failed to get airborne at the end of the runway and crashed into the ocean.

"All six aboard fatal, little wreckage recovered, no remains… the following items are suspected causes…structural failure, loss of thrust, dragging brakes, life raft inflation and a list of other things. Nothing about the wing falling off although that could be what they mean by structural failure."

"I'm telling you, the fucking wing fell off," said Melvin. "Charlie Couples was standing in the hung bomb area at Pati Point and he swears the right wing just folded up over the fuselage when the pilot tried to rotate. It folded just like you would fold a piece of paper. You know who Charlie Couples is, he's the major who flips slides at the briefings. You've seen him, he says he gave a statement to the board."

Nobody in the room knew the gunner who was killed in the accident, but the grapevine provided details. He was an old head out of Fairchild AFB. Left a wife and four kids. Legend said he once bailed out years ago when there was nothing wrong with the airplane. Some instructor pilot accidentally hit the bail out switch when he was playing around with something on the center console.[41]

The story reminded Sam of how many similar stories he had heard. Sometimes the gunner made it, sometimes he didn't. It was like poker. Some days you drew out and some days you didn't. The difference was that in poker you could always fold and wait for another hand.

Meanwhile, Cathy tried without success to get the three professors to deal with Sam's absence. Two trips to the college didn't provide any relief and she felt frustrated with being given the run around. The admissions office said, "Talk to the professors." The professors said "It's up to the dean and Sam will just have to talk to her when he gets back." The one bright spot was Sam's accounting instructor. Maybe because he wasn't a full-time faculty member he was willing to listen. He told Cathy he was willing to consider working out an arrangement for Sam to finish his course work without starting over. Of course, this too would need the approval of the dean. The whole thing was a mess.

In peaceful Iowa, Bobby D. Olsen, who was thirteen when Melvin flew his first mission, attended a draft party. His cousin, who was called Aardvark because of his gloriously oversized nose, had organized the party for his nineteen-year-old friends. Each would listen as the numbers, based on exact birthdays such as March 9th, were broadcast over a local radio station as they were drawn in Washington. Those with low numbers could expect to be called in the draft and sent to Vietnam after they completed basic training. Bobby D was now almost eighteen, and instead of playing soccer and thinking about sex he was having sex and thinking about soccer. His ignorance of the Vietnam War, his feelings that it didn't concern him at all, ended suddenly as he watched the reaction of his older friends as the numbers were called. When Aardvark drew a thirty-two in the lottery, the alcohol-induced noise suddenly stopped and the room became eerily quiet. Not knowing what to say, Booby D looked away and thought, "It's not to long before it's going to be me sitting here wondering."

Chapter Twelve

ELLSWORTH AIR FORCE BASE, SOUTH DAKOTA

Sam's crew returned from Guam via commercial airline under contract to the government. Not being as scruffy as some of the army troops in the back, he got put in first class with his officers. Twelve comfortable hours later they landed at San Francisco International Airport. It was somewhat of a shock to get off and observe the war protesters. It was the first time Sam had been face to face with the anti-war movement and he was surprised at the number of people carrying signs. He wasn't sure he liked what he saw. He'd read about the controversy the war was generating, but it had been difficult to understand the magnitude and depth of the opposition to the war until he walked the gauntlet between the foul-mouthed protesters and had to listen to their chants.

A chain link fence protected him from several hundred people with fury in their eyes. Later he told Cathy about it. "I was in my khakis while most of the people on the airplane were army troops in fatigues. They got most of the abuse and several of them looked like they were going over the fence. One soldier, when asked how he could kill women and kids replied, 'It's easy, you just don't lead them as much'—"

"What does that mean?" asked Cathy.

"It's like when you shoot in front of a fast-moving pheasant. That's called leading. If you shoot exactly at the pheasant the bullets would pass behind it because of the time it takes for the birdshot to travel. Women and kids are slower, therefore you don't lead them as much. Anyway, this set off a major confrontation, with the cops caught in the middle. Several protesters were beaten with nightsticks and roughly hauled away before order was restored. It really pissed me off when one young girl not more than fifteen was dragged into a paddy wagon by the hair. It wasn't pretty and sure didn't help the protesters' attitude towards the government."

After going to his squadron to check his schedule, Sam stopped at the small office the college maintained on the base. It was pretty much bad news at the school. "They're going to let me take the accounting final, but it looks like the other two courses will be dropped with failing grades," he said to Cathy when he got home. "So out of nine hours work I started I end up in the hole by six, and along the way sink my GPA to a 2.79. That's assuming I can max the accounting test."

Compared to what Sam told Cathy next, this was the good news. He struggled to find the words. "I don't know how to tell you this, but there's something I learned at the base. "We've got short notice orders to Abilene Texas. Dyess Air Force Base is getting ready to deploy and I'm being to be sent to fill a hole in the crew roster.

"You just got home," said Cathy, as she started to cry. "I don't think I can stand another separation."

U-TAPAO AIR FORCE BASE, THAILAND

Officially, Melvin was assigned a bed in one of the new prefabricated modular rooms built for the gunners, but he stayed in a bungalow he maintained off base. This came with various creature comforts in the form of beautiful and demure Thai girls who accepted Melvin for what he was and never questioned him about his frequent absences. For a while, Melvin even maintained two bungalows and commuted, but with his flying schedule this took too much time away from the New Moonlite, the bar where he liked to spend his time. Its ownership, while questionable, left little doubt it was being run for gunners. Daily flying schedules were posted on the wall behind the bar, as soon as, if not earlier, than they went up on base.

A gunner could eat, get his haircut and have his laundry picked up and delivered there.

The New Moonlite had been Melvin's hang out of choice since he discovered the bar while exploring an area called Newland. It had been established after the King of Thailand expressed his irritation at the collection of bars and whorehouses located in a small fishing village south of U-Tapao Air Force Base.

Constructed on empty land, this new collection of bars and whorehouses served the same purpose, but was eight miles further down the road from the main gate. Transportation to either of its two streets by Baht bus cost the American equivalent of five cents. Mixed drinks ran from thirty-five cents to one dollar, depending on the level of table service requested.

If a GI monitored his schedule astutely it was possible to get trapped by the midnight base curfew and be forced to spend the night with little to do except drink and carouse with beautiful Thai and Eurasian women. Sleeping accommodations were available in bungalows located at the rear of many of the bars and all-night companionship could be arranged for five dollars.

The proprietress of the New Moonlite was a small black-haired Thai woman who depending on the light could have been anywhere from thirty to fifty years old. Nicknamed Mama Moon, her waist was not quite as thin as the hostesses on her staff although she was still tiny and quite attractive. She provided wall space for a large gunner logo and encouraged gunners to check off their attendance on the name board under the gunner bulldog.

Specials were offered, including a round trip Bhat bus ride, a steak dinner, unlimited drinks and a girl for the night, all for ten dollars. Thanks to the KC-135 boom operators who imported them on aircraft transiting Japan or Okinawa, most of the bungalows surrounding the elaborately manicured garden, behind the bar, contained air conditioners.

It was tacitly understood that unescorted officers were not welcome and the few strays that showed up were usually refused service. The gunners who visited the Moonlite were a mixed lot. Most came for a beer or two and to catch up on the latest gossip. In general the clientele was laid back, and with missions almost every day they couldn't afford to get too screwed up.

While on the premises, Melvin pretty much drank for free because of his status as an old war dog and as someone who could answer questions about how the wing worked and make introductions or set up bungalows. In some ways Melvin was the New Moonlite's mayor and when necessary he performed duty as an unofficial bouncer. This didn't take much of his time after he took on a drunken green beret in uniform who was bad-mouthing gunners.

Melvin walked up to him and quietly said, "Nice hat, can I have it?"

This drew the expected response from the elite Army man who truly believed the publicity about his status as a member of an unequaled fighting unit. "If you want it you're going to have to take it," he said.

"Okay," Melvin calmly said. "It'll look good in my collection."

And it did.

Hard partying took a strong constitution and while some gunners tended to get a little wild, Melvin seldom gave them trouble. "What the hell, it's a war and if they want to get crazy that is their business," he thought. "A few are just out to sample the available pleasures anyway. It's a scientific fact that being fired up helps their search."

OFFUTT AIR FORCE BASE, NEBRASKA

Meetings between chief master sergeants at SAC Headquarters and their counterparts from the Military Personnel Center at Randolph AFB were held in building 500. This resulted in a decision to drop the requirement of four years' service to enter the gunnery field. The war made it difficult to locate volunteers and the career field was top-heavy with rank and years of service. The subject wasn't without controversy and it took pressure from above to overcome the resistance to change.

Resigned to the inevitable the chiefs began to sort out the mechanics of selecting volunteers from Basic Training. Much of the discussion centered on high qualification scores with emphasis on the electronic portion of the test.

"You guy's got it all wrong," said one grizzled chief master sergeant with 139 missions. "What we should be looking for is kids who have speeding tickets in excess of one hundred miles an hour. We don't need scientists, we need people with balls."

This was not the consensus reached by the panel, which decided to concentrate on recruiting only those with flawless backgrounds and test scores in the high percentile. Attitude was a major concern and the panel decided that a senior gunner would interview each candidate.

LACKLAND AIR FORCE BASE, TEXAS

Bobby D. Olson was in his third week of basic training when he reported to a building called the "Green Monster" for placement in an Air Force career field. When queried about becoming a gunner he admitted he hadn't given it much thought. He didn't mention to the staff sergeant clerk that the only reason he joined the Air Force was a strong desire to avoid the draft.

The way the draft worked, Bobby knew if he just hung around and waited to be called he would be forced to go in the Army. This probably meant sleeping in the mud and slogging through rice paddies. It was better to volunteer for the Air Force. At least he'd probably get clean sheets.

During his interview with a chief from Barksdale AFB Bobby D learned he would receive flying pay as a gunner. With simple math he converted this to payments on a motorcycle. The war was never mentioned. Bobby was to become one of the first "baby gunners" of the Vietnam War. [42]

CASTLE AIR FORCE BASE, CALIFORNIA

Most of Jim's job involved transitioning experienced G- and H-model gunners to fly in the tail. The course was short and each gunner only flew four flights. Jim enjoyed teaching and it was something he was proud of. He knew his war experience added to his value as an instructor and his motivation to prepare his students for combat never faded. Jim continually crusaded to get more of the student gunners to exercise and build up their endurance. "You never know when you might need a little extra," he would tell them.

He didn't just talk about physical fitness; he made it his mission to stay in shape. He worked out every day, often spending time in the weight room of the base gym. He could run three miles in less than twenty minutes.

"Not bad for an old man," he thought. "I'll bet there aren't many others my age that can do one hundred push-ups. I just wish I could convince more people how important being ready is."

Jim spent a lot of his free time with the new baby gunners. He spent hours with them making sure they knew what to do in any situation they encountered. He believed there was nothing wrong with them that a little experience wouldn't cure. They would get that quickly enough.

Jim's girls were in high school and absolutely beautiful, a perfect matched set with red hair like their mother. They were truly fine young ladies who stuck together. Their grades were awesome to a father who never did much better than a C when he was their age. Elizabeth was a great homemaker and their base house always smelled of something baking in the oven. Life couldn't be much better.

The squadron gunners set up a baby gunner adoption program and instructors frequently invited the young men into their homes for a meal or just conversation in a friendly environment. Elizabeth welcomed Jim's "orphan" into the family and made sure he understood the door was always open. The first time Jim saw his daughters look at Bobby D, he felt his fatherly instincts rise, but he didn't need to worry. The girls quickly accepted Bobby and treated him like an older brother.

By the middle of 1972, when Bobby D graduated, the war was having a significant impact on the B-52 forces. Morale reached new lows as Strategic Air Command entered its seventh year of providing bombers to support the Vietnam conflict. Many of the crewmembers were losing confidence in SAC leadership and thought the whole effort was misdirected.

SAC was in a desperate scramble for crews. Even the Combat Crew Training School at Castle was not exempt. Jim's crew was picked to deploy on two weeks' notice.

Two nights before he left, Jim was sitting alone in the house with Elizabeth when she asked, "I've heard a lot of stories. Did you ever get tempted with all the girls running around the last time you were in Thailand?"

"Sometimes maybe, but I know what I've got at home," said Jim.

"I know I shouldn't have said it. I trust you. It's just that I've heard so much about some guys running around over there and I know you're human. I want you to know I'll love and pray for you while you're gone."

Sam's time at home sped by as he tried to prepare himself for another combat tour. There was no sense in trying to sign up for the two courses he needed. The TDY would just screw them up and he couldn't stand any more hits to his GPA. He thought that maybe he could do something with correspondence courses. He'd completed everything he could with end of course exams. He needed core subjects. Six hours and so close, but…

Sam departed for Guam the day before his anniversary and tried to figure out when was the last time he had been home for one. Or for Christmas for that matter. "How many birthdays have I missed?" he wondered. "How many things we should have done as a family and I was either gone or on alert?"

Cathy reconciled herself to being alone again. One week she took the boys out of school and went to visit Sam's parents in Minnesota. She had forgotten how cold it got there and twice the car wouldn't start, but the trip was good for the boys. She also spent some time catching up with her brother Randy who still lived close to where Sam and Cathy grew up. He expressed disbelief when she told him how many times Sam had been gone.

"Is this going to be Sam's last trip or is he going to have to go again?" he asked.

"I honestly don't know and I don't think he does either. It would be a lot easier on me and the boys if we knew there was an end in sight."

"How are you handling it?" Randy asked.

"It has its days, but mostly we're coping. If nothing else we've learned to fend for ourselves. We're doing a lot better than some of the families I know."

ANDERSON AIR FORCE BASE, GUAM

Sam was drafted to sit in on a meeting on ways to improve fire control system reliability. It quickly deteriorated into a bitch session between two senior master sergeants. Sam didn't know the black gunner with the seven stripes but he was laying it on.

"It's rare for a gunner to complete a flight without some discrepancy. Distorted scopes, weak target returns, no video on one or both scopes, hydraulic failure and the one that really burns my ass, guns that won't fire out. I know you're on your ass, but you might as well take the guns off and leave the gunner home. Seventy percent reliable is like one out of three is no good shit."

"You're right...shit," glared the maintenance sergeant through tight jaws. "Thirty percent may have problems, but in no way does that mean one out of three is no good. If your damn gunners write up a bug spot on the window, it's charged against the system, it doesn't mean it won't work. I've seen more half-assed write-ups than I can count. Maybe if you taught some of your buddies to work the thing, we could stop chasing ghosts and fix the real problems.

"One of your damn gunners wrote up turret failure in all modes. He'd been questioned about this at debriefing and said he'd checked everything possible and no luck. Two of my people worked all through the night trying to duplicate the problem and in exasperation we hunted him down in his trailer. It seems he left the turret disable switch out on preflight. Rather than admit an error he blamed the problem on maintenance."

The sergeant's face got redder and redder as he continued. "Now before you decide to go whip on that gunner of yours you'd better think about if you can whip nine of your troops. I have statistics that prove over half our discrepancies come from just nine gunners." He went on to tell how undermanned and underskilled his fire control shop was. "Most of my troops haven't been out of school more than a year and they are tired, just plain tired. Some of them have been forty-six days without a break and a lot of them work twelve- to sixteen-hour days."

Sam listened as the two senior NCOs went at each other, and when the meeting broke up nothing was solved. Sam could see both sides of the story. Most people didn't believe the guns would ever be used and just couldn't see a reason to go through all the bullshit for nothing. Gunners were down on maintenance and maintenance was down on gunners, particularly those who wrote up the system. Yet those few gunners who took the time to identify discrepancies might be the only ones who were doing their job. With too many gunners the care factor was about zero.

Some were on their fifth TDY and they never got over their aches from one flight before it was time to go again. It looked like nobody was going to get a shot at a MiG. "Why give a rat's ass?" was the general sentiment.

A few days later a handout was circulated inviting crewmembers to a formal "Dining In." The speaker was going to be an Army lieutenant general, and several VIP's would be in attendance. Nobody thought to exclude the gunners because this was going to be a full mess dress affair and it was probably apparent to the officer making the plans that none of the gunners would have one.

"Why the hell do they say crewmembers when they mean officers only?" said a gunner from KI Sawyer Air Force Base in Michigan. "I wonder what would happen if we got some mess dress uniforms and showed up? What about the full dress blue uniforms they make us carry so there is something to send our body home in. Why can't we get white shirts and black ties and dress up like we do for the fancy NCO stuff?"

Someone produced a better idea which resulted in twenty-three gunners showing up at the officers' club for the formal dining in. The effect was stunning. The officers, resplendent in their white mess dress, looked pale in comparison to "gunners' formal."

The perfectly tailored dress uniforms procured at one of the many low-cost tailor shops in Bangkok matched the officers in every detail, right down to the ruffled shirt and stripes down the pants' legs. It was perfect in every detail, except one—everything was in camouflage. Even the cummerbund was camouflage and a close observer could see the camouflaged wings and miniature medals on their chests.

The wing commander appeared about to explode until a visiting congressman grinned as he stood up to greet the gunners and lead them to the open bar. Some of the officers who recognized their own gunner were roaring with laughter as they began to cheer. Most of them would have paid money to hear what the wing king was going to say to his wing gunner.

Sam regretted missing the gala event because he was flying, but it was something he would have like to have seen. "It's not often a bunch of raggedy-assed gunners get to reshuffle the officers' deck. I hope that if I ever get commissioned, I don't walk around with my drawers in a knot like some of the colonels do."

BACK IN THAILAND

On the first night of a three-day break, Melvin was in Bangkok and at first he didn't realize the guy he was drinking with was a major. The balding, slightly overweight officer was beyond slightly drunk. "Come on, let's go out to the Animal Bar at Naked Fanny and I'll show you the officers' club," he said to Melvin who thought this seemed reasonable and saw no reason to mention he was an NCO. "I've been kicked out of better officers' clubs than this dude has ever seen," he thought.

The officers' club at Nakon Phanom (NKP) was torn up to the point it would have embarrassed a west Texas roadhouse. Apparently the wing commander told his fighter pilots he didn't give a shit what they did as long as they kept flying sorties. Holes were kicked in the walls and the ceiling was covered with multi-colored graffiti. "You see the series of round spots up there, " said the officer conducting the tour. "Those were made by inking the bare bottom of a female personnel officer and then lifting her upside down like a rubber stamp."

"Interesting concept," thought Melvin.

The major went on, "About two months ago some general came through and raised holy hell so the walls were fixed and everything repainted. That lasted about two days before the pilots kicked new holes and replaced the graffiti. Somebody found the personnel officer, inked her up again and it's been this way ever since."

It was daylight before they left the club and Melvin had a new appreciation for officers—at least fighter pilots anyway.

The night before Melvin's scheduled rotation back to Guam, Cal's wing gunner came by the New Moonlite. "Cal will be on the same KC-135 you are and I need you to be sure he doesn't get in trouble while he's on Guam," he said. "He usually does okay as long as we keep him flying, but it doesn't take much to turn him into a regular skid row type. I expect you to watch out for him."

"Why me, he's not my baggage," said Melvin.

"First off, because he's a gunner and we take care of our own. He's getting way too much attention from the wing commander and others. Next, he's flown more missions than anybody around here and if somebody's looking for a spare in the middle of the night, he's first on the volunteer list. And lastly, because I'm a chief master sergeant and I just told you to."

When Melvin saw Cal coming into base operations dragging his bags, he said. "You need a better class of undertaker. You look terrible. Is your face allergic to a razor?"

"I just got off a flight," said Cal. "What the hell do you expect me to look like? Some split tail who works in an office?"

"Well, our tanker's broken and they told us to hang around. It sounds like a couple of hours. Why don't you go get some coffee, I'll find you when it's time to go."

Three hours later Melvin found Cal in the terminal restaurant drinking beer. He was so intoxicated that the boom operator didn't even bother to put him in a seat when they got to the tanker. He just strapped him to the top of a cargo pallet.

BACK ON GUAM

Immediately after landing, Melvin went to his room, emptied his bags and took a quick shower. After putting on a pair of Levis and a Hawaiian shirt, he left for Mama Nening's. When the official 1 a.m. Guam closing time came, Mama Nening let down the canvas curtains normally used to keep the rain out and hung out a hand-lettered sign that said "PRIVATE PARTY." Melvin continued to drink with the five other gunners who had been there since late afternoon. Somebody asked, "Where's Cal?"

"He'll be in the sack by now," said Melvin. "He had a little too much cool aid before we left Okinawa and whenever he's had enough he just ends up in bed. Doesn't matter if we're on the far end of the island with no car, he still ends up in bed. People used to spend a lot of time looking for him in ditches until they learned this. I don't know how he gets home sometimes, but if there is a car he's likely to disappear with it so you've got to watch your car or get stranded."

"Does he always make it to his bed?"

"Mostly, sometimes it's somewhere else like the lawn or some vehicle, but he usually ends up in bed. In the past that's been a real problem with Cal. He'll come home, pass out in his bed and somebody will forget to watch him and he'll wake up sober," said Melvin with exaggerated seriousness.

Speaking of bed, it's time to get out of here," said Melvin as he popped the top on another beer. "Does anybody think they can find the steering wheel?"

On the way home they pulled over for a piss stop and one of the wheels dropped over the edge of the narrow roadway. The Datsun from HURTS rent-a-car was stuck in the mud and teetering precariously above the thick jungle ten feet below them. Everyone got out to push except one person who remained in the car looking for his beer.

The uncoordinated effort went bad when a gunner by the name of Murphy started rocking the car from side to side. It rolled over and out of sight into the dense foliage below. After rescuing their fellow gunner, the six drunks hitchhiked a ride back to the base with an awestruck airman in a blue Air Force metro van.

Melvin declared an emergency, gathered up two cars from the HURTS fleet and woke every gunner he could locate to assist in manhandling the blue Datsun out of the jungle. After the group successfully returned to base an informal accident board was held just prior to daybreak. As expected, Murphy was unanimously convicted.

News travels fast and Sam heard about the car before he got back to the room from his flight. Even though he no longer had a financial interest in HURTS he volunteered to go see the insurance agent since he was the one who set up the original contract. He had a little difficulty explaining to the agent that the driver was not in the car when it rolled over. "A guy in the back seat," didn't seem to go over very well so he amended the facts and provided Murphy's name as the driver. This was more satisfactory and the agent signed off on the repairs.

SOMEWHERE OVER SOUTH VIETNAM

Any time they were over South Vietnam the radio calls on the guard channel (Universal Distress Frequency) were usually interesting, and Jim was listening to a helicopter working a rescue.

"Roger, this is jolly green one-niner, it looks like the pilot's out and has a good chute, it looks like he's going to land to the right of a small clearing here. Ah, Paris, this is one-niner, we're picking up some small arms from our zero-four-zero quadrant. Could you bring us in some guns?"

"Roger, one-niner, can you get the pilot?"

"Negative...that's ah, negative, we are receiving more small arms fire and are going to back out until the guns get here..."

Two A1E's from Da Nang were on the way when the helicopter called Paris Control again. "Paris, this is one-niner... we can see the pilot and there are about a dozen people on the ground moving towards him ...ah, we are taking some hits and are breaking to the south...it appears we are going down." There was a long pause and then a very calm voice came back on the air.

"Paris this is one-niner... ah... this is a Mayday."

Jim crossed himself as he thought about the pilot on the ground.

U-TAPAO AIR FORCE BASE, THAILAND

When Jim landed and got back to the mod it offended him to find Hog Jaw sitting on one of the beds talking to Bobby D in the small room with four beds and two tables. As usual Hog Jaw was gross. He was telling Bobby D about Thai bingo.

"If you go downtown you need to know the whores in Thailand are required to wear numbers, such as 1837 on their outer clothing. When a girl is identified as being infected with VD, the Armed Forces television broadcasts her number.

"If you're smart you'll keep track of the identification number of the girl you sleep with. Then watch one of the four daily TV shows in the day room. If your numbers match, you yell bingo!"

With exaggerated politeness Jim asked Hog Jaw to step outside so he could tell him something he didn't want Bobby D to hear. "This place is small enough already without a foul motor mouth in it," said Jim through clenched teeth. "I arranged for the kid to stay with me so I could watch out for him. He doesn't need any of your bullshit. If I ever catch you talking to him again I will consider it a personal insult."

While Jim was straightening Hog Jaw out, Sam was spotting a familiar figure walking across the ramp. With his short round figure, Scotty was hard to miss. The last time Sam talked to him over two years ago they mentioned they were together at gunnery school when President Kennedy was shot. Sam had been sleeping after a night mission when Scotty woke him and gave him the news.

"It's funny you can go so long without seeing someone and still remember the last conversation," Sam thought as he asked Scotty about how the war was treating him.

"You should ask my wife, this is my fifth trip over here," said Scotty. "She's a little agitated about how much I've been away. At least you and I have the same wife we started with. That's a lot better than some of the guys. We just had one where his old lady sold his stuff, took the car and lit out for parts unknown while he was overseas. I don't have enough fingers to count the crewmembers I personally know that have split the sheets.

"Flying isn't too much fun either. We've had SAM missiles on my last two flights and they scare me so bad I'm not going to look at them anymore. From now on I'm going to lower my seat, slide it all the way to the back and put the helmet bag over my head. If the pilot wants to know what's behind us, I'm going to tell him I'm not looking out anymore."

Sam realized Scotty was kidding about covering his head, but he understood how he felt. Since the bombers started hitting the North more often, SAM sightings were becoming common and it wasn't hard to figure out that the crews' exposure was increasing. Everything was pointing to something bigger in the future.[43] If for no other reason then the number of crews and aircraft that were arriving on Guam, Sam suspected it would mean raids even deeper into the North. This was a game he had no interest in.

162

Chapter Thirteen

RAMEY AIR FORCE BASE, PUERTO RICO

The G-model was a tough airplane to get used to after the relative luxury of the reclining seat in the D. Andy rode in a rear-facing ejection seat to the right of the EW and his seat could not be tilted. To sleep he leaned forward in his straps. This got grossly uncomfortable in a hurry. Sitting in a windowless space in the rear of the upper deck wasn't pleasant, but Andy had to admit the ride was smoother and there was something to be said for having an ejection seat rather than try to struggle way out of the tail for bailout. He liked not being alone. It was better to have somebody to help if he experienced a problem. This came with a price. As the only enlisted man he was the dedicated gofer. If somebody needed a cup of coffee, he was the one who delivered it.

Even though Andy was legally still married, the marriage was obviously over. He tried to entice Rosalie in his letters by describing the beauty of the island, with its white sand beaches. He sent her brochures on the tropical rain forest and the fort at El Morro and described the fish in Phosphorescent Bay. The response was always some version of, "You have to come home, I'm not leaving here and if you want to ever see your little girl again you better listen."

Andy took up golf; it was something to do with his off time. By playing whenever he wasn't on alert or flying he got his handicap down to a five. One morning he teed up with Linda, a beautifully tanned blonde in blue shorts and a white tank top.

Linda was married to a captain in the Hurricane Hunters, a unit that shared the base with the bombers. Her husband was gone a lot and she frequently used that time to improve her game. Andy liked playing golf with her. She was fun and no slouch on the course. He knew if he had any sense it should end there, but they got in the habit of going to the nineteenth hole after their round. They would drink a beer or sip on a Pina Coladas. Neither drank much and they would talk for a while before leaving.

When they parted she often gave him a quick kiss. These innocent kisses started to get a little longer and one day she suggested going to the beach. That afternoon they parked at Ramey NCO club and walked down the steep jungle trail to Survival Beach. They were the only ones on the deserted and pristine strip of white sand surrounded by coconut palms. They spent the afternoon snorkeling and lying in the sun. It was an idyllic time and when Linda suggested they come back after dark and build a fire, Andy agreed without much hesitation.

That night, sitting in the glow of the fire, she asked him, "Have you ever done it on a beach before?"

Andy had some quick misgivings about what he was getting into, but his indecision ended when she spread a bath towel on the sand and pulled her muumuu over her head. He could see her naked body in the firelight.

Afterwards Andy felt guilty about what they'd done. "I don't feel married anymore," he thought, "but she still is. Did I take advantage of a good girl who has spent too many lonely nights without her husband?"

U-TAPAO AIR FORCE BASE, THAILAND

Hog Jaw was up to his normal mischief. Sometimes this was benign, like when he escorted a group of Navy cadets on a tour of the B-52 ramp. As he walked up to each airplane he would snap to attention and salute the bomber's nose. The cadets did the same thing and were impressed with how similar Air Force protocol was to the way a Navy ship was boarded. This was just good clean fun, but Hog Jaw's actions were sometimes more mean-spirited and had the potential to cause real trouble, as was the case on this occasion.

An obnoxious electronic warfare officer from Westover frequented gunners' rooms in the mod to bum drinks. When the pint-size lieutenant got some booze in him he wanted to take on the world. He once offered to fight three gunners who knew better than to get into it with an officer. He was generally insufferable and insults didn't run him off. Attempts to escort him out just stirred him up. Lately his visits were becoming a regular event.

Hog remembered a feisty gunner from Grand Forks who would wrestle a running chain saw if had enough alcohol in him, so he arranged a meeting between the lieutenant and the gunner in one of the rooms. To warm them up he provided a bottle of Jim Beam and then walked out of the room to let nature take its course. Somehow nobody got a court martial, but the EW lost a chunk of ear and the gunner had deep teeth marks in the fleshy part of his chest.

Hog Jaw will go too far one day, thought Sam as he walked to his airplane.

The first thing Sam noticed when he got to the airplane was its odd angle and that the tail was sitting in a ditch behind the parking ramp. A captain maintenance officer named Ron Smith was explaining to the pilot:

"It was raining and one of my overworked maintenance crews was running engines at full power when the bomber started to slide on the wet surface. They immediately shut down, but one of the front trucks ended up on top of a sixty-foot-long ground interphone cord. Rather than call for a tow truck, my genius in the left seat figured that since the ramp sloped all they had to do was release the brakes and roll the bird off the cord.

"So far so good. Even with the hydraulic pumps not running there should have been enough pressure stored in the accumulator for three brake applications. The first brake release was a check to see if the system worked. The second press on the pedals released the brakes, but the aircraft didn't move because the aft chocks were still in place. The third release wasn't long enough to move the airplane off the cord and the fourth released the brakes as advertised, but the system was out of pressure. I was driving down the ramp when I saw what happened. I continued radioing aircraft status to Job Control—you know, '589 in commission, 083 in commission' and finished my call with 'and 697 is in the klong'." Klong was a

Thai word for waterway. Some were fairly clean, but as far as the GI's were concerned klongs were nothing but sewage-filled ditches. Several of these ran behind the aircraft parking spots.

Looking at the awkward nose-up angle of the B-52 in the klong, Sam couldn't help but wonder who was going to get their lips ripped off for this. It hadn't been a week since he taxied by a KC-135 sitting on its tail with the nose gear twelve feet in the air because somebody forgot to install the tail stand.

It turned out there was more to the story. It started with the crew chief losing his airplane. He landed in Guam, refueled, accomplished the post-flight inspection, installed the covers and checked into billeting. Sometime in the middle of the night another tanker was needed and his airplane was sent to Okinawa.

When he got up in the morning and tried to find his airplane, nobody knew where it was. Finally he traced it to Kadena and went through the transportation hassle and caught a ride on a C-141. By then the tanker was at U-Tapao. Had he been there he could have told them the bird had a recurring problem with fuel seeping through a check valve. Fuel had to be transferred out of the aft tank daily to keep the airplane from becoming tail-heavy.

Sam found it painful to think about the tough life the maintenance people had. Some of them were on their fourth or even fifth tour and they didn't get the R&Rs or long breaks between flights like gunners did.

Sam's sympathy changed when he found himself gurgling blood in his oxygen mask shortly after take-off. It had been dumb to accept the bad seat on the airplane that replaced the one in the ditch. On preflight he noticed several nuts and washers alongside the gunner's seat and showed them to one of the assistant crew chiefs who said, "Oh yeah, they were working on your seat and couldn't get it fixed so they locked it in the down position."

Not wanting to press the tired-looking airman, Sam went ahead and finished his preflight. Everything was okay until the aircraft broke ground and the free-floating seat rammed his helmet into the windows above him, causing him to bite his tongue. His oxygen mask rapidly filled with blood and when he tried to talk to the pilot all he could do was gurgle.

Later he decided it was mostly his fault. He was becoming too complacent. He didn't even check to confirm the seat was locked down. He took somebody else's word. That was like trying to bet on a hand without looking at the hole cards. He was so tired of flying missions he didn't even take the time to think anymore. At least he would be going home shortly.

But Sam's complacency was nothing compared to Cal's continued drinking problem. He had passed four hundred missions, but he was on another slide into the bottle.

He'd quit drinking for a while and then drink just one beer. The resulting binge would add to his problems and more than once he almost missed a flight. People were getting tired of trying to rescue him from himself.

On one occasion he had to be literally rescued. He was walking with another gunner when he either tripped or dove into one of a series of klongs that ran along side many of the roads on U-Tapao. The gunner who rescued him was bitter.

"I've had it with that skinny son of a bitch," he said. "I thought I was doing him a favor bringing him home from the club and the next thing I know I'm in shit up to my ears trying to get him out of the water. I don't care how many missions he's got, somebody got to fix his ass."

DYESS AIR FORCE BASE, TEXAS

Cathy Jackson was talking to Patty Baker whose husband Earl was a gunner in the same squadron as Sam. They'd known each other at Ellsworth and became close when the wing deployed in 1966. They often leaned on each other when their men were gone and their friendship grew when both families moved to Dyess. Linda was telling Cathy her husband was going to get out of the Air Force after sixteen years.

"It's not worth it any more. I've got to the point I resent it when he comes home and I lose the car keys. The kids don't know him and I'm not sure I do either. He's so different when he gets back from Arc Light that it takes months before he adapts to being home. It's like he doesn't know what to do and has forgotten what I do while he's gone. I get used to running the show and all of a sudden he tries to change things. He spends too much time just sitting around when

167

I want to go out and enjoy life. I told him that as much as I love him, if he didn't get out, I was leaving. His enlistment is up in a month and he isn't going to re-up."

"What will you do?"

"I don't know, go back to Ohio, I guess. Earl thinks he can get on with the Post Office like his dad. It's not as much money, but it's got to beat this life."

The conversation bothered Cathy because she was hearing the same sort of thing from other gunners' wives. Many of them were becoming afraid to answer the door for fear it might be an officer in a blue uniform and they were tired of being single parents.

Some wives, although surprisingly few, considering the extended absences of their mates, were doing the bar scene and leaving their kids to fend for themselves. Mostly they coped in their own ways. Cathy found a small job as a clerk in a downtown drug store. She found this a great way to keep her mind off Sam and it left her plenty of time for the boys. She was continually thankful they were doing so well since she knew many wives were having troubles managing their children without a father to help with the discipline.

Money was a problem for many of her friends, particularly those in maintenance whose husbands didn't get flying or combat pay. With geographic separation one paycheck didn't go far. If too much got spent on booze and partying while overseas, some families back home were left close to destitute. She was lucky Sam was able to live on his poker money and could send every paycheck home. But this didn't give her much solace.

Cathy did the best she could to keep thinking that it would all work out. She tried to avoid thinking how different it would have been had Sam been able to get his degree. Nights were the hardest for her and she had recurring nightmares about Sam being trapped in an airplane that was on fire.

U-TAPAO AIR FORCE BASE, THAILAND

As they both sat on a long bench outside the mod, Scotty Burns said to Sam, "Did you hear another BUFF went down out of Guam? We've lost so many I can't keep score anymore. I hear they got most of the crew with some wild-ass rescue effort that involved an armada of rescue planes and no less than two submarines.[44]

"From what I learned they were about three hundred miles from the island when they bailed out directly into Typhoon Rita because of some sort of instrument problem. Somebody said the winds were 145 miles per hour and the waves were mountainous. Rescuers dropped tons of rafts, but no one could come up with a way to get any ships to them. Somebody finally got smart and diverted two subs to pick them up. It took about twenty-four hours and everybody including the Navy got the shit banged out of them on the rolling sea. Best I know they got the gunner who I think was one of the new baby gunners on his first tour. If so he sure got a hell of a baptism."

As Sam and Scotty were talking, Hog Jaw walked up and began to spout. "You sorry fuckers look like you got ate by the alligators. I'll tell you it can't be as bad as the whores in Newland are going to feel when they hear I'm leaving. They're just going to have to find a new orgy master. I'm getting out of this sorry war for good and SAC can stick the whole thing up its ass for all I care. Come next Tuesday I'm making tracks to the land of the big BX and I'll think about you hired guns and goddamn war heroes when I read you got your ass killed."

"We'll miss you," said Sam sarcastically as Hog Jaw walked away. Then turning back to Scotty, he said, "I don't know how he lasted as long as he did. More than once I've wanted to break his neck. He's half the reason Cal's been in trouble and he thought it was funny when he started paying Thai hookers to get in the beds of gunners coming off night missions. There's a departure that sure will change the morale around here and I see improvement already."

Every day Sam saw more new gunners he didn't know. Crews were coming from SAC bases all over the country and someone said that crews from a dozen bases were spread between Guam and Thailand.

When Sam first started flying out of Guam there were only two wings and thirty-some aircraft involved. Now he would estimate the number of bombers to be five or six times that. Okinawa was now only being used for emergency recoveries so aircraft parking space was a problem, particularly at U-Tapao, and sorties were frequently delayed because of snarls on the taxiways. It was deja vu to listen to the new folks grumble about the heat and humidity.

Sam remembered the first time he walked off the airplane and the Pacific heat struck him like a wave. "Life was simpler then and we pretty much knew everybody," he told Scotty. "Now it's a bunch of strangers who only worry about themselves. Now the colonels don't even know each other, let alone who they are sending out on sorties. It's just one big numbers game trying to keep the headquarters happy, and I haven't the slightest idea what's coming next.

"Cathy writes and asks questions I can't answer. She's got to be frustrated beyond belief. It's not fair to her that she married somebody that's gone all the time and it's not fair to the boys to grow up without a father. I've had about all the fun I can stand and about all I can hope for is that maybe the President will declare victory and pull out. I don't think either Cathy or I can handle this much longer."

Scotty left for home two weeks before Sam and time continued to drag while Sam thought about how often he'd been to the war. "How many missions does that make?" he wondered. "It's got to be over three hundred and I'm just tired of dragging bags and flying my butt off. It wouldn't be quite so bad if it was all one stretch, but this not knowing is like playing blind baseball and getting trapped with a lousy hand."

RAMEY AIR FORCE BASE, PUERTO RICO

Andy was surprised when Rosalie wrote and said she wanted to come to Puerto Rico. He had no way of knowing about her fight with her sisters and he wondered why she relented. He told Linda that Rosalie would be coming and they decided to stop seeing each other and find other golf partners. Andy was apprehensive about having his wife with him on the base. It was just that he'd got used to living by himself and liked the freedom and the absence of bitching. But the deciding factor was Kathleen. "I want to see her again so bad I'll put up with a lot," he thought.

When Rosalie and Kathleen arrived, the three of them moved into a three-bedroom concrete base house with surprisingly attractive government-provided rattan furniture. The lush corner yard contained two coconut palms and a large flamboyant tree whose bright red flowers made it resemble a huge poinsettia.

Getting Rosalie away from her mother and sisters turned out to be a good thing. Without their influence she became a more rational and loving person. A year and two months after she arrived on the island, Kristin Lynn was born. Andy and Rosalie were doing well as a couple and often went shopping and to the movies together. Andy thought the two girls were wonderful and he even changed their diapers.

Two days before Thanksgiving, Andy received the formal word. He thought this would never happen because the G-model, although somewhat longer-ranged and faster than the older D-model, was designed only to drop nuclear weapons. Its bomb bays hadn't been modified so it couldn't carry as many conventional bombs as the D.[45]

When Andy heard about the deployment, he wondered why anyone would want to use the G when the D could hold over three times as many bombs. It didn't have the structural beef-ups of the D's and in polite terms its electronic counter-measures sucked. It didn't seem logical to think the G-model, with its limited capability, would be sent to fly Arc Light missions.

As long as he was riding in the G-model, Andy never expected to go back to the war. He'd been sitting fat-dumb and happy on the tropical island of Puerto Rico and assumed that since he was on a controlled tour, he wouldn't be moved until he had three or more years on station. He felt safe until he heard G-models were starting to be sent overseas. Then he pretty much knew he was going to be back in the war. This time Rosalie accepted it without crying and bitching. Not that there weren't some tears, but they weren't selfish ones like the last time.

On the long ride from Ramey Air Force Base to Guam, Andy went through five hot TV dinner-type meals provided by the flight kitchen before take-off. He got at least twelve hours of sleep, most of it stretched out on a mattress positioned on the upper deck. After parking he was met by two maintenance troops who wanted to know if there was any milk left over. They were looking for real milk, not the reconstituted chalk-flavored stuff that was all they could get on Guam.

171

Chapter Fourteen

ANDERSON AIR FORCE BASE, GUAM

It was difficult for Andy to comprehend what he saw when he arrived back on Guam. With the addition of aircraft and crews from eleven stateside bases the base had grown from three thousand people to over eleven thousand. Almost 150 B-52's filled the three parking ramps. Huge steel dirt-filled revetments had been erected on two of the ramps, obviously to protect the BUFF's from each other, since nobody was going to bomb Guam.[46] Even with the large number of revetments there were more aircraft than protected spots to park them in. Numerous aircraft were parked on taxiways while others were kept airborne awaiting parking space.

Some crews were living in converted base housing and hundreds of tents were situated around the base. The gym was surrounded with olive drab canvas six-man shelters, and a large village of hastily constructed corrugated metal buildings had been erected on the old tennis courts. It was easy to see why it was called Tin City or the "Turkey Farm". At least he had air-conditioning. Andy empathized with the poor maintenance troops that worked nights and then tried to sleep in a hot tent during the day.

Gilligan's Island was gone, paved over on the instructions of some colonel who didn't like to see crewmembers drinking there. This was probably the same asshole that stopped the maintenance people from drinking beer outside, during the day, when heat in the tents got unbearable. At least there was still a "hat colonel"; in fact now there were several of them with their clipboards, keeping everyone from forgetting how important uniforms and haircuts were to the war effort. GI's were crammed everywhere.

Offices built for four people held twelve and front panels had been removed from gray steel government-issued desks so that each desk could accommodate two NCOs sitting face to face. Makeshift was the name of the game, except in serious officer country and even that was cramped. In some cases full colonels were living four to a room. The number of B-52G's on the ramp was surprising. There must have been fifty, with more on the way.

Andy was disappointed in how few gunners he recognized. There must have been two hundred crews sent from bases all over the States to support the Bullet Shot and Linebacker missions. If you discounted crews from Ramey he didn't know many of the people. He looked around for Sam and Melvin without success.

Some gunner he'd never met before told Andy that Cal had been sent home from U-Tapao after a series of booze-related incidents. Apparently he missed two flights in a row and some commander just had enough. "Imagine that, more than four hundred missions and they kick him out of the war," Andy thought as he shook his head.

DYESS AIRFORCE BASE, TEXAS, NOVEMBER 1972

By Cathy's count Sam had been home for thirty-five days when he received notice that they were going back. The ten days before he left went by unbelievably fast. Sam was still bone weary, and even after long uninterrupted sleep he couldn't rid himself of a feeling of constant fatigue His time at home was so short he never really adapted to being a father again. The boys were ten and eleven now and although obviously glad to have their father back, they had developed interests in things that he wasn't part of.

Cathy hovered over him and tried her best to be solicitous. She quit the job which had helped her deal with the loneliness during Sam's absences, and when Sam went back on alert she visited with him in the parking lot every night. Sometimes she brought the boys with her, although she and Sam knew it was boring for them. One night they sat in the car and talked about all sorts of dreams until after midnight.

When Sam retired they would build a cabin on Little McGraw Lake, six miles across the Minnesota-Wisconsin border and less than a hundred miles from where he was raised. He would change his major to education, finish his degree and get a job teaching in one of the small schools in northern Wisconsin. They would need the money since his retirement check would not be close to what it would have been had he not been cheated out of a commission by the war.

The last four days at home were the hardest. Sam sat down with his boys and tried to explain why he was going again. He wrestled with different ideas of what to say. "I know you don't understand everything I have to do," he began, "but going away is just part of my job. It doesn't mean I don't love you and your mother. While I'm gone it's your job to be the men of the house. Do what your mom asks you to and give her lots of hugs and kisses."

When it was time to leave, Sam couldn't bear having his family go to the flight line with him. It was better to say good-bye in the house, not among all the noise and activity on the flight line, and he didn't want Cathy to have to look at the bomber taking him away again.

ANDERSON AIRFORCE BASE, GUAM

For over an hour Sam's crew moved in a stream of six B-52's making their slow "elephant walk" as they waited to park on a taxiway in front of several fuel pump houses. When he climbed out of the tail the smells and the humidity were the same, but Guam looked different to Sam than it had less than two months ago. More airplanes, more people, more everything.

Once he settled in he set out to find Andy, whose name he'd seen on a roster. It turned out he was living in one of the trailers just two down from Sam's. "Goddamn sleeping beauty," Sam said when he visited him, "you need to get up when one of your superiors is present. What he heck do you think this, a rest camp? Hasn't anybody told you there is a war on? I didn't think you cabin stewards needed to rest."

"Hey, my seat doesn't fold into a bed like you aft compartment commanders have," Andy replied, and then added, "Jesus, it's good to see you. How's Cathy?"

"I don't think you could call her thrilled about me coming back and she's not the only one. I don't know if you know it, but I was home about seven weeks before I got tagged again. I'm not exactly overjoyed with this war hero stuff."

The two grown men hugged in a blatantly unmilitary manner and held each other for a few moments. Breaking apart, they sat on the bed and talked for a long time, catching up with each other's news. They talked about their families and some of the bomber crashes that had happened since they last saw each other. Sometimes they knew who the gunner was, but usually they didn't. "There have been a lot of accidents since you were over here, including several off the runway at Guam, and a few in Thailand," said Sam. "As far as I know, other than the one B-52 that went in at U-Tapao after being damaged by a SAM missile, none have been lost to enemy action. Just tired airplanes and tired inexperienced crews that probably didn't always have the smartest leadership."

"Let's get off this serious crap and talk about something else," said Andy, who didn't like to be reminded of the dangers of their mission. "Did you hear about Cal?"

"Yeah, I was here when he got sent home. Somebody said he's working in the base commissary stocking shelves. It's proof that you can screw up and be rewarded. Hell, I'd do that if I was sure it would get me out of the goddamn tail."

"I'm offended you think us important people who are allowed to ride up front with the officers in first class like it any better than you do," said Andy in mock seriousness. "It's comforting to sit and watch gray snow on television and not worry about getting sunburned like some of the lower-class folks who have windows."

"That bad?"

"No, it's worse than bad," replied Andy. "Anytime ECM cranks up it wipes out the radar and I get to see snow on two screens. Remember when we used to talk about gunners being useless because of lousy guns and no targets anyway. You can't question the fact that guys in the back have prevented a lot of mid-air collisions by being able to see. How many times has a tail gunner called evasive action for a SAM? If you are in a G-model you might as well be in a closet with the lights out."

"Have you seen Mama Nening?" asked Sam.

"Yeah, she's doing good and is still the Mama for wayward gunners. I've been there a couple of times and the Rum Shack is so busy you can't find a seat. There's even a batch of gunners living downtown in a hotel that's within walking distance of the Rum Shack. Everybody claims they found it first and there are several guys who never got over here until 1968 who are claiming to have the first bean. By the way, did you know Jim is here? I thought he was teaching at Castle until I saw him in the parking lot."

"Yeah, he either transferred or they sent him from the school-house, "said Sam. He came over before I left for my short break. I ran with him once in a while and I never even asked if he was still at Castle. I do know he got promoted to master sergeant and by now has been here or in Thailand for almost six months. He must be getting ready to go home."

U-TAPAO AIRFORCE BASE, THAILAND, NOVEMBER 1972

Melvin didn't know what he liked the least, the long missions out of Guam, followed by some time off, or the short ones out of Thailand that came every day. "I'm getting too old for this shit," he thought. "My ass gets to dragging so bad I feel like I'm fifty. I'd never thought I'd say this, but I'm tired of the war and I need to change the way I'm living."

His last girlfriend worked in a strip club and she always seemed to be working when he was off, so a lot of the time he was alone in the bungalow. Without a girl, there weren't many amenities available in the small concrete house and he missed the long hot showers he could get on base. Life would be simpler if he just lived in the mod and it would sure make the early goes a lot easier.

There was another reason Melvin decided to move back on base. He was beginning to think he was in love with an olive-skinned Eurasian girl more than fifteen years his junior. He met her in the NCO club, not downtown, and she enchanted him. It wasn't just her beauty. Thailand was filled with truly beautiful Thai and Eurasian women available for a small fee.

But Yuphen wasn't for sale and other than a few simple kisses Melvin never touched her body. She worked on base more to improve her English than because she needed a job. She was clearly educated and carried herself with an elegant gracefulness that no bar girl could touch. He talked to her casually for months and often kidded her about how he'd like his eggs cooked in whiskey. She wanted to know about the United States and his job as a gunner.

"Why you not afraid?" she would ask, and he could never answer. He didn't like to think about it. Most of the time he didn't worry, but she made him realize that lately a lot of his carousing was because he needed to escape from reality.

Anybody with half a brain could figure out that the new "press on" missions, where all bombers were required to continue on to the target regardless of malfunctions or enemy threats, had greatly increased their risk. Melvin realized that the big build-up going on wasn't just to continue to pummel targets in South Vietnam or the relatively undefended ones in the North. One of these days the shit was going to hit the fan and it was not going to be pretty.

Melvin and Yuphen began to go for walks around the base and one Sunday they rode a Baht bus to Pattaya Beach, a Thai resort on the ocean ten miles south of the base. He couldn't remember a single time in his life that had been more pleasant and he didn't want the day to end. He talked more deeply with Yuphen than any other woman he had ever known, including his three ex-wives. He was in love, and when Yuphen asked to see where he lived on base he knew it was time to move out of the bungalow for good.

After completing six uneventful missions out of Guam, Sam's crew landed in Thailand on the backside of a mission twenty miles north of the DMZ which separated North and South Vietnam. He wasn't originally scheduled to rotate to U-Tapao until later in the month, but there was a new push on to make more B-52D's available to fly the shorter missions possible out of Thailand. This rapidly grew to sixty or more bombers that saturated the smaller U-Tapao ramp. Aircraft were even parked nose to tail on the south taxiway.

Melvin pre-arranged for Sam to share his room in Mod 5, and left him a note on the bed that said, " I'm flying—be back in the morning."

Melvin almost made it back, but on the post-target turn his airplane was hit by a surface-to-air missile. They were flying just above a tall cloud deck and Melvin could not see the ground, nor did he see the missile until it exploded without warning twenty-five yards under the right wing. From his seat in the tail it looked like an enormous sparkler and it was only microseconds before he heard the boom. Surprisingly, it did not dramatically shake the airplane and it felt more like they had hit a small speed bump than a missile strike. They remained flying and the pilot leveled the wings without problems.

From what Melvin heard on the crew report, no one was injured and neither compartment had suffered an explosive decompression. Number eight engine had shut down and a number of warning lights were illuminated, but other than that it appeared that the aircraft was sound.

Melvin thought about taking his oxygen mask off so he could smoke a cigarette, but then thought better of it. He decided to wait until they crossed into Laos since they were at 35,000 feet and still over North Vietnam.

It was going to be about an hour before they landed back at U-Tapao and there was not much to do. He had repeatedly checked the portions of the aircraft he could see and saw no visible damage. There was no sign of smoke or fuel vapor trailing from the wing and the spoilers appeared to be working correctly. His first indication of trouble was when he noticed that the red cabin low pressure light on the panel in front of him was blinking brightly. The light, which was designed to go on somewhere between 13,980 and 16,020 feet, caused him to immediately check his cabin altimeter. It showed the pressure in his compartment was at a little over 15,000 feet.

Melvin suspected that the aluminum wall of his compartment had been punctured by shrapnel or the bleed air system in the right wing had been damaged. There was no way to know for sure, but he decided bleed air was the most likely cause. His air conditioner used engine bleed air from the number three nacelle to pressurize his compartment and there did not seem to be much air flow coming from the ducts.

Pressure slowly continued to rise until his cabin pressure was equal to the bomber's altitude of 35,000 feet. Since he was on oxygen this had little effect on Melvin except for the slightly uncomfortable nature of pressure breathing. Instead of breathing in he had to breath out against the force of oxygen under pressure higher than his compartment.

Wanting a cigarette badly, Melvin thought about Yuphen. Did she have a premonition? Two weeks ago she brought a pair of Buddhist monks to his room. They had shaved heads and were wearing bright orange robes. They ritually sprinkled and blessed him with water from a bowl that had a special name that Melvin could not pronounce. Melvin sat through this ritual without understanding it, but he hoped it brought luck.

Before he took off on this flight, Yuphen again visited him in the mod and this time brought four monks with her. They went through the same ritual.

Shortly after the descent began, the pilots reported an overheat warning light in the 47-section had illuminated and the controls were somewhat sluggish in left banks, indicating a hydraulic problem on the right wing. They continued the descent and when they finally crossed the threshold to the U-Tapao runway they were aligned to the left of their planned touchdown point. A rapid decision to go around was made and the co-pilot pushed the throttles for the seven operating engines to the firewall.

Unfortunately, the thrust of the remaining three engines was reduced due to a series of massive bleed air leaks caused by the damage from the missile. This and the fact that they had more engines on the left side caused the aircraft to yaw to the right directly at a hill alongside the end of the runway.

They might have made it if the pilot who was flying the airplane had longer legs, but he was unable to push the left rudder pedal far enough to stop the drift. The aircraft was destroyed, and all six people on board were killed.

When Sam heard the news he swore softly. After looking around he found the note Melvin had written. He crushed it and threw it

179

at the wall. Then standing silently, lost in his thoughts, he tried to figure out how long he had known Melvin. It had to be more than six years since they first flew combat together. Mother was part of their room then. "When the hell did he go down? Somewhere around sixty-nine. Fuck!"

ANDERSON AIR FORCE BASE, GUAM, DECEMBER 1972

Before the large influx of bombers arrived, Anderson Air Force Base was like a small American city. Families lived in base housing and kids attended school while their moms shopped in the base exchange or commissary. This sometimes created a sense of unreality in the crews flying combat, but it was a pleasant environment to spend the time off between missions.

When the base population tripled in size, many of the permanent party resented the TDY troops taking over their clubs and activities. Guam was becoming less friendly to crewmembers. It was a strange feeling going to church and watching fathers hover over their daughters.

Jim packed and got ready to depart for home two days before he was due to leave. He would be home for Christmas and couldn't wait to see Elizabeth and the twins again. He'd lost a lot of idealism on this trip and as far as he was concerned he didn't like the way the war was going. It had gone on too long and except for a few targets in North Vietnam they didn't seem to be doing anything more than going through the motions. The big Bullet Shot build up generated some excitement for a while, but nothing substantial happened. He wondered how much truth there was to the rumor of a draw down. Would SAC would actually bring most of the airplanes and crews home? What a waste that would be.

His time in Thailand bothered him. It was not that Jim was a prude, but there were too many distractions. This was supposed to be a war, not an extended R&R. His brother talked about slogging in the mud and ice in Korea and about night patrols behind enemy lines. The GI's in Korea lived in leaky pup tents with a straw floor.

It embarrassed Jim to think about how different his life was here. When they were at U-Tapao they were living four to a room with regular beds and maid service. If he wanted to it was easy to find a beer night or day. Guys bragged about how they spent the night in town and then went to fly. That irked Jim. There were rules about not drinking before flight. When his fellow NCO's did it that was bad enough, but when some of the officers did the same thing it was even worse. It went against the grain of everything he believed in. He would be glad to leave this war.

Still thinking about the trip home, Jim went to the base snack bar for a hamburger. It would be good to get something with a different brand of grease. After waiting in a long line he finally was served and sat down with some maintenance guys at the only open table. They were talking about a park they were building. When Jim asked about it one of them explained.

"You know where the big POL tanks are, well if you go out behind them you'll find a path into the jungle. That's the entrance to Ramp Runner Park. It's the only place we can drink beer without having somebody all over our ass. When we get off the night shift the tents are too damn hot.

"We used to hold sunrise services on the baseball field until somebody got upset about the sight of a bunch of grubby maintainers laying on the grass and drinking beer. Anyway, we chopped this clearing in the jungle and put up four chamorro huts made out of bamboo and palm fronds. It's pretty neat and we can sit around in our underwear if we want to. It's a hell of a lot better place to sleep than the goddamn tents."

"Doesn't anybody know about it?" asked Jim.

"The only one I know for sure is our OMS Commander.[47] He's an old ex-enlisted guy and I think he talked to POL and told them to cool it."

About this time two air policemen in uniform walked into the snack bar. The shorter of the two asked loudly, "Are there any B-52 crewmembers in here?"

"Yeah, I'm a gunner," said Jim as he looked around to see if any others responded. The tall cop walked over to him and said, "You're directed to stop drinking and report to your quarters."

"I hear you, but I'm not drinking, unless you count Coke," said Jim. He wondered what the hell this was all about. Could some of the crews be going home early?

Lack of information was not a new problem for gunners. Most of what they learned required effort to ferret out. None of the leadership put the gunners together and said, "here's the big picture," so what they learned always came in erratic ways. The best source should have been their aircraft commanders, but usually this meant waiting until they got together at briefing or on the crew bus.

Hunting them down was an option, but with the gunners living in the trailers it could require walking a half-mile to the officer's room only to learn they were gone. This could mean any number of places. There was no way to find anybody on the golf course and the officers' club wasn't exactly friendly to visits from enlisted gunners.

Early in the war wing gunners were a good source of information because they spent time hanging around the staff in officer country. Now, with three hundred gunners in the Pacific, it was a problem figuring out who the hell they were.

There must have been more than a half dozen frazzled chief master sergeants who carried the title wing gunner. In his own way Hog Jaw probably said it the best. "The organization is so fucked up the VC could light a fire on my balls and I still couldn't tell them what the chain of command was."

Jim wasn't able to hunt somebody down for information even if he wanted to, since the cop had taken his name when he told him he was restricted to quarters. He decided to get back to the trailers and see if anybody knew anything.

It didn't take long, listening to the large number of gunners starting to congregate around the trailers, to learn that something big was up. "It's another stand down and maintenance is loading bombs on everything on the ramp," he heard someone say. "It's got to be Hanoi."

After being told his return home was cancelled, Jim went out and ran for over an hour in the hot Guam sunshine. By the time he got to the top of the hill, coming up from Tarague Beach, he was drenched in sweat and his eyes stung from the water pouring off his forehead. When it started to rain it felt good, and when Jim got back to his trailer he did a hundred push-ups and the same number of sit-ups.

Bobby D watched quietly until Jim finished his exercise routine and then asked, "Have you ever had any MiG's when you've gone north?"

"It's amazing to think you were in the eighth grade when I flew my first combat mission," replied Jim. "Now you're sitting on the bed across from me asking about fighters. To answer your question, I think the couple I've seen were probably scouts getting our formation altitudes and headings to send back to ground missile stations. They were never close enough to shoot at and I used to doubt any MiG pilot with any sense would attack a B-52 from the tail.

"I think it's going to be different this time. This looks like it's going to be a big push. You need to be ready. Pay attention to where you are and listen to the 'bulls eye'[48] calls. This will tell where the MiGs are in relation to downtown Hanoi. My advice is to stay cool and be damn sure you've got a real target before you pull the trigger."

"What about missiles—is it possible to shoot one down?"

"Anything is possible, but I don't think so. I've seen quite a few and they were all moving too fast to get a lock on even if I had my head in the scope, and in my opinion that's not where it should be when SAMs are flying. You need to keep your seat up and your eyes out the window so that you can call evasive action. I know you've heard this before, but when you call 'break left' make sure it's the pilots left and not yours.

"One more thing. It could get pretty wild up there. Be damn sure what you've shooting at. You don't need some bomber pilot screaming, 'Do I look like a MiG?'"

"You think we're going to Hanoi tonight?"

"It's going to be downtown Hanoi or somewhere close, but I don't think it'll be tonight. It takes too long to crank up for a big mission and from what I hear, every bomber on the flight line is being generated. My advice is to get all the sleep you can and stay away from the whiskey. I'm going to early mass in the morning if we're still around. You're invited if you want."

On December 18, 1972, the first sorties of Linebacker II missions were launched from Guam in three separate waves approximately fours hours apart. They met up with other aircraft out of U-Tapao to

strike airfields, rail yards, communications and storage facilities in the Hanoi area. Andy was fifteenth in the first group of bombers that took off from Anderson. For him it would be a long sixteen-hour flight and he was terrified, listening to all of the SAM calls. In the environment of chaff and electronic
counter-measures, Andy's radar was marginal, and in the dark his small television was useless. With no windows in his compartment, he could not get a sense of situational awareness as he felt the aircraft maneuver and climb, apparently to avoid SA-2's.

The last four minutes to the target were the worst of Andy's life. He knew from the briefings that the airplane had to be flown completely straight and level for the bombing system to work accurately. There were visual SAM sightings in all quadrants and the radios were jammed with warning calls. He heard his co-pilot talking about two missiles that had missed them by less than fifty feet. The EW sitting next to him was a flurry of motion as he moved switches and pressed buttons, trying to jam whatever was chasing them. All Andy could do was watch and try to see something on his scope or television screen, but nothing made sense. From where he sat he had no reference to what was going on outside of the airplane and he could do nothing except anticipate the worst. He expected to die any second. His eyes stung from sweat running down from his forehead and he felt the pain in his crotch from the tight parachute straps. He pulled on them again, not knowing what else to do as he thought about what would happen to Rosalie and his daughters after he was killed.

Coming off the target they made a steep turn and he heard his navigator say, "Eighty knots, would you believe the headwinds are eighty fucking knots." This was the first time Andy heard the captain, a devout Mormon ever say anything stronger than "Oh, my heck," and he understood they were facing increased exposure until they got out of North Vietnam.

Back on the ground, Andy found it difficult to get his bearings. Even walking wasn't automatic any more. He needed to consciously tell his legs what to do. Nothing would make his dread go away. He was so nervous he couldn't hold a cup of coffee without using both hands.

Rumors were circulating that on the first night three bombers were shot down and many others damaged. Typically, this was neither officially confirmed or denied, and the rumors were impossible to pin down. Several crews did not return to Guam after the mission. Nobody seemed to know whether they had been shot down or had just landed somewhere else.

The word that several gunners were claming MiG's created a sense of elation among the gunners, and the fire control technicians who maintained the guns were ecstatic.[49] Mechanics who had been working twelve-hour shifts for weeks on end had to be ordered off the flight line. Systems were tweaked and re-tweaked. Gunners saw a subtle change in the officers, who seemed to be more interested in their welfare than before. Even the chow hall was different. Gunners, recognizable by the lack of rank on their flight suits, were being offered steaks cooked to order. For a short time it felt good to be a gunner. But it didn't take long for the sense of euphoria to wear off.

It turned out that three airplanes and nineteen airplanes had not come back from the mission over Hanoi. This was a high price to pay, and it was not over yet. Most gunners were resigned to going to Hanoi again. Nobody really believed Linebacker II would be over in a few days, even though it was hard to see how SAC could take another night like the previous one. The atmosphere became serious. The macabre ritual in which gunners divided up their possessions before they went to North Vietnam stopped. People were too superstitious to ask, "Can I have your stereo if you don't come back?" There were already too many who hadn't come back to tempt fate. It just wasn't funny anymore.

Andy didn't go on the second night mission. But what he heard about it added to his apprehension about going again. Information about how many SAM missiles were fired at the formations trickled down to the gunners. Although there was no official confirmation, some estimates said two hundred missiles were fired at the more than ninety bombers that flew.

Now they were going to try it again for a third night using exactly the same plan as the first two nights.[50] Didn't anyone in the command leadership chain catch onto the concept that this might in some small way help the North Vietnamese track the bombers and bring their guns and missiles to bear?

Andy started several letters to Rosalie but always gave up before he completed them. He couldn't concentrate. He would write a couple of sentences and then tear the letter up because he couldn't think of what to say. He was overwhelmed by the thought of not coming home.

He wondered how they would tell her. Would it be somebody from his squadron who stayed behind? What about the base house? Would she have to move out of it right away? Would she go back to Rapid City with her mother and sisters? Would Kathleen even remember him? What would Rosalie tell Kristin Lynn about him?"

Bobby D's thoughts were quite different. He was excited by the feeling of being in combat. "How many missiles do you think they fired at us?" he asked Jim.

"It was pretty wild. At one time I physically counted eight missiles airborne at the same time and from the radio calls it sounded like dozens of SA-2's were being salvo launched at us. I told you it would get interesting."

"Yeah it was," said Bobby D. "My pilot just disregarded everything they said at briefing about not maneuvering between the IP and target. A SAM locked on and tracked us. When I called 'break left' the ace stood it up on its wing so hard the nose started to drop. That was the first time I'd seen an angle like this and I thought he'd lost it. Coming off the target I was lucky again. When we started our post-target turn I saw one coming right at us. If I hadn't hollered, 'stop turn' I think it would have got us. It didn't miss by over fifty feet. It was a good thing I unstrapped and put my seat up and as far back to the tail as it would go. If I hadn't been right up in the windows—"

"You ready to do this again?" asked Jim.

"Sure, why the hell not? I'll be there," said Bobby D. " You bet I'm ready. I want to get a MiG."

"One thing about Bobby D, he's too young and dumb to know any better," thought Jim. "He's eager and I guess so am I. We've been at this too damn long, it's about time somebody got serious about winning."

As Jim's bomber taxied for take-off, maintenance people were standing at attention at every empty parking spot they passed. They held their proud salutes as the heavy bombers slowly rolled by. When the B-52's turned onto the runway there were dozens of trucks and busses parked on the grass alongside the hammerhead. They waved flags and held their right hands to their foreheads as the bombers rumbled down the runway, in an unbroken stream, bellowing black smoke from the water used to increase thrust for take-off. Even with earplugs the noise was deafening.

Everything went smoothly for Jim's crew until, coming off the target, his aircraft banked to begin its post-strike turn. This increased the size of its radar cross-section and decreased its ECM coverage as the wings masked the ECM antennas. Before they completed the turn, the bomber was struck by two SA-2's fired from a missile site within the city limits of Hanoi.

Jim had little time to react before the airplane exploded and started to break up. He was surrounded by fire as he pulled the turret jettison handle and rolled out of the tail. The cold wind tore at him as he descended in a free fall. He managed to pull the green apple on his right side that activated his emergency oxygen bottle and he tried to put his arms out to stabilize himself and stop the uncontrolled spinning. This tore his gloves off before his parachute automatically opened at 14,000 feet. As the chute opened he was almost on his back and it violently tugged him upright. When he caught his breath and looked around he could see what might be three other parachutes, but it was hard to tell in the dark, even though portions of the sky were lit up from SAM's still being fired.

He hit the ground hard and was pretty sure his right arm was broken. At least it hurt like hell when he removed his parachute by opening the buckles holding the risers to his harness. Everything around him was lit up, and from the small depression he was lying in he observed a surface-to-air missile launch with a deafening roar from a site on his right. He estimated the distance at more than two city blocks. His first thought was for the rest of his crew, but he had not seen where they landed and was not about to stand up and look.

As he struggled to hide his parachute and survival kit he could hear voices speaking Vietnamese coming closer to him. He remembered he had in his chaps a .38 snub-nose pistol with six bullets. "Maybe the right thing to do is go down in a firefight," he thought. "I don't think being a POW will be much fun."

But then he thought about Elizabeth and his girls. He stood up and put his hands over his head.

For Elizabeth, a warning of the bad news came in a four a.m. phone call. It was Meg Browne, the wife of Jim's aircraft commander.

"You had better sit down before I tell you this," she said. "You know how rumors are, but I just got a call from a friend in Guam that said my husband's airplane was shot down over North Vietnam. If so Jim would have been with him. I woke up the wing commander, but he said he hadn't heard anything and not do anything unless there's something official."

Elizabeth woke Susan and Sharon and brought them into bed with her to tell them the news. "We probably need to pray and then get dressed," she said. "I'm deathly afraid we are going to see a blue staff car in the driveway."

The bad news didn't come in a blue staff car, but in a white Volkswagen bus. All six of the crewmembers on Jim's crew were married and lived in base housing. Emergency notification checklists called for simultaneous action so that no wife learned about the tragedy before the others. This meant six vehicles and six notification officers along with hospital and chapel support. Time was of the essence, and the acting commander, who had just returned from Arc Light himself, wisely decided not to delay while he rounded up Air Force staff cars.

When Elizabeth looked at the vehicle that had pulled into her driveway, her heart stopped and she hugged the twins with tears running down her face. A master sergeant she casually knew was driving and in the right front seat there was a captain she didn't know, in a khaki uniform. In the back was a medic in whites. Her friend Katherine Daily got out and held her as the captain read from a piece of paper.

It took a moment, but she finally grasped that Jim was missing and not necessarily dead. This gave her some hope. She closed her eyes and prayed for God in his mercy to bring her husband home safely.

Bobby D was inbound to the target when his navigator asked over the interphone, "Are you listening to the bulls eye calls?"

"Roger sir," said Bobby D who already knew MiG's were in the area.

"I've plotted them at our two o'clock, they're at about twelve miles and could be working our way…they may have an angle on us."

Bobby D glanced up from his scope and pressed his face against the side window, trying to spot the suspected bandits. When they were reported within seven miles he put his head back in the scope and concentrated on trying to pick them up on radar. At about four thousand yards he saw one bogie and then the other as small blips on his radarscope. He could tell by their position and movements they were not part of the bomber formation.

"Gunner, this is nav. Have you got the bad guys? I show them at about our five o'clock closing fast…"

Without answering the navigator, Bobby D said over the intercom. "Pilot, gunner. Break right, keep going hard right. I've got two bogies at about six o'clock, they're still turning with us and about twenty-five hundred yards. Request permission to fire when they get in range."

"Roger, gunner, you're cleared if you can confirm the target," said the aircraft commander.

Bobby D observed the targets swap lead and went to second target mode. At four thousand yards he observed the beginning of a pass and locked on. At two thousand yards he fired a ten-second burst. The first fighter fell off his scope and the second dropped rapidly back.

Someone on the radio was talking about a fireball and Bobby D looked up in time to see what looked like a roman candle plunging towards the earth.

Chapter Fifteen

U-TAPAO AIR FORCE BASE, THAILAND,
DECEMBER 1972

Sam was bewildered. "God, how did I get in this mess? Melvin dead, Jim down over the north, along with something like a dozen other gunners. I don't even know how many total people are down, at least eighty or ninety I figure. I don't even know who is left."

Sam had been in the room when an unsmiling lieutenant came to pack Melvin's belongings. The way things were scattered in the room it was hard to tell what belonged to Melvin, but the lieutenant went through everything, reading every letter to insure nothing a wife shouldn't see was packed. Since Melvin no longer had a wife this was a wasted effort.

Military gear to be turned in was put in one pile, personal belongings were stacked in another. The lieutenant didn't miss a thing and even took the laundry tickets. When he was done he asked Sam to sign a statement that said, "To the best of my knowledge there is no property belonging to Sergeant Cunningham remaining in the room."

"What an impersonal way to go, all your shit just dumped in a big cardboard box," thought Sam. He supposed some fresh new lieutenant had been assigned to pack Jim's stuff. But he would be wasted his time reading the mail. Jim was the straightest arrow he knew.

He was distressed by the heavy losses. One mission with thirty-seven people down. At least eight dead, if the chute counts were accurate. He'd heard that three men had been picked up by rescue but the fate of the rest was unknown. Of the four chutes from Jim's airplane there was no way to know what crew positions made it. Several survival radios were being tracked on the ground, but these could be from any number of bombers down over the north. The clouds in the area were stopping any more rescue attempts for the time being.

Sam wondered why the rescue couldn't be as efficient as that goddamn room packer. He must have had a plan—typical SAC—a checklist for everything. It was a pretty shitty deal though. Like a stranger coming in and packing your wife's things the day after she died without so much as a fare-thee-well. Didn't that lieutenant understand that Melvin and Jim were like family to him? No doubt about it—he'd probably spent more time with them over the last six years than he did with Cathy.

Sam sat on the edge of the GI bed rubbing his head, trying to make his headache go away. It seemed like he'd been up forever, but it was only eight hours. Worse, he was due at first briefing in less than two hours for a mission he knew would be deep into North Vietnam.

How in the hell could they do this again? he wondered. The attrition must be better than five percent, anyway you cut it.

Sam had been flying combat on and off for over six years and he'd never seen anything as bad as his first two Linebacker II missions. He knew about odds, and even before they started going north every day, it was pretty easy to figure out that his butt was on the line. But nothing prepared him for the lousy cards he had been dealt.

That night would be his third time over the Hanoi area. The first time, his airplane had been hit but not badly damaged. On his second mission Sam watched a missile pass between the wing and the horizontal stabilizer. Then another SAM exploded within four hundred yards of the airplane, creating a fireball the size of a house. Sam could clearly see the red-hot shrapnel spinning off the cone-shape explosion. "That's close enough," he thought, just before a missile he hadn't seen exploded close enough to the airplane that he could hear the blast and smell the cordite.

When they landed, a maintenance count indicated several hundred fragments from the blast peppered his BUFF from just aft of the nose wheel well doors to the drag chute door almost directly under his seat.

This had to be an omen of an impending bad hand. No way to draw out again. He'd never been as fearful as he was now, sitting and sweating on his bed. His head hurt and he felt queasy, like he might throw up. Maybe the flight surgeon could…Nah, he would go. He'd been at this business too long to take the cheap way out.

In poker terms this meant Sam was "all in"; he'd staked his last dollar, and unlike poker, he couldn't fold his hand. He told himself he couldn't keep sitting there, he had to get started. There was a lot to do in the next two hours and it was no use putting it off any longer.

Getting ready to fly combat was a ritual Sam had practiced since his first mission. First he would take a long hot shower and then stand naked a couple of minutes to drip-dry. He would always put on clean underwear, white socks and a clean flight suit that did not contain any personal information the enemy could use. He placed his dog tags with the chain outside of the collar and the tags themselves tucked inside next to his white tee shirt, with nothing touching the skin.

He took two packs of Winston's, one in his pocket on the left sleeve and the other in the right pants' leg. He placed one glove in each leg side pocket. That way they were easy to get at and also provided padding if the plane hit turbulence.

Next he placed his ID card, Geneva Convention card and a few dollars in the right front pocket in case they had time to stop at base ops. That wouldn't happen that night, but he put the money in anyway. He then put a ballpoint pen in the right sleeve along with an emergency penlight. Two pencil flares he'd stolen from the equipment section shared the pockets with the Winston's.

Then he realized he had forgotten matches. They should have come with the cigarettes. He wondered if that was a sign. He'd never missed spreading out six books, one to a pocket.

Boots would come last. It would be a while before Sam was ready for them and his feet were sweaty enough as it was.

He put his helmet on the bed and took it out of its canvas bag. Getting a bottle of alcohol out of his locker, he used a cotton swab to wipe the mask clean. It was unbelievable how dirty a mask could get on one flight. He couldn't stand a sticky mask and the last thing he needed was for dirt and goo to block the inhale or exhale valves.

Sam continued his preparation: checklist; flashlight. He made sure that his flashlight worked, and also checked that two eight-amp fuses were taped to it. Too many times he'd needed a spare fuse, only to find none on the aircraft.

He picked up the spare bayonet connector. There was no real need for it since there was one on the oxygen hose connected to the mask, but several years ago he left one on the aircraft and didn't know it was missing until he started his preflight for the next mission. It was embarrassing to have one brought out to him so the next time he got a chance he'd stolen a spare. That would go in the helmet bag side pocket along with the flashlight, checklist and two filters—one red, one green—used on the Aldis light for signaling.

The B-4 bag was next. Sam wouldn't inventory the large green bag, since he knew what it contained—just stuff like parka, heavy pants and heavy boots, carried in case of loss of heat in the tail. It even contained a pillow and blanket so he could get stretches of rest on the longer flights if it wasn't too goddamn bumpy. This wouldn't be the case tonight. His adrenaline was too high. Maybe that was what was making him sick, he thought as he looked into his leather briefcase which contained his flight manuals. "Watch…" was his next thought. "Where the hell's the watch? It should have been laid out with the boots. I've never been this squirrely."

Rummaging through the top locker shelf he found the silver pocket watch. Tied to a white cord around his neck, the watch would be slipped into a top front pocket until preflight, when he would hang it from one of the flash curtain rails running under the top of the green house. It was easy to see there and it made a pretty effective turn and bank indicator. For a seven-dollar watch it was surprisingly accurate.

Over the years Sam had left behind so many damn watches on airplanes that every crew chief must have one. He was sure he never got twenty flights per watch. He'd do okay for a while and then lose two in a row. He'd started taping his name and rank on the back, but it didn't seem to do much good. A watch could still disappear between the airplane and the bus. He would go back and look for it, but he never seemed to find it. He always seemed to encounter a couple of the most innocent two-stripers who just gave the maintenance salute—a palms up shrug.

The last item in his ritual was always his gunner bean. He rubbed it between his fingers, then along the side of his nose. Then he securely zipped it in the front pocket on the left side of his flight suit. If he ever needed luck it was tonight.

"That's about it," he thought. He stood in his stocking feet and patted himself down. Then he remembered one more thing, the knife. This was an orange switchblade with a cutting hook that was always open when it went into the flight suit leg pocket designed for it. To be used for cutting parachute lines, it was connected to a three-foot-long piece of parachute cord and tied to the flap above the pocket it went into.

Out of habit, Sam thought about bringing a book but quickly dismissed the idea. There was no way he could read. If he had any spare time he would be better off reviewing manuals and going over emergency procedures.

The ritual of getting ready calmed Sam down. It had been good for him because it was something he knew and a procedure he had gone through hundreds of times. A lot of it was busy work, but he always felt better when he had done it. Normally when he finished, he would drink a cup of coffee and bullshit with the guys in the trailer until it was time to go. But this time the trailer was empty. He guessed he'd go sit on a picnic table until it was time for first briefing.

ANDERSON AIR FORCE BASE, GUAM, DECEMBER 1972

Andy seriously thought about refusing to go north again. He didn't know how he'd do it, but there had to be some sort of procedure. Probably the smartest way was to go to the flight surgeon. From what he'd heard he wasn't alone in his thoughts. So many crewmembers had declared themselves sick that a DNIF[51] cap was made up to cover for people grounded for medical reasons and three people on standby for each crew position. There was no way to know whether story of an aircraft commander who declared himself a conscious objector was true, but Andy believed an untold number of people had taken themselves off flying status in one way or another. He just wished he had Jim or even Mother to talk to. They would get him through this and know what to say. He thought about Jim and all his courage and flag waving. He would have talked him blue before he'd let him quit like that damn Hog Jaw. He was not afraid of the officers if he quit, but he'd be letting down Jim and Mother. Somehow they would convince him to do it for the gunners. Quitting meant somebody else would have to fly in his place.[52]

U-TAPAO AIR FORCE BASE, THAILAND, DECEMBER 1972

When Sam arrived at first briefing the first thing he noticed was the complete absence of horseplay. Normally first brief had a lot of grab-ass before everyone got seated. This had gone way down since they started going north to Hanoi, but tonight was like a funeral. Even the latest "hat colonel" at the door just looked straight ahead without apparently noticing any uniform flaws.

If nothing else, the sober attitude of the crews drove home the point that the fun and games were over. There was no more playing at war. And if the missions of the previous two nights were any indication, some of the people sitting in the briefing room wouldn't be at the debriefing.

Briefing went fast. It was almost like the officers doing the talking couldn't face the crews any longer than necessary.

The mission was targeted against a rail marshalling yard within the city of Hanoi. Sam had studied the area many times before and was intimidated by the number of SAM rings around the city. There was no single place where they did not overlap. He guessed there would be about fifteen minutes of continuous SAM coverage, and that was how it was briefed. They could expect Triple A or anti-aircraft artillery anytime they were over the North Vietnam land mass, with a hell of a lot in the Hanoi area. Sam hoped the flak suppression provided by chaff-laying Navy fighters would keep it down. MiG cap would be F-105 and F-4's out of bases in Thailand that would patrol the skies along their route. Weather would be overcast.

One more thing was briefed and it was not new. Sam had heard it on every combat mission he'd ever flown, It vividly reminded him of the nature of this war, where every son-of-a-bitch with a gun or a missile would be shooting at them. "Routes from IP to target must be flown straight and level," said the officer, "and unless the target is positively identified, visually or on radar, there will be no drop. Either racetrack on it for positive identification or retain the bombs."

Sam knew these instructions to orbit in a racetrack pattern and not drop the bombs unless the target was positively identified was designed to reduce civilian casualties. It was not just to fill a square. Photos from each aircraft would be checked, and woe to the dumb shits who chugged off their bombs for some simple reason, like it being the only way to avoid a SAM hit.

When the briefings ended, the room was called to attention and a lieutenant general was introduced. He was in his fifties and his short hair was almost totally gray. He started out by talking about haircuts and then switched to talking about how his World War II experience proved that crews could not bomb accurately unless they remained perfectly straight and level between the IP and target. Several crewmembers, with experience in successfully striking targets after maneuvering their bombers away from SAM's, began to hoot, and the general left the stage. A colonel who then got up and threatened disciplinary action was shouted down by cries of "What are you going to do, send us to Hanoi? Read him the patch." (If you haven't been there. Shut the fuck up.) [53]

Take-off was normal and once they got in the air Sam looked around. He pushed out with his elbows and touched the sides of the compartment. Earlier he'd prayed they would have to abort, and now his eyes swept the wings like they had thirty times since take-off. Nothing, no fuel leaks, no smoke, not a single thing that would cause the big bomber to return to Thailand.

Things didn't get bad until they reached the IP, fifty-eight miles due south of Hanoi, and turned north. At seven miles a minute this meant they were a tad more than eight minutes from the target.

Sam's navigator had just called IP when a voice saying "SAM launch…SAM launch…" broke through the radio garble loud and clear, blocking out the rest of the navigator's transmission. Then Sam heard the emergency channel (guard) broadcast, "SAM launch! SAM launch—Hanoi!" followed by "SAM launch! SAM launch… Cream Cell…"

Sam wasn't overly superstitious, but it was eerie to hear what sounded like his name being called when something was being shot at him. It was too much coincidence for his comfort and he worried that on his last three missions he'd used up too much of his luck. He turned, trying to see in front of the airplane, knowing he was in Ruby One directly behind Cream Cell with only three miles between them.

"SAM visual!…Cream Cell…two SAM's!" cut in some unknown voice and then repeated the same message, "SAM visual! SAM visual!…Cream Cell!"

Too many SAM warnings to count were saturating the radios. The North Vietnamese were launching them like artillery without even trying to use the radar guidance to track specific aircraft. Proximity fuses were set to explode at the altitudes of the inbound formations with a force of 350 pounds of TNT.

"Holy shit," thought Sam as he scanned the haze for any sign of what he knew would look like a flying telephone pole in the daylight. "They're going to get us." It was like he had an eight high and was looking at three Kings straight up. There was nothing to do except play it out.

"No visual," Sam said over the intercom, trying to keep his voice under control. He'd seen SAM's on each of the last two missions and knew what to expect. In the dark they looked like a rapidly moving, expanding, incomplete halo of fire.

"SAM…visual!…Cream Cell…two SAM's…one o'clock, climbing to three o-clock," said a high-pitched voice that could have been Lou Zable, the gunner on Cream Two. The echo was blocked out by another SAM call, and then another, and then one identifying Maroon Cell. Sam was trying to figure out how many surface-to-air missile warnings were being broadcast. Things were happening so fast it was hard to tell, and the fact that several aircraft and ground

197

stations were calling out warnings on the same missile just added to the confusion. Then he heard, "SAM visual! Ruby One."

"Shit, we're Ruby One," he thought as he tried to figure out who was speaking. It had to be one of the pilots on his airplane, but Sam didn't recognize the voice. "Ruby One...SAM! visual...four SAM's visual, eleven o'clock...SAM visual two o'clock." A voice he was pretty sure was his co-pilot started another warning call on guard when he was interrupted by a voice Sam knew was his aircraft commander: "Shut-up co-pilot, I'm trying to count."

This was immediately followed by a soft thump that felt like something had hit the aircraft. The bomber started to shake and it felt like the tail exploded. Fourteen SA-2's had been fired directly at them, and four of them either struck or exploded close to the bomber. The tail was a whirlwind of flying dust and smoke, mixed with fog generated as a result of the explosive de-compression when the atmospheric pressure in the compartment instantly went to 35,000 feet.

Sam was badly dazed and having trouble figuring out where he was. He could feel the g-loads building as the shuddering bomber started to fall. Even with the mask on he could smell cordite and his eyes burned. The movement of the tail was more violent than anything he'd ever experienced and he was fiercely hanging to the rope straps. If he let go to bail out he was afraid he wouldn't be able to reach the turret jettison before he was knocked senseless.

Up front, things were worse. Every officer on the crew was injured to some degree when one of the missiles exploded between the left wing root and the cockpit, creating an explosive de-compression and causing portions of the side panel to collapse against the pilot's ejection seat. Among other things this panel held the controls for the radios, hydraulics, attitude and directional gyros.

Tornado-like wind whistled through the cockpit, stirring up trash and pieces of metal from the damaged aircraft that threatened to cause more injuries as the upfront crewmembers hunkered down in their seats trying to avoid decapitation. All four engines on the left side had stopped and two of them appeared to be on fire. The asymmetrical thrust forced the bomber into a sharp left turn and it was rapidly descending from 35,000 feet, while swaying from side to side like a leaf in the wind. The noise combined with the velocity of the thin air blowing through numerous gaps in the fuselage suggested the stricken bomber was about to disintegrate.

Resigned to probable death, Sam regretted that he hadn't written Cathy in the last four days except for one short note where he didn't say much. At least his last line said, "I love you." Not that this was close to expressing how he felt. She was the best person he had ever known and they had so many plans together. If only…

The only one on the airplane not preparing to die or get marched through Hanoi on a string was Sam's aircraft commander, Major Trevor Tyler, or TT to his friends. He had only been Sam's AC for about two months, but Sam liked him. He was slightly overweight and joked that he had been on one type of diet or another his entire career. When some of his crew expressed concern about going again after being hit on the first two Hanoi missions, he promised them they wouldn't get hit on this mission. That would turn out to be false, but TT was going to fly the airplane until it proved it couldn't be done.

The B-52 was one tough old bird and Major Tyler was pushing its right rudder pedal with all his strength. He knew his co-pilot was doing the same. Fighting the control column to cut down on the side-to-side roll, the pilot attempted to signal his co-pilot using hand gestures since his interphone was not working, and with a mask on, he couldn't mouth the word throttles. His right-seater didn't get the message so he relaxed his grip just long enough to reach over with his right hand and pull the throttles on engines five, six, seven and eight back to flight idle. Then he regained his hold on the control column and started pulling it towards his stomach.

The pilot felt the bomber start to respond and some of the pressure on his quivering right leg started to relax. With careful movements he leveled the bomber at 21,000 feet. About the same time the radar navigator tried the interphone call function which was designed for emergencies.

"Pilot, this is radar, how you read?'

"Stand by, he's a little busy," replied the co-pilot, turning the interphone switch on his side panel to the call position. The spring-loaded call button had to be continually pressed in order for it to work. Actually, the aircraft commander was a lot busy and one hand short of doing everything he wanted to do, starting with trying to push some of the sheet metal from the side panel that was painfully cutting into his left thigh.

It looked like the fires might be going out because right after they were hit, the pilot managed with considerable difficulty to pull the fire T-handles on the left engines that were dead or dying. They now were flying with the wings reasonably level, but a new problem occurred. The aircraft was in a nose-to-tail porpoise. It would climb and then dive, and the altitude was dropping with each dip. The pilot knew they were losing airspeed with the throttles back and he worried about stalling the airplane. He also needed to try to respond to whoever was trying to get information about Rose One on UHF.

The radar navigator, knowing the pilot was overloaded, responded twice, but he couldn't tell them much. With nothing working downstairs he couldn't even exactly determine their location. Maybe if the optics were operational he could have looked at the ground.

Major Tyler could hear interphone conversations but didn't respond using the call button since it was somewhere in the wreckage on his left side. It was too noisy to talk across the cockpit even if he dared to take his oxygen mask off, so he needed to be creative. Taking a grease pencil from his shoulder pocket he pulled the laminated work sheet off his knee and quickly wrote:

"EASE REMAINING THROTTLES UP.
BACK OFF IF IT GETS TOO WORMY."

It was taking all the effort and concentration he could muster to keep flying the bomber. But Major Tyler knew he had to find out the condition of his crew and start thinking about bailout. Motioning for the co-pilot, who had just pushed the throttles up another notch, to return the worksheet, he wiped it semi-clean with his hand and wrote:

"CREW REPORT/I CAN HEAR I JUST CAN'T TALK"

The co-pilot took quick action. "Crew, this is co-pilot on call," he said. "The pilot is able to hear...he just can't work his call button. He wants a crew report...make it abbreviated. If you're okay, on oxygen and nothing is burning in your area just say okay, unless you've got something the pilot absolutely needs to know." Every person on the faltering B-52 had some sort of injury caused by either shrapnel or larger pieces of the airplane hitting them. But to a man they reported "okay."

With the power on the remaining engines increased, the bomber felt a little more stable, even though this increased the need for rudder pressure. It was time to use the radio, but nothing worked from the aircraft commander's position. It was less than ten minutes since they were hit, although it seemed like hours.

The whole time somebody—probably many somebody's— kept calling for Ruby One. Major Tyler heard the radar navigator's brief responses and knew it was time to expand on them. Afraid his only usable radio was the survival one in his chaps, he tried the radio switch on his control column again. This time when he pushed the switch he could hear a back tone over the noise in the cockpit. He shouted into his mike, "Co pilot. . . you read me?" Receiving a nod he continued, "Radio calling Ruby One... this is Ruby One with a Mayday...we're about sixty miles west of Hanoi. Altitude nineteen thousand...Ah...Four engines shut down...aircraft in a porpoise... losing altitude...bailout imminent...you copy?"

"Ruby One, this is Paris Control...we copy...have you on radar...will contact rescue...can you make the MeKong River?. . . Over."

Major Tyler had been holding the aircraft with not much more than the force of his will. He felt he could hold it a little longer if nothing else went wrong. He just needed to stop losing altitude with every porpoise. "Paris Control...this is Ruby One...Roger that... We'll give it a shot...over."

Then Sam, and everyone else monitoring the emergency, heard the pilot say, "We're over the mountains so I think we should be out of SAM range. I'm going to try to hold this beast together until we get out of North Vietnam."

Sam didn't have much confidence. He was sure the vibration and brutal side motion he felt was a sign the bomber was in its last moments of flight. The porpoise continued to bottom out every few moments, not violently, but with a distinct shudder. It was impossible for Sam to tell what the exact situation in the cockpit was, but he sensed the frequent changes in power meant the pilots were fighting the throttles as well as the rudder in an attempt to achieve a balance between conflicting aerodynamic forces.

It was turning daylight and looking upward Sam could see the rudder shake as it was displaced to his left. There were several damaged areas on the tall tail fin and two major holes in the rudder itself. Looking forward he could tell not all the spoilers were working and smoke or fuel vapor was streaming from the left wing.

Sam was as sure as an Ace beats a King that they would never get to the MeKong River. "What about fighters," he thought, "we're all by ourselves and at our present altitude and speed it would be easy for them to jump us."

Major Tyler deduced by the feel of the throttles that the number seven engine had also quit. Without gauges it was hard to determine whether it had just lost power or stopped completely, but he kept fighting to keep the three-engine bomber in the air. There was no way for him to know how much fuel, if any, the co-pilot was able to transfer to the right wing, but it felt like it was taking less effort to hold the left wing up.

Sam felt a rush of relief when they were out of North Vietnam. After they struggled across Laos, he finally saw the MeKong River below him. They were below 15,000 feet now and the 5,000-foot mountains below him appeared close. Bailout would not be far off. The pilot ferociously flying the airplane was becoming seriously concerned about stalling it, particularly if he tried to trade speed for altitude. Paris Control suggested, ". . . Ruby One...If you can hold it a little longer you can make NKP?" (Nakon Phanom Air Force Base, Thailand.)

Major Tyler had held it so long he figured he could hold it a little longer, but the BUFF he was flying was too ragged to consider landing. His first concern was getting the gunner out. He could tell the rest to punch out and would know when they went, but the gunner was a different story. There was no way to completely ensure the gunner was gone.

The pilot also worried about the damage around his ejection seat. "I'll be the last to go," he thought. "I've held it for them for so long, who is going to hold it for me if my seat doesn't work?"

But that could come later. Right now he needed to get Sam and everybody else ready to go. He would do this over the UHF radio that was monitored by everyone on the airplane. Everybody and their brother on the ground could also hear his transmission. "Crew, this is pilot on UHF…as I call your position give me a click if you can hear me"

After he heard five clicks as he called out the crew positions, he began talking again. "Crew, this is pilot…We're about eight minutes from NKP…I want you to be ready to go…look around your seats for anything that might cause trouble…sequence is going to be everyone except the co-pilot go when they hear the alarm bell… radar, wait a couple of seconds for the navigator to clear…I will also announce bailout bailout bailout on this radio…co-pilot, you stay until we are sure the gunner's gone…Break, Break…gunner, we're under ten thousand and you're cleared to jettison your turret…Call me when it's gone…"

Sam attempted to jettison his turret, but the inertia reel holding the parachute to his seat would not unlock and he couldn't lean forward enough to reach the yellow handle. He moved the unlocking lever several times and the harness still wouldn't come free. He loosened his shoulder straps, enabling him to lean forward enough to rotate the jettison handle. Immediately he heard a small pop, over the noise in the tail, and everything in front of him began to drop back.

"Pilot, gunner…my turret is gone."

"Roger gunner…" Because the pilot was still on UHF he continued, "Station calling Ruby One…say again." Two people on different radios were trying to talk at the same time and he was having difficulty understanding the transmission. The part he caught was, "Don't get out of it over the base…we don't want it down here…"

Sam's emotions spiked when the turret departed the aircraft. He'd felt relief when they crossed over the MeKong river and left North Vietnam. Now, looking at the large hole in front of him, he was euphoric about the probability of survival.

It was starting to get light and below him Sam observed rice paddies, roads and houses. They were very low now and he knew the bailout order would come soon.

When he heard the bailout tone in his headset, he yanked hard on the integrated harness release handle on the left side of his seat and tried to roll forward. Pulling the handle should have completely released his parachute from the inertia reel cable holding it to the aluminum seat. But even using all the force in his left arm it wouldn't work, so he tried both hands. Nothing. He was firmly attached to the airplane. Sam was still struggling when he watched the EW's seat pass over the top of him and turn into an open parachute.

"Shit, I'm so close and now the law of averages gets its revenge," thought Sam.

"Gunner, this is pilot…Are you gone?"

"Negative…I'm trapped in the seat…I've tried everything and can't get loose…You guys forget me and get out of the airplane…" Sam knew that if the pilots stayed much longer they would die too. They had to get out…

"Gunner, this is your aircraft commander…I'm not going until you go…If you have to, take the fire axe to your seat…don't give up. Co-pilot, go ahead and punch…"

Major Tyler was doing his best to keep the crippled bomber airborne long enough for Sam to free himself. At his suggestion Sam took the crash axe from its holder on the left side panel and slashed at the mechanism under the integrated release handle. The chute would still not release, but then he had a final thought. He unbuckled his parachute, thinking "Fuck it…no guts…no glory." Then he slid the seat back on its rails so he wouldn't be quite so close to the gaping hole left by the departed turret, and partially stood up as he turned around. With one slash he severed the cable holding his chute to the seat. Back in his straps he called the pilot, "Pilot…I…got free…am going now."

"Roger that Sam…I'll see you on the ground."

Sam rubbed his gunner bean through the fabric over his breast pocket and rolled out of the tail. The zero delay lanyard pulled the pilot chute out of its bag and a beautiful parachute opened above Sam. At almost the same moment Major Tyler pulled the handles on the seat he was concerned was too damaged to work. The explosive charge hit him in the butt, just like advertised.

Sam's landing was softer than expected and as he pulled the chute off of his head he saw he was in a dry field and there was a blue truck on a road about fifty yards to his right. Not just any truck, a blue United States Air Force truck. Sam had just drawn four cards to a Royal Flush.

The next night would be Christmas Eve.[54]

END

EPILOG

The war ended for Sam on that fateful day. He spent two days in the U-Tapao Base hospital getting treated for the wound to his right leg. It required twenty-eight stitches to repair the damage caused by one of the SAM missiles that hit his aircraft. The missile exploded and sent pieces of the tail compartment's thin aluminum structure tearing into him. Probably because of adrenaline he never felt much pain. But for the blood he might not have known he was hit.

For ten days after he got out of the hospital, he hung around the base. Before he left he went to see Yuphen, who was still working at the NCO club, and told her about Melvin. "I know when he no come back, he dead," she said. "He good man."

Sam received an age waiver for Officer Training School and was commissioned on November 10th 1973. He retired as a major in 1987 and is now dealing Blackjack at the Hole in the Wall Casino in Danbury, Wisconsin, twelve miles from his cabin on Little McGraw Lake. Cathy works with crafts she sells at local fairs in the summer.

Melvin was buried in the National Military Cemetery at San Bruno, California. Two of his three ex-wives attended the graveside ceremony which was held with full military honors. He left his Serviceman's Life Insurance to Yuphen Dang.

Jim was released from prison camp on May 16th 1973. He was given a two-stripe promotion on his release and retired as a chief master sergeant in 1986. He and his wife Elizabeth live in Merced, California, where he works part-time in a mobile home dealership owned by his son-in-law Mathew. He has three grandchildren.

Andy went on to finish a long career in the Air Force and retired as a chief master sergeant in 1984. He works for the telephone company in Rapid City, South Dakota. He and Rosalie continue to enjoy Emily Allison, born May 16th 1976.

Cal struggled with alcohol until his retirement as a staff sergeant in 1973. He has not been heard from since.

Diane Vinroot never remarried and now lives in Omaha, Nebraska.

Hog Jaw retired in 1972 and now lives in Ogden, Utah, where he converted to the Church of Latter Day Saints.

Bobby D. Olson got out of the Air Force after four years. He lives in Prescot, Arizona.

Mama Nening, whose real name was Antonia Muna Guzman, died on Guam on March 24, 1998. She was 79.

ACKNOWLEDGEMENTS

Judy Larsen is my wife. She scared me when she read my first chapter and said, "That's gross." Her cheerful support kept me going on this project.

Jack Rachels (Lieutenant Colonel USAF retired) is a close friend. We've been partners in a number of adventures where he has tried to kill me in the air, on land and at sea. Jack is a high-time B-52 aircraft commander who also flew O-2's (Birddogs) in the Vietnam War. He was a participant in the rescue made famous by the book and movie *Bat 21*. He worked out aircraft performance capabilities for me, checked my facts, fixed my spelling and offered me much encouragement as I went along.

Peter (Scotty) Burns (Master Sergeant USAF retired) provided several stories for this book and led me to a number of websites about B-52 crewmembers. We met at USAF survival training in 1963 and have kept in touch over the years. For the record, Scotty flew 435 combat missions between 1966 and 1973.

James Siendenburg (Senior Master Sergeant USAF retired) was my partner when the HURTS rent-a-car was established on Guam. He spent hours (if not weeks) telling me about his life as a B-36 gunner.

Melvin Hay (Master Sergeant USAF retired) is an old friend who provided stories about his life as a gunner.

Lynn Chase provided me with the story of his bailout after a mid-air collision. I was in awe of Lynn's calm description of this extraordinary experience.

Willy Hoff (Chief Master Sergeant USAF retired) is a gunner and a master storyteller. I've known Willy for thirty-five years. Many of his stories did not make this book due to their extremely colorful nature.

Jim Merrell (Chief Master Sergeant USAF retired and former head gunner for Eighth Air Force) walked me through the "Baby Gunners".

Randy Jackson tore up my first draft like only a brother-in-law could.

My daughter-in-law, Vanessa Larsen designed the cover.

And last, but not least, Bryan Aubrey, Ph.D., a truly professional editor who awed me with his quick responses. His questions were always valid and his suggestions were invaluable. I am in his debt.

Many others provided stories and encouragement over the years. I would like to acknowledge the following people:

Dale Anderson
Elizabeth Anderson
Elizabeth Branch
Norm Clinton
Iggy Cruz
John Cunningham
Gill Elmy
Bill Foster
Betty Foster
Ben Godwin
John Graham
Bob Herrings
Bobby D. Johnson
Norm Lake
Rich Martin
Jackie Merrell
John Mize
Paul Murr
Vic Perez
Jim Savage
Tom Schrantz
Lila Siendenburg
Ron Smith
Grance Thompson
Roger Tollerud
Jack Quay

Endnotes

Chapter One

[1] The B-52 has fourteen large hydraulically powered flat panels on the top of the wing that act as both wing spoilers and airbrakes. If a pilot needs to slow the airspeed down he can put these panels up in increments from one to six. Airbrakes one and two are the only positions generally used for in-flight refueling. Their use, since they change the aerodynamics of the wing, requires immediate counteracting control column pressure to prevent a violent pitch change. Position six is normally only used for emergency descent or aerodynamic braking on the ground. In flight they are eased in to prevent violent pitch up of the tail.

[2] This trick known to many tail gunners is not as ridiculous as it sounds. The crapper in the tail is behind the gunner's seat, and its use requires removing the straps, folding the seat down, going off interphone, unloading bags and junk off the can and sliding it out from the compartment sidewall. Then crap while hanging onto wire bundles, bent over by the low ceiling in the compartment. Rules are: "if you use it, you clean it."

Will power was the best solution, but it was possible for a gunner to remove his shoulder straps without getting out of the seat, strip his flight suit down around his ankles and hang onto the side rails as he slid the small cardboard box in under his ass. It was simpler and neater and it left a nice little package that was easy to get rid of after flight. It was best to take out the lunch first. More than one scrounging ground crew member out after left over pickles came upon a little surprise. "Oh well, the gunner paid for the lunch."

[3] At the OQ Range outside of Shilling Air Force Base in Kansas, gunners in training shot at propeller-driven drones launched from a circular runway that provided targets for gunners using four M3 fifty-caliber machine guns mounted in a ground based B-52 tail. The gun fed by a 600-round magazine fired 200 rounds of ball ammunition a minute. It reminded many of a World War II movie where they fired short bursts until pieces started flying off. When the firing was over the drone was dropped by parachute and unless the damage was too severe, it would be repaired and re-used.

[4] A high point for every gunner was shooting the M-61 Vulcan Cannon. This six-barrel monster used B-52H models until they were removed in 1991.It puts out 6,000 rounds of high explosive 20- millimeter ammunition a minute and its ASG-21 fire control system was years ahead of the older B-52's. It sounded like a very noisy truck starting up, just a loud burp and an instant ball of flame. After they fired gunners wondered, "Where the hell did all the shell casings come from?"

5   Depending on how sick the electrons and hydraulics were, it could take up to twenty-three different set-ups to control the guns. At the high end a computer solved the gunnery problem and at the low end there was an emergency mode generally known as "spray and pray." In this case the gunner didn't even know which way his guns were pointed.

6   This program was established by General LeMay during the years he was building SAC. The potential for temporary promotion derived from the aircraft commander's position on the wing commander's preference list. A number of things went into this, including how well the crew refueled, bombed and generally performed on training missions under a complex scoring system devised by SAC headquarters. When spot promotions were around it was possible for a gunner to be temporally promoted by as much as two grades. Some staff sergeants actually wore the stripes of a master sergeant and earned time in grade for E-6, E-7 and E-8 all at the same time. Several gunners actually made tech, master and senior master sergeant in three consecutive cycles.

7   Every combat ready B-52 crew assigned to a bomb wing was given a number prefixed with an S, E, or R that among other things rank ordered them. "S" or Sierra was derived from select and identified the elite few who were the highest qualified, with "R" or Romeo crews being the least. Romeo came from the R in ready crew as they were actually called. E or Echo crews fell in the middle and were the most numerous. There was no apparent logic behind the Echo tag except that it came from the phonetic pronunciation of the letter E. It should have been "L" since they were also designated as lead crews. Probably some pointy-headed staff officer in headquarters didn't want a set of Lulu crews.

Chapter Two

8   Gunners universally applied the term Zero to all officers. It was derived from the flight rosters. In front of each name, officers had the letter O for officer, just as the enlisted gunners had E for enlisted. Gunners interpreted the letter O as a zero and among themselves all officers were routinely called Zeroes.

Chapter Three

9   On long missions, except for refueling and the bomb run, many crews slept in shifts. The radar operator slept with his head on the table in front of him or shared with the navigator a tight space in the lower deck called the "Wine Cellar." This space was always cold, but they didn't have far to commute to work. It was almost directly under the RN's table. Pilots and co-pilots could split their time on a small mattress on the upper deck, although many pilots just slept in their seats.

The electronic warfare officer could sleep anytime he could sell off monitoring the single HF radio he was assigned to listen to. As low man in the pecking order he didn't have much of a designated sleeping space. He normally stretched out on the hard aluminum floor of the upper deck alongside the small mattress the co-pilot used.

Except for turbulence, erratic heat and lack of arm rests, the gunner's seat in the tail provided the best sleeping accommodations on the airplane. It reclined to semi-level and brave gunners used their B-4 bag and an air mattress to create a semblance of a bed. In the narrow compartment the mattress would curve up against the side panels and become a hammock of sorts. By sleeping with his feet towards the front of the airplane the gunner didn't have the worry of waking up upside down in entrance door "hell hole," although he still could come to pasted on the greenhouse windows. Since this was dark, cold and somewhat deep it could be fairly frightening trying to figure out where you were, as more than one gunner learned. Not too bad if you added a pillow and blanket, but there was no way to really strap in. If something happened it took time to deflate the mattress, fold the seat back up and get buckled back in the parachute.

It was usually hard for a gunner to fell into a deep sleep. Occasional bounce and Dutch-Roll, along with the constant din of the interphone and three, sometimes four, radios didn't make for peaceful slumber. Most gunners never got into much more than a twilight zone when sleeping.

[10] This actuates two explosive thrusters' separating the turret from the aircraft.

[11] The gunner's chute serves as a shoulder harness when clipped to the back of the seat.

[12] Emergency interphone override position.

Chapter Four

[13] This sometimes releases ammunition binding in the link feeds.

[14] Charging is accomplished with air pressure controlled by a toggle switch on the gunner's left side panel. This recycles the bolt and operates the recoil system. If there is a round in the chamber it is ejected out the bottom of the airplane.

[15] The basic 50-caliber gun had been around a long time but it still experienced problems, mostly in the recoil operation or in the link-belt feed. Periodically, aircraft were scheduled for test fire, not as a measure of accuracy but as a test to ensure the guns worked and all 2,400 rounds fired. This was done over open water and when the Pacific Ocean is the only target, it's hard to miss. Fire-out percentages were a "special interest" item closely tracked by the wing commander.

16 Radar time out is essentially a warm-up of the fire control electronics. It normally takes three to five minutes.

Chapter Five

17 This seldom-violated rule said there were to be no military duties, including training, in the twelve hours prior to flight. Technically, even an official phone call reset the timing.

18 Survival radios were part of the basic gear all crewmembers scheduled to fly combat missions were issued. These were carried in chaps worn around the upper legs and thighs and contained basic survival gear, signal flares, a 38-caliber snub-nosed pistol. Designed for escape and evasion, these chaps essentially duplicated the equipment carried in the cumbersome global survival kit seat pack strapped to the bottom of the parachutes. If necessary the crewmember could drop the kit, run and still have the wherewithal to survive and operate in hostile territory.

19 In April 1966 Strategic Air Command B-52's struck North Vietnam for the first time. Thirty bombers were used in this historic raid on Mu Gia Pass and although the success of the mission would be debated it showed that SAC had truly entered the war. It highlighted, probably for the first time the confusion and fog of war that the B-52 crews would face as the war dragged on.

20 Classified briefings at the time indicated North Vietnam owned about a hundred MiG's including 15, 17 and 21's. Their range was limited so bases like the one north of Hanoi (Kep) were probably too far away to be a danger. It was more likely any bandits would come from the airfield in the south (Phuc Yen).

The surface-to air missiles mentioned were SA-2's with a range of 31 miles and a speed of mach 3.5. They were advertised to be effective at altitudes in excess of 75,000 feet.

21 Radio Silence created several challenges for the crews. If taxi was not accomplished exactly as directed, it was possible for two B-52's to meet nose to nose on a taxi way. With several bombers or tankers in trail this could be a nightmare to sort out. This happened on numerous occasions throughout the war. Radio silence missions required that pilots' director lights positioned on the belly of the tanker replaced the radio. This was in lieu of Boom Operator call outs that identified distances such as "forward fifteen" or "back five." With director lights it was harder for some pilots to judge the spacing necessary to engage the boom.

22 This is how and when Mama Nening presented the first "Gunners Bean". The gunners present were all from Ellsworth and consisted of Bill Whitenmier, Bob Netzger, Bob Herring, and the author. Dale Anderson, Jim

Siendenburg and Don Murphey were most likely the other gunners there and if not they became early bean holders. To this day there are gunners who didn't get to Guam until much later that will swear they have the first bean...

Chapter Six

[23] This was accomplished using written and oral examinations and observing the gunners as they accomplished their preflight. Then prior to engine start the evaluator would move to one of the jump seats in the forward compartment and monitor the gunner in-flight. These checks given on both a notice and no notice basis included a detailed review of gunner's checklist and the flight manuals carried in the tail for currency. It was said, "A good evaluator could look at a manual containing several hundred pages and immediately open it to the one improperly filed page it contained."

[24] In the wisdom of Strategic Air Command, real in-flight emergencies didn't count as practice.

[25] Any time the bombers were in formation, it was the tail gunner's job to monitor the aircraft behind him for spacing so the airplanes didn't collide. He could do this by looking out the windows that made up what was called the "green house" or by using the radar on the MD-9 fire control system that was used to search for targets.

Chapter Seven

[26] This military rest area on the China Sea offered a small room for seven dollars a night. Most of its residents were Marines on R&R directly from the trenches of Vietnam. Besides a dining room and casino the rest camp offered massages and hot baths. It was not like the Paris Steam Bath in Koza, which for a small fee provided somewhat more than a basic massage. This spa was strictly run under the supervision of the U.S. Government. The door to the room had to remain open while the young girl soaped and rinsed her customer. Touching the help was strictly forbidden.

[27] This story was adapted from a written summary provided to me by Lynn Chase, the gunner who survived this incident.

Chapter Eight

[28] "The Carousel" wasn't the official Air Force name for the rotation between Guam, Okinawa and Thailand, but it sure was descriptive. Crews would spend a month in each location and then move to the next one. Every move meant packing up your belongings, checking out of the room and getting set up all over again. The missions would change too. While it took over twelve hours to get to the target and return to Guam, the round trip from Okinawa would take less than seven, and missions from Thailand averaged just over

three hours. The use of Kadena ended when Okinawa was handed back to Japan in early 1972.

[29] It would be interesting to count how many successful Bonus Deal bomb runs were accomplished during the course of the Vietnam War. This was something the gunners never got much credit for, yet this concept saved a lot of B-52 sorties from failure.

Chapter Nine

[30] Urban legend says this happened on more than one occasion. I tend to believe this.

[31] To minimize fatigue damage to the B-52 wing structure, a rolling take-off was required when the aircraft was heavy. When done correctly this meant the aircraft was already moving at fifteen knots as it turned onto the runway, and from that point on things got busy. The first concern was water augmentation. In the first 110 seconds after full power was applied, over 300 gallons of water was injected into the eight engines to increase take-off thrust. The pilot checked this by noting that the four water pressure lights were out and confirming there was a rise in fuel flow and EPR (Engine Pressure Ratio).

[32] On the B-52D there were three upward firing ejection seats, one for the pilot, co-pilot and electronic warfare officer. The radar navigator and the navigator had downward firing seats. The gunner rolled out of the tail. The bailout sequence was: gunner, navigator, EWO, co-pilot, extra crewmember(s), if applicable. They could escape through the navigator's hatch which could also be used if for some reason one of the ejection seats failed to work. In theory the radar navigator stayed until there was no need to assist people exiting through the navigator's open hatch. By long tradition the aircraft commander was the last to go. In an uncontrolled bailout the sequence might be governed by who could pull their handles the fastest.

[33] <u>RULES OF THE GUNNER COINS (BEAN))</u>

1. BULLDOG COIN AND BEAN ARE EQUAL AND INTERCHANGABLE. I.E. HAVING A BEAN IS LIKE HAVING A COIN. HAVING A COIN IS LIKE HAVING A BEAN.

2. COIN OR BEAN MUST BE CARRIED AT ALL TIMES. YOU CAN BE CHALLENGED FOR IT ANYWHERE ANYTIME. YOU MUST BE ABLE TO PRODUCE THE COIN OR BEAN WITHOUT TAKING MORE THAN THREE OR FOUR STEPS.

3. WHEN CHALLENGING, THE CHALLENGER MUST STATE WHETHER OR NOT IT'S FOR A SINGLE DRINK OR A ROUND OF DRINKS.

4. UNDER NO CIRCUMSTANCES CAN A COIN OR BEAN BE HANDED TO SOMEONE. IF A GUNNER GIVES HIS COIN TO ANOTHER GUNNER, THAT GUNNER CAN KEEP THE COIN—IT'S HIS. HOWEVER IF A GUNNER PLACES THE COIN DOWN AND ANOTHER GUNNER PICKS IT UP TO EXAMINE IT, THAT IS NOT CONSIDERED "GIVING" AND THE OTHER GUNNER IS HONOR BOUND TO PLACE THE COIN BACK WHERE HE GOT IT. HE CANNOT CHALLENGE WHILE HE HOLDS THE OTHER GUNNER'S COIN.

5. IF A GUNNER HAS NEVER BEEN GIVEN A COIN OR BEAN HE CANNOT BE EXPECTED TO PLAY THE GAME.

6. RULES OF THE GAME MUST BE EXPLAINED TO ALL NEW COIN HOLDERS.

7. LOST COINS OR BEANS, OR FAILURE TO PRODUCE SAID COIN, RESULTS IN THE CHALLENGER BEING BOUGHT A DRINK OR A ROUND OF DRINKS. THIS TYPE OF TRANSACTION COULD BE EXPENSIVE, SO HOLD ONTO YOUR COINS. ONCE THE CHALLENGED HAS BOUGHT YOU A DRINK YOU CANNOT CONTINUE TO CHALLENGE HIM.

8. IF A COIN IS LOST, REPLACEMENTCOST IS UP TO THE INDIVIDUAL'S OWN GUNNERS ASSOCIATION. A NEW COIN SHOULD BE REPLACED AT THE EARLIEST POSSIBLE TIME. LOSING A COIN AND NOT REPLACING IT DOES NOT RELIEVE A GUNNER OF HIS RESPONSIBILITIES.

9. GUNNER'S COINS SHOULD <u>BE CONTROLLED AT ALL TIMES</u>. GIVING THEM TO JUST ANYONE IS LIKE OPENING UP THE VARIOUS ASSOCIATIONS TO ANYONE. IT'S UP TO THE INDIVIDUAL ASSOCIATION AS TO WHO, OUTSIDE THE ACTIVE MEMBERS, THEY WANT TO HAVE THE GUNNER COIN OR BEAN. IT'S CONSIDERED AN <u>HONOR</u> TO BE GIVEN A COIN AND LET'S TRY TO KEEP IT THAT WAY.

10. LOCAL BASE RULES APPLY TO LOCAL GUNNERS ONLY.

11. THE ABOVE RULES PERTAIN AND APPLY TO ANYONE WHO IS WORTHY TO HOLD THE POSITION OF A DEFENSIVE AERIAL GUNNER,(OR) HAS HELD THE POSITION OR HAS BEEN SELECTED AS AN HONORARY MEMBER BY AN ACTIVE ASSOCIATION.

12. THE COIN WILL NOT BE DEFACED – I.E. DRILLING A HOLE IN THE COIN.

SOURCE: BULLDOG BULLETIN-FALL 1985.

Authors note: I believe the coin did not come into existence or common use until years after Mama Nening presented the first bean to a gunner. The first coins I saw were scrounged from MAC truck dealers because of the similarity of their Bulldog logo to the Bulldog on the gunner's patch. Later, someone set up production of the coins and they are still available for purchase by qualified individuals through the Gunners' Association. ($2.00) Today many Air Force specialties, including test pilots and bomb loaders, have specially designed coins. Of interest is how similar their rules are to the ones developed by the Guam gunners in 1966.

Chapter Ten

34   Prior to WAPS (Weighted Airman Promotion System) a gunner could do very little to control his destiny. Crew gunners regardless of rank held essentially the same job and there was no way to build a case that one gunner had more responsibility than another. An aircraft commander could hurt you with a bad ticket, but since most Airman Performance Reports were equally inflated, there wasn't much a pilot could do to help move his gunner move up in grade.

It was a system that didn't work very well when it came to handing out a limited number of stripes. It all came down to too many gunners, too few stripes and maybe some politics that was over their head.

Under WAPS an individual could compete for promotion on factors other than just performance reports. Points were added for time in service, time in grade, medals and test scores.

35   The Bootstrap Commissioning program allowed some military personnel to attend college full time for up to a year to complete their degree.

36   Beau Rae is a Cajun card game sometimes played on alert. It's not for the faint hearted because pots double rapidly

Chapter Eleven

37   By 1970 problems with the SAC crew force were becoming more apparent as new crews were continually being formed. A lot of the older officers retired or moved up as they got promoted, and transfer between D-model bases increased as the command began to "share the wealth" among those who had not been to the war. Where once the same numbered crew stayed together for years this basic tenet of Strategic Air Command was undergoing subtle revision as Arc Light missions continued unrelentingly. With the exception of the gunners, the composition of the crews was also becoming younger as the old heads were replaced and to some degree the humorless discipline of SAC was shifting to a less rigid variety.

SAC decided to allow those assigned to B-52 G&H wings a chance to fly the D-model since now only the D's were flying Arc Light. This provided new blood and at least in theory let the war come around less often for some. Because of the differences between the aircraft a Combat Replacement Unit (CRU) was established at Castle AFB.

System differences were taught in classroom settings, and because the D-model had variations in the way it flew this was followed by a flight phase. None of this was difficult for the navigators and electronic warfare officers or for that matter the pilots. Performance characteristics were not the same, but as a general rule their transition was not tough. The challenge for gunners was somewhat greater. First it meant moving from an ejection seat in the forward compartment to the tail. This by itself was an experience for many who had last ridden in the tail during their initial B-52 training ten or more years ago. Then there was the control of the guns. The G-model contained essentially the same MD-9 fire control system as the D, except in place of optics and the windows in the green house there was a small black and white television receiver. Those gunners coming from H-models had to adapt from an entirely different system, the ASG-21. The four 50- caliber machine guns on the D would be a step back from the H-model with the six-barrel 20-millimeter Vulcan Cannon.

It took a while for G-model gunners to get used to the ride in the tail. It was like moving from the front of a luxury sedan to the back of an old farm truck. But one thing about it was they didn't have to get coffee or cook some officer's TV dinner. And even the skeptics agreed the view was a lot better.

[38] The impact of the war was taking its toll and more critical components were failing in flight. The B-52 was a solid, well-engineered airplane, but as parts became harder to get, maintenance had to work with what they could get. Sometimes this meant re-build rather than replace. It also meant some things didn't get done.

[39] I use the term BUFF here for the first time, because by early 1970, it was universally used to describe the B-52. It was not in existence or at least not commonly used at the start of the war. Senior leadership failed in their vigorous attempt to stop the use of what they felt was a derogatory term.

[40] Gunners were removed from B-52's on October 19, 1991 at the direction of General Lee Butler, Commander and Chief, Strategic Air Command.)

[41] This happened to a gunner at Ellsworth AFB while I was stationed there. The gunner was uninjured on bailout. People said it was difficult to figure out how you could accidentally activate a switch with a plastic guard over it, but that was the IP's story and he stuck to it. The bailout light only remained on a few seconds before he switched it off and seconds later the tower called and said something fell off the back of the airplane. One of the navigators

crawled back to the tail to check and there was nothing except a hole where the turret had been.

The gunner must have been spring-loaded. The airplane was at less than five hundred feet and his chute only swung once and he was on the ground. Turned out he wasn't injured and not hard to find He landed on the overrun and was standing next to his parachute smoking a cigarette.

Chapter Twelve

42   Concerned about the aging and rank-heavy gunnery force, SAC broke with precedent and began recruiting gunners on their first enlistment. This was a first for the B-52 field and a number of old gunners worried it was a mistake. The term "Baby Gunner" was used to describe these young airmen who were selected to attend gunnery school directly out of basic training.

43   Strategic Air Command's Vietnam effort enlarged as the buildup for Bullet Shot and Linebacker began. Its motto "Peace is our Profession," no longer held the same meaning. As the Vietnam War persisted, SAC became more involved even as the draw down of Army forces continued. To support the need for more bombers, nuclear sorties were being taken off alert and crew turbulence was becoming even more prevalent. Crewmembers were also becoming much more aware of the country's mood about the war. Some of them began to question many of the basic assumptions they held, but continued to endure the long deployments.

Chapter Thirteen

44   Written up in a Readers Digest article, "Submarines to the Rescue," December 1973.

45   The B-52 G could carry a maximum of 27 500 or 750 pounds internally. The B-52D could carry 84 of the same bombs along with twelve under the wings.

Chapter Fourteen\

46   A side note about these revetments. When I was serving as a maintenance squadron commander on Guam in the 1980's, much of the graffiti had resisted the weather, and their walls still displayed a lot of history about the Air Force bases on temporary duty to Guam during the Vietnam war. As in: "McCoy Sucks, Carswell Sucks" There was considerably more about some of the leadership during that same period. As in: Colonel so-and-so Sucks, Sergeant Blank Sucks.

47   Organizational Maintenance Squadron.

48   Distance and headings of enemy aircraft.

[49] The claims of two gunners, Staff Sergeant Samuel O. Turner and Airman First Class Albert E. Moore, were later confirmed by Strategic Air Command and 7th Air Force messages. Several other claims were disapproved by the 7th Air Force Enemy Claims Board due to lack of a visual witness. I've always wondered how, if you are the last bomber in a stream, and the one most likely to draw fire, do you get a visual witness?

[50] The first three days of Linebacker II were flown using exactly the same mission package Strategic Air Command headquarters staff officers had prepared for Day One. This brought bombers over the targets at the same times, altitudes and headings as the previous day. This resulted in unprecedented losses. On day three, six B-52's were shot down.

Chapter Fifteen

[51] Duty Not Involving Flying

[52] A B-52 gunner became ill at the last minute and was replaced by Jim Cook. Cook was literally still in the flight he wore on the mission he just landed from when he climbed into the tail without even meeting the crew. He was shot down over the North and spent the rest of the war in a North Vietnamese prison camp.

[53] This story comes from an urban legend related to a briefing during Linebacker II. It has been in the grapevine since the end of the war. Supposedly General John C. Meyers, The Commander and Chief of SAC traveled from Omaha to Guam to brief combat crews and was booed off the stage.

[54] Under the urban legend category there are two stories about Christmas Eve 1972 and the clubs on Anderson Air Force Base. 1. Several fights broke out in the NCO Club after two gunners were told they didn't belong there, "the club is for Permanent Party people only." Things calmed down then got ugly again when some Permanent Party member said gunners were just a bunch of a prima donnas in flight suits. 2. The Officers' Club held a Christmas Party for B-52 crewmembers that didn't include gunners. Some mischief occurred including the removal of several large potted plants for the entrance foyer, which were then placed in more suitable locations.

Made in the USA
Coppell, TX
28 August 2021

61319276R00136